French Harpsichord Music
of the 17th Century

Studies in Musicology, No. 11

Other Titles in This Series

French Harpsichord Music of the 17th Century

A Thematic Catalog of the Sources with Commentary

VOLUME THREE
Catalog Inventories 37-68

by
Bruce Gustafson

RESEARCH PRESS

Produced and distributed by
University Microfilms International
Ann Arbor, Michigan 48106

Library of Congress Cataloging in Publication Data

Gustafson, Bruce, 1945-
French harpsichord music of the 17th century.

(Studies in musicology ; no. 11)
Includes bibliographies and index.
1. Harpsichord music—Thematic catalogs. 2. Music,
French—Thematic catalogs. I. Title. II. Series.

ML128.H35G9   016.7864'04'210944   79-23567
ISBN 0-8357-1069-6 (set)
ISBN 0-8357-1068-8 v.3

INTRODUCTION

All abbreviations are explained in the *List of Abbreviations* (Volume I, pages xvii-xliii). An *Explanation of the Catalog* is found as the last chapter of the Commentary (Volume I, pages 147-154).

Provenance: France, post 1694.

Location: Paris; Bibliothèque nationale, département de
   la musique, fonds conservatoire, Réserve 475 (<u>olim</u>
   Conservatoire de musique 24827).

Description: 1 p.ℓ., 180 p., 1 ℓ.; 23 quires (A^1, B-U^4,
   V^{10}, W^1); oblong quarto format, 18 x 25 cm. Watermark #64. Original full sprinkled calf binding,
   gilt-tooled spine, 18.8 x 26 cm.

Notation: Keyboard score (two 5-line staves, 3 systems per
   page, written page by page). Clefs usually F^3, G^2.

Scribe: One unidentified hand.

Marginalia: "Liure des pieces de clauessin de Tous les
   Tons /Naturels et transposéz, de Jean Nicolas geoffroy
   /Organiste de St Nicolas du Chardonnet a paris /et
   depuis Organiste dela Cathedralle de /St Jean de per-
   pignan En Catalogne ou Il est mort," ℓ. 1r. The identical notation is written inside the back cover and
   crossed out. Inside front cover, almost totally
   scratched out, in another contemporary hand, "A la
   maitrise / ...."(cf. same notation in same hand in
   40-Rés-476).

Summary:
   Composer:
      GEOFFROY, Jean-Nicolas (d. 1694).
   Contents: 255 pieces (213 different, 42 transpositions),
      arranged in 24 harpsichord suites or key groups (20
      different, 4 transpositions), with miscellaneous
      pieces for solo harpsichord, solo organ, violes, or
      violes with keyboard(s); some interspersed, most at
      the end of the volume. In the following list of

key groups, "&" denotes mixture of new and trans-
posed pieces; omitted numbers indicated miscellaneous
pieces:

1 (c) #	1-10		13 (B♭)	145-152
2 (C)	12-22		14 (b)	153-158
3 (d)	23-33		6& (F)	159-168
4 (D)	34-46		7 (g)	169-176
5 (e)	47-57		14 (a)	177-183
6 (E)	58-60		15 (C)	184-194
7 (f)	61-68		16 (d)	196-204
8 (F)	69-80		17 (F)	205-212
9 (g)	81-90		18 (g)	213-219
10 (G)	91-109		19 (G)	220-225
11 (a)	110-129		20 (a)	226-229
12 (A)	130-143		12& (G)	235-250

<u>Inventory</u>:

ℓ 1^r [see "Marginalia"]

ℓ 1v$^{1-3}$ 4e couplet, vous trouueréz la commence-
               ment de la chaconne En dlare page 9 [#11]

1   [GEOFFROY: <u>Allemande la confidente</u> (c)]
    Allemande En csolutbmol. Appellée la Confidente Tirée
    des pieces de /son Opera de clauessin |Reprise
     p 1$^{1-3}$ ₵|18|21|

    ED: Campbell p 48.

    p 2   Suitte En csolutbmol [#1-10]

2 | [GEOFFROY: <u>Allemande</u> (c)]

Autre Allemande. |Reprise |vous trouueréz Encor vn
Tombeau En csolutbmol En forme d'allemande page i44
[#230]

p 2$^{1-3}$ ^{C}|7|10|

ED: Campbell p 50.

---

3 | [GEOFFROY: <u>Courante</u> (c)]

Courante En csolutbmol |Reprise |vous trouueréz vne
autre courante page 6 [#8]

p 3$^{1-3}$ $3[^6_4]$|8|13|

ED: Campbell p 52.

---

4 | [GEOFFROY: <u>Sarabande</u> (c)]

Sarabande En csolutbmol |Reprise

p 4$^{1-2}$ $3[^3_4]$|8|16|

ED: Campbell p 54.

5 | [GEOFFROY: <u>Gavotte</u> (c)]

Gauotte |Reprise

   p 4³   ¢|4|8|

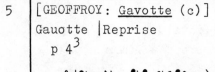

ED: Campbell p 56.

6 | [GEOFFROY: <u>Menuet</u> (c)]

Menuet En csolutbmol |Reprise

   p 5¹⁻³   ³[$\frac{3}{4}$]|8|8|

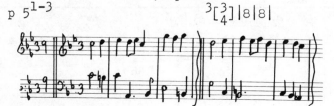

ED: Campbell p 57.

7 | [GEOFFROY: <u>Rondeau</u> (c)]

Iʳ couplet /Rondeau qui Est Escrit Encor En Esimi,

page 35

   p 5²⁻³ $\frac{6}{4}$|4|4|4|4|

CO: 37-Geoffroy #55 [e]

ED: Campbell p 58.

8 | [GEOFFROY: Courante (c)]

Autre Courante En csolutbmol |Reprise

p 6$^{1-2}$ $^3[^6_4]$|6|8|

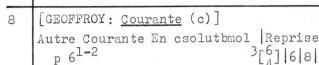

ED: Campbell p 59.

9 | [GEOFFROY: Gigue (c)]

Gigue En csolutbmol |Reprise

p 6^2-7^3 $^3[^3_4]$|25|36|

ED: Campbell p 60.

10 | [GEOFFROY: Chaconne (c)]

Chaconne Encsolutbmol /I^r Couplet ... 4

p 8^1-9^2 $^3[^3_4]$|8|13|15|16|

ED: Campbell p 63

11 | [GEOFFROY: Chaconne (d)]

I^r Couplet /Chacone /endlare ... 5 |Retournéz pour

la Suitte au premier fueillet [ℓ 1v]

p 9$^{2-3}$, ℓ 1v$^{1-3}$ $^3[^3_4]$|8|11|6|21|12|

p 10   Suitte En csolut [#12-22] /vous Trouueréz
              encor dautres pièces /en Csolut page i2i
              [#184-194]

---

12 | [GEOFFROY: <u>Allemande</u> (C)]

Allemande
p 10¹⁻³   C|8|10|

ED: Campbell p 66.

---

13 | [GEOFFROY: <u>Courante</u> (C)]

Courante En CSolut |Reprise
p 11¹⁻²   3[$\frac{6}{4}$]|8|11|

ED: Campbell p 68.

---

14 | [GEOFFROY: <u>Sarabande</u> (C)]

Sarabande |Reprise
p 11²⁻³   3[$\frac{3}{4}$]|8|16|

ED: Campbell p 69.

15 | [GEOFFROY: Gavotte en rondeau (C)]

Gauotte En Rondeau En CSolut
     p 12$^{1-2}$ ¢ |8|8|

ED: Campbell p 71.

16 | [GEOFFROY: Gavotte en rondeau (C)]

Autre gauotte En Rondeau
     p 12^2 ¢ |4|8|

ED: Campbell p 72.

17 | [GEOFFROY: Menuet (C)]

Menuet qui Est Escrit encor page i24 |Reprise
     p 12^3 $^3[^3_4]$ |8|8|

CO: 37-Geoffroy #193 [C]
ED: Campbell p 73.

18 | [GEOFFROY: Menuet (C)]

Autre Menuet En CSolut |Reprise
     p 13^1 $^3[^3_4]$ |4|8|

ED: Campbell p 74.

19 | [GEOFFROY: <u>Rondeau</u> (C)]

Rondeau En CSolut /I.^r couplet ... 3

p 13¹⁻²   ¢|8|8|8|

ED: Campbell p 75.

20 | [GEOFFROY: <u>Bourrée</u> (C)]

Bourée en CSolut |Reprise |la mesme bourée est Escrit
En dlarebquar page 28

p 13³   ¢|5|10|

CO: 37-Geoffroy #43 [D]
ED: Campbell p 76.

21 | [GEOFFROY: <u>Canarie</u> (C)]

Canaries En CSolut |Reprise |Vous trouueréz vne cha-
conne En CSolut Sur 4 nottes page 146 [#231]

p 14¹⁻²   3[3/4]|8|22|

ED: Campbell p 77.

22	[GEOFFROY: <u>Menuet</u> (C)] Autre menuet |menuet |Reprise p 14$^{2-3}$ $^{3}[^{3}_{4}]$|8|16|  ED: Campbell p 78.

	p 15 Suitte En Dlare. [#23-33] Vous Trouueréz
	                encor dautres pieces /en dlare page i26
	                [#196-204]

23	[GEOFFROY: <u>Allemande</u> (d)] Allemande |Reprise p 15$^{1-3}$ ^{C}|9|10|  ED: Campbell p 79.
24	[GEOFFROY: <u>Courante</u> (d)] Courante En Dlare |Reprise p 16$^{1-2}$ $^{3}[^{6}_{4}]$|8|11|  ED: Campbell p 81.

25 | [GEOFFROY: <u>Sarabande</u> (d)]

Sarabande |Reprise

   p 16³-17¹   ³[³/₄]|8|16|

ED: Campbell p 82.

26 | [GEOFFROY: <u>Gavotte</u> (d)]

Iᵉ gauotte En Dlare |Reprise

   p 17¹⁻²   ¢|4|8|

ED: Campbell p 84.

27 | [GEOFFROY: <u>Gavotte</u> (d)]

2ᵉ gauotte |Reprise

   p 17²   ¢|4|8|

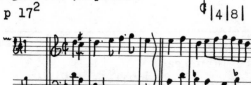

ED: Campbell p 85.

28 | [GEOFFROY: <u>Menuet</u> (d)]

Menuet endlare |Reprise |vous trouueréz le double page

   2i [#33]

    p 17³   ³[³/₄]|8|16|

ED: Campbell p 86.

29 | [GEOFFROY: <u>Rondeau</u> (d)]

Rondeau En Dlare /I[r] Couplet ... 3
p 18[1-2]   ¢|8|4|4|

ED: Campbell p 87.

30 | [GEOFFROY: <u>Gigue</u> (d)]

Gigue endlare |Reprise
p 18[2]-19[3] $3[\frac{3}{4}]$|30|43|

ED: Campbell p 88.

31 | [GEOFFROY: <u>Canarie</u> (d)]

Canaries En Dlare /I[r] Couplet ... 4
p 20[1-2]   ¢|8|4|4|5|

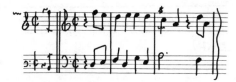

ED: Campbell p 91.

32 | [GEOFFROY: <u>Chaconne</u> (d)]

Chaconne /I.^r couplet |2. La mesme chaconne est mis en Esimi /page 37 |... 5 |Vous trouueréz vne autre cha-conne En dlare page 9 [#11]

p 20^3-21^2 [$\frac{3}{4}$]|4|10|4|10|16|

CO: Geoffroy #57 [e]
ED: Campbell p 92.

33 | [GEOFFROY: <u>Double</u> (to #28) (d)]

double du menuet |Reprise. vous trouueréz le simple page i7 [#28]

p 21^3 ^{3}[$\frac{3}{4}$]|8|16|

ED: Campbell p 95.

p 22   Suitte En Dlarebquar [#34-46]

34 | [GEOFFROY: <u>Allemande</u> (D)]

Allemande |Reprise

p 22$^{1-2}$ ^{C}|7|7|

35 | [GEOFFROY: <u>Allemande</u> <u>de</u> <u>la</u> <u>plaisante</u> <u>gaye</u> (D)]

Autre Allemande dela /plaisante gaye, Tiré des
pieces deson opera /de clauessin |Reprise
p 22³-23³   ¢|14|28|

36 | [GEOFFROY: <u>Courante</u> (D)]

I.ᵉʳ Courante En Dlarebquar |Reprise
p 24¹⁻²   3[$\frac{6}{4}$]|7|11|

37 | [GEOFFROY: <u>Courante</u> (D)]

2ᵉ Courante En Dlarebquar |Reprise
p 24³-25¹   3[$\frac{6}{4}$]|5|8|

38 | [GEOFFROY: Sarabande (D)]

Sarabande En Dlarebquar |Reprise

p 25$^{2-3}$ ^{3}[$\frac{3}{4}$]|8|12|

39 | [GEOFFROY: Gavotte (D)]

Gauotte En Dlarebquar |Reprise

p 26^1 ₵|4|8|

40 | [GEOFFROY: Menuet (D)]

Menuet En Dlarebquar |Reprise

p 26^2 ^{3}[$\frac{3}{4}$]|8|8|

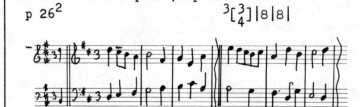

41 | [GEOFFROY: Gigue (D)]

Gigue En Dlarebquar |Reprise

p 26^3-27^2 $\frac{6}{4}$|13|15|

CO: 37-Geoffroy #152, Gigue [variant (B♭)]

42 | [GEOFFROY: <u>Bourrée</u> (D)]
Bourée En Dlarebquar |Reprise
p 27³   ¢|8|8|

---

43 | [GEOFFROY: <u>Bourrée</u> (D)]
Autre bourée en Dlarebquar. La mesme bourée Est Escrit
En CSolut page i3 |Reprise
p 28¹   ¢|5|9|
CO: 37-Geoffroy #20 (qv) [C]

---

44 | [GEOFFROY: <u>Rondeau</u> (D)]
Iʳ couplet /Rondeau en dlarebquar
p 28²⁻³   ¢|7|6|8|

---

45 | [GEOFFROY: <u>Canarie</u> (D)]
Canaries En Dlarebquar |Reprise
p 29¹⁻³   ¢3[³/₄]|8|20|

46 | [GEOFFROY: Danse villageoise (D)]
Danse villageoise En Dlarebquar. Tirée deson Opera de
pieces de claussin /Ire couplet ... 3 |vous trouuerez
vne chaconne /En dlarebquar Sur 4 nottes pag i48 [#232]
p 30$^{1-3}$ ₵ |4|12|14|

---

p 30^{3} Suitte de l'allemande la sans pareille en
                   gresolbquar page i38x [#220] /vous trou-
                   ueréz le reste page 6i.

p 31   Suitte En Esimibmol [#47-57]

47 | [GEOFFROY: Allemande (e)]
Allemande |Reprise
   p 31$^{1-3}$ ₵ |6|9|

48 | [GEOFFROY: Courante (e)]
Courante En Esimibmol |Reprise
   p 32$^{1-2}$ $3[^6_4]$|8|10|

49 | [GEOFFROY: <u>Sarabande</u> (e)]

Sarabande En ESimibmol |Reprise

p 32³-33¹   ³[³/₄]|8|16|

50 | [GEOFFROY: <u>Gavotte</u> (e)]

Gauotte en ESimibmol |Reprise

p 33²   ¢|4|8|

51 | [GEOFFROY: <u>Gavotte</u> (e)]

Autre gauotte en ESimibmol |Reprise

p 33³   ¢|4|8|

52 | [GEOFFROY: <u>Menuet</u> (e)]

Menuet En ESimibmol |Reprise

p 34¹⁻²   ³[³/₄]|8|16|

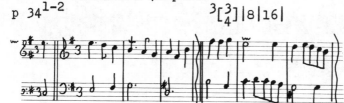

53 | [GEOFFROY: <u>Menuet</u> (e)]

Autre menuet En Esimibmol |Reprise

p 34$^{2-3}$ $^3[\frac{3}{4}]$|8|16|

---

54 | [GEOFFROY: <u>Rondeau</u> (e)]

Rondeau En ESimibmol

p 35^1 ¢|8|8|

---

55 | [GEOFFROY: <u>Rondeau</u> (e)]

Ire couplet /Autre rondeau qui est Escrit encor /En
dlare page 5 ... 4

p 36$^{2-3}$ $\frac{6}{4}$|4|4|4|4|

CO: 37-Geoffroy #7 (qv) [d]

---

56 | [GEOFFROY: <u>Gigue</u> (e)]

Gigue en ESi/mibmol /Il faut couler les nottes |Re-
prise

p 36^1-37^2 ¢|17|20|

| 57 | [GEOFFROY: <u>Chaconne</u> (e)] |
| | I^r couplet /Chaconne En ESimibmol ... [6e] |vous trouueréz la Suitte page 43. |

57 | [GEOFFROY: <u>Chaconne</u> (e)]
I^r couplet /Chaconne En ESimibmol ... [6e] |vous
trouueréz la Suitte page 43.
    p 37^3, 43^3 ^{3}[$^3_4$]|10|4|6|12|8|
CO: 37-Geoffroy #32 (qv) [d]

---

p 38   Suitte En ESimibquar [#58-60]. vous trou-
              ueréz la mesme Suitte en futfa page 100
              [#159-161]

---

58 | [GEOFFROY: <u>Allemande</u> (E)]
Allemande |Reprise
    p 38$^{1-3}$ ¢|8|13|

CO: 37-Geoffroy #159 [F]

---

59 | [GEOFFROY: <u>Courante</u> (E)]
Courante En ESimibquar |Reprise
    p 39$^{1-2}$ ^{3}[$^6_4$]|7|12|

CO: 37-Geoffroy #160 [F]

60 | [GEOFFROY: Sarabande (E)]
Sarabande en ESImibquar |Reprise |Vous trouueréz vne
gauotte En ESimibquar page 9i [#144] et vn Rondeau
aussy En ESimi♮ page 94 [#149]
p 39$^{2-3}$ $^3[^3_4]$|8|16|

CO: 37-Geoffroy #161 [F]

---

p 40   Suitte En futfabmol [#61-68]. Vous trou-
                ueréz la mesme Suitte en /gresolbmol page
                i06 [#169-176]

---

61 | [GEOFFROY: Allemande (f)]
Allemande |Reprise
    p 40$^{1-3}$ ¢|9|10|

CO: 37-Geoffroy #169 [g]

---

62 | [GEOFFROY: Courante (f)]
Courante En futfabmol |Reprise
    p 41$^{1-3}$ $^3[^6_4]$|10|11|

CO: 37-Geoffroy #170 [g]

63 | [GEOFFROY: <u>Sarabande</u> (f)]

Sarabande En futfabmol |Reprise

    p 42¹⁻² $^3[\frac{3}{4}]$|8|16|

CO: 37-Geoffroy #171 [g]

64 | [GEOFFROY: <u>Gavotte</u> (f)]

Gauotte /en futbmol. |La mesme gauotte est /Escrite
en gresolbmol page i35 et i08 |Reprise

    p 42³   ¢|4|8|

CO: 37-Geoffroy #172 [g]
    37-Geoffroy #214 [g]

65 | [GEOFFROY: <u>Menuet</u> (f)]

Menuet En futfabmol |Reprise

    p 43¹ $^3[\frac{3}{4}]$|8|8|

CO: 37-Geoffroy #173 [g]

66 | [GEOFFROY: <u>Rondeau</u> (f)]

Ire couplet /Rondeau En futfabmol ... 3

     p 43^2 $^3[\frac{3}{4}]$|4|4|8|

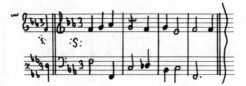

CO: 37-Geoffroy #174 [g]

---

     p 43   5e Couplet. Vous trouueréz le commence-
ment de la chaconne page 37 [#57] /Vous
trouueréz la mesme chaconne En Dlare
page 20 [#32]

---

67 | [GEOFFROY: <u>Gigue</u> (f)]

Gigue En futfabmol |Reprise

     p 44^1-45^3 $^3[\frac{3}{4}]$|37|52|

CO: 37-Geoffroy #175 [g]

---

68 | [GEOFFROY: <u>Chaconne</u> (f)]

Chaconne En futfabmol /I^r couplet ... 5

     p 46^1-47^3 $^3[\frac{3}{4}]$|8|13|8|12|21|

CO: 37-Geoffroy #176, Chaconne [g]

ED: Haas app B.

p 48   Suitte En futfa [#69-80]. Il ya une pe-
              tite Suitte En futfa page i30 [#205-212].
              ... Vous trouueréz aussy une Suitte En
              futfa qui estoit # En Simibquar page i00
              [#159-168]

---

69 | [GEOFFROY: <u>Allemande</u> (F)]

Allemande. Il y a **vne** autre allemande La resueuse
page 55 [#80]
   p 48^{1-3} ^{C}|7|10|

---

70 | [GEOFFROY: <u>Courante</u> (F)]

Courante En futfa |Reprise
   p 49^{1-3} $^{3}[{}^{6}_{4}]$|10|14|

---

71 | [GEOFFROY: <u>Courante</u> (F)]

Autre Courante En futfa |Reprise
   p 50^{1-2} $^{3}[{}^{6}_{4}]$|7|10|

72 | [GEOFFROY: <u>Sarabande</u> (F)]

Sarabande En futfa |Reprise

$$p\ 50^3-51^1 \qquad\qquad {}^3[\tfrac{3}{4}]\,|8|16|$$

73 | [GEOFFROY: <u>Gavotte</u> with <u>Double</u> (F)]

Gauotte En futfa |double |Reprise |Double de la re-
prise

$$p\ 51^{2-3} \qquad\qquad \mathcal{C}\,|4|4|8|8|$$

74 | [GEOFFROY: <u>Gavotte</u> (F)]

Autre gauotte en futfa |Reprise

$$p\ 52^1 \qquad\qquad \mathcal{C}\,|4|8|$$

CO: 37-Geoffroy #191 [C]

75 | [GEOFFROY: Menuet (F)]

Menuet En futfa |Reprise

   p 52^2 $^3[\frac{3}{4}]$|8|12|

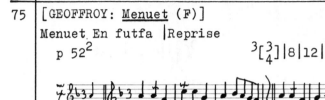

76 | [GEOFFROY: Rondeau (F)]

Rondeau /en futfa

   p 52^3 ¢|8|4|

77 | [GEOFFROY: Gigue (F)]

Gigue En futfa |fin |Reprise

   p 53$^{1-2}$ $^3[\frac{3}{4}]$|16|12|

78 | [GEOFFROY: Rondeau (F)]

Rondeau En futfa

   p 53$^{2-3}$ ¢|8|8|

79 | [GEOFFROY: <u>Chaconne</u> (F)]

Chaconne En futfa /I^r couplet ... 4

   p 54^1-55^1 $^3[\frac{3}{4}]$ |8|14|8|14|

---

80 | [GEOFFROY: <u>Allemande</u> <u>la</u> <u>resueuse</u> (F)]

Allemande En futfa La Resueuse, Tirée deson Opera de
pieces de clauessin |Reprise

   p 55$^{2-3}$ ¢|13|15|

---

p 56   Suitte En greSolbmol [#81-90]. vous trouueréz encor dautres pieces En gresolbmol
page i35 [#213-219]

---

81 | [GEOFFROY: <u>Allemande</u> (g)]

Allemande |Reprise

   p 56$^{1-3}$ ^{C}|8|11|

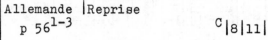

82 | [GEOFFROY: <u>Courante</u> (g)]

Courante En greSolbmol |Reprise
p 57¹⁻² $^3[^6_4]$ |7|7|

83 | [GEOFFROY: <u>Courante</u> (g)]

Autre Courante En greSolbmol |Reprise
p 57²⁻³ $^3[^6_4]$ |7|9|

84 | [GEOFFROY: <u>Sarabande</u> (g)]

Sarabande En greSolbmol. |Reprise
p 58¹⁻² $^3[^3_4]$ |8|12|

85 | [GEOFFROY: <u>Gavotte</u> (g)]

Gauotte en greSolbmol |Reprise
p 58²   ¢ |4|8|

86 | [GEOFFROY: Menuet (g)]
Menuet En greSolbmol |Reprise
  p 58³-59¹ $^3[\frac{3}{4}]$|8|16|

87 | [GEOFFROY: Gigue à l'Angloise (g)]
Gigue a l'angloise En greSolbmol /Ire couplet ... 3
  p 59¹⁻³ $^3[\frac{3}{4}]$|16|12|8|

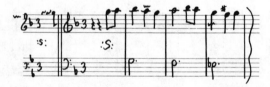

88 | [GEOFFROY: Rondeau (g)]
Rondeau En greSolbmol /I^r couplet ... 7
  p 60¹-61¹ $^3[\frac{3}{4}]$|8|8|6|8|8|8|

89 | [GEOFFROY: Rondeau (g)]
Autre Rondeau EngreSolbmol
  p 61²⁻³ $^3[\frac{3}{4}]$|8|14|

p 61   le reste delallemande la sans pareille en
              /greSolbquar vous trouueréz le commence-
              ment page i38 [#220]

---

90 | [GEOFFROY: <u>Chaconne</u> (g)]

Chaconne Sur 4 mesures EngreSolbmol /I^r couplet ... 13

p 62^1-63^3 ^{3}|5|8|[etc] [$\frac{3}{4}$|63|]

---

p 64   Suitte En greSolbquar [#91-109]. Vous
              trouueréz encor des pieces en /greSolbquar
              page i39 [#220-225]

---

91 | [GEOFFROY: <u>Allemande</u> (G)]

Allemande |Reprise

p 64^1-65^1 ^{C}|12|13|

---

92 | [GEOFFROY: <u>Courante</u> (G)]

Courante /en greSolbquar |Reprise

p 65$^{1-3}$ ^{3}[$^6_4$]|9|12|

93 | [GEOFFROY: <u>Sarabande</u> (G)]

Sarabande En greSolbquar |Reprise

p 66[1-2] $^3[\frac{3}{4}]$|8|12|

94 | [GEOFFROY: <u>Gavotte</u> (G)]

Gauotte en greSolbquar. |Reprise

p 66[2-3]   ¢|4|8|

95 | [GEOFFROY: <u>Gavotte</u> <u>serenade</u> (G)]

Gauotte Serenade en greSol♮ /Tirée de son Opera |Reprise

p 66[3]   ¢|4|4|

96 | [GEOFFROY: <u>Menuet</u> <u>serenade</u> (G)]

Menuet Serenade EngreSolbquar /Tiré de Son Opera |Reprise

p 67[1] $^3[\frac{3}{4}]$|8|8|

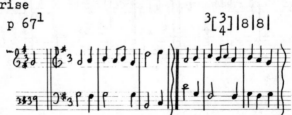

97 | [GEOFFROY: Menuet serenade (G)]

Autre menuet Serenade |Reprise
p 67^{1-2} $\frac{3}{[4]}$|8|8|

98 | [GEOFFROY: Menuet (G)]

Autre Menuet En greSolbquar |Reprise
p 67^{2-3} $\frac{3}{[4]}$|8|16|

99 | [GEOFFROY: Gigue (G)]

Gigue En greSolbquar |Reprise
p 68^{1}-69^{1} $\frac{6}{4}[\frac{3}{4}]$|34|38|

100 | [GEOFFROY: Canarie (G)]

I^{r} couplet /Canaries En greSolbquar ... 3
p 69^{2-3} $\frac{3}{[4]}$|8|8|8|

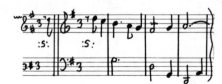

101 | [GEOFFROY: <u>Rondeau</u> (G)]

petit rondeau en greSolbquar
   p 69³   ¢|4|4|

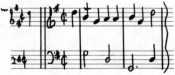

102 | [GEOFFROY: <u>Rondeau</u> (G)]

Rondeau En greSolbquar tiré de Son opera |I^r Couplet
... 3
   p 70¹   ¢|4|4|4|

103 | [GEOFFROY: <u>Rondeau</u> (G)]

I^r Couplet /Autre Rondeau en greSol♮ tiré de son opera
... 3
   p 70²⁻³   ¢|4|4|8|

104 | [GEOFFROY: Rondeau (G)]

Autre petit Rondeau /en greSolbquar

p 70³   ₵|4|4|

105 | [GEOFFROY: Danse paysanne (G)]

Danse paysanne En greSolbquar Tirée de Son Opera de
pieces de Claussin /I^r couplet /paysan paysanne
fricattant lamour Ensemble ... 5

p 71$^{1-3}$ ₵|4|6|4|8|8|

106 | [GEOFFROY: Air de bergère (G)]

I^r. Air de Bergere En greSolbquar qui eStoit En Amilabquar. Ces 3 airs de bergere /sont tirées de Son
Opera de pieces de claussin. |Reprise

p 72$^{1-2}$ ³[³⁄₄]|8|12|

107 [GEOFFROY: Air de bergère (G)]
2ᵉ Air de bergere qui estoit En A mi la b quar |Reprise

p 72²⁻³   ³[3/4]|8|16|

108 [GEOFFROY: Air de bergère (G)]
3ᵉ Air de bergere. Rondeau. En greSolbquar qui estoit
En A mi la b quar /Iʳ couplet ... 4
p 73¹⁻²   ¢ |4|4|4|4|

109 [GEOFFROY: La Musette (G)]
La Muzette /Tiré de /Son Opera./En greSolbquar |Reprise |Vous Trouueréz vne Chaconne En gresolbquar sur
4 nottes page i50 [#233].
p 73³   ³[3/4]|8|16|

p 74   Suitte En Amila [#110-129]. Vous trouueréz encor dautres pieces en Amila page
              i4i [#226-229]

110 | [GEOFFROY: Allemande (a)]

Allemande |Reprise
p 74$^{1-3}$ C|7|10|

111 | [GEOFFROY: Courante (a)]

Courante En Amila |Reprise
p 75$^{1-2}$ $^3[^6_4]$|6|9|

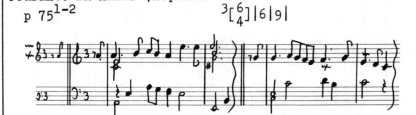

112 | [GEOFFROY: Courante (a)]

Autre courante En Amila |Reprise
p 75$^{2-3}$ $^3[^6_4]$|7|9|

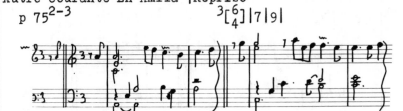

113 | [GEOFFROY: Sarabande (a)]

Sarabande En Amila |Reprise
p 76^1 $^3[^3_4]$|8|16|

114 | [GEOFFROY: <u>Gavotte</u> (a)]
Gauotte En Amila |Reprise
p 76[3]   ¢|4|8|

115 | [GEOFFROY: <u>Gavotte</u> (a)]
Gauotte En Amila |Reprise
p 77[1]   ¢|4|8|

116 | [GEOFFROY: <u>Gavotte</u> <u>en</u> <u>rondeau</u> <u>l'aimable</u> (a)]
Gauotte en Rondeau l'aimable En Amila
p 77[2]   ¢|8|8|

117 | [GEOFFROY: <u>Gavotte</u> (a)]
Gauotte En Amila.|Reprise
p 77[3]   ¢|4|8|

118 | [GEOFFROY: <u>Gavotte</u> (a)]
gauotte En Amila |Reprise
p 78^1 ¢|4|8|

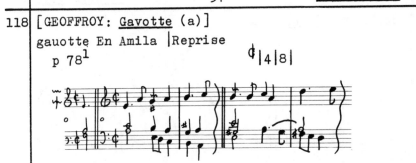

119 | [GEOFFROY: <u>Gavotte</u> (a)]
gauotte en amila |Reprise
p 78^2 ¢|4|8|

120 | [GEOFFROY: <u>Gavotte</u> (a)]
Gauotte en amila |Reprise
p 78^3 ¢|4|8|

121 | [GEOFFROY: <u>Menuet</u> (a)]
Menuet En Amila |Reprise
p 79$^{1-2}$ ^{3}[$^3_4$]|8|16|

122 | [GEOFFROY: Menuet (a)]

Autre.menuet en amila |Reprise

p 79² $^{3}[\frac{3}{4}]|6|8|$

123 | [GEOFFROY: Rondeau (a)]

Rondeau /en amila. /Vous trouueréz encor vn autre
page 83 [#129]

p 79³ $^{3}[\frac{3}{4}]|8|8|$

124 | [GEOFFROY: Canarie (a)]

Canaries En Amila /I^{r} couplet ... 3

p 80$^{1-2}$ ¢|4|8|8|

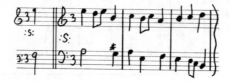

125 | [GEOFFROY: Basque (a)]

I^{r} couplet /Basque En Amila. Tiré deson opera ... 3

p 80$^{2-3}$ ¢|8|8|8|

126 [GEOFFROY: Gigue (a)]

Gigue En Amila. |Reprise

p 81$^{1-3}$ $\frac{6}{4}$|13|17|

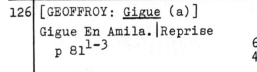

127 [GEOFFROY: Passacaille (a)]

passacaille EnAmila

p 82$^{1-3}$ ^{3}|4|4[etc] [$\frac{3}{4}$|36|]

128 [GEOFFROY: Chaconne (a)]

Chaconne Sur 4 nottes |Vous trouueréz encor vne autre
chaconne /en Amila page ii8 [#183] qui estoit en Bfasi

p 82^3-83^1 ^{3}|4↓4|[etc] [$\frac{3}{4}$|24|]

129 [GEOFFROY: Rondeau (a)]

Rondeau EnAmila

   p 83$^{2-3}$ $^3[{3\atop4}]$ |11|24|

---

   p 84   Suitte En Amilabquar [#130-143]. ... Vous
                    trouueréz la mesme Suitte mise en greSol-
                    bquar page i6i [#235, 238-250].

---

130 [GEOFFROY: Allemande (A)]

Allemande |Reprise

   p 84$^{1-2}$ ^{C}|9|11|

CO: 37-Geoffroy #235 [G]

---

131 [GEOFFROY: Courante (A)]

Courante En Amilabquar |Reprise

   p 84^3-85^1 $^3[{6\atop4}]$ |8|9|

CO: 37-Geoffroy #238 [G]

132 | [GEOFFROY: <u>Sarabande</u> (A)]

Sarabande En /amilabquar |Reprise
   p 85$^{2-3}$ $^3[{}^3_4]$|8|16|

CO: 37-Geoffroy #239 [G]

133 | [GEOFFROY: <u>Gavotte</u> (A)]

Gauotte En A milabquar |Reprise
   p 86^1 ¢|4|8|

CO: 37-Geoffroy #240 [G]

134 | [GEOFFROY: <u>Gavotte</u> (A)]

Autre petite gauotte /en amilabquar |Reprise
   p 86^2 ¢|4|4|

CO: 37-Geoffroy #241 [G]

135 | [GEOFFROY: <u>Menuet</u> (A)]

petit Menuet en amila♮ |Reprise

p 86$^{2-3}$ $^3[\frac{3}{4}]$|6|6|

CO: 37-Geoffroy #242 [G]

136 | [GEOFFROY: <u>Menuet</u> (A)]

Menuet en a milabquar |Reprise

p 86^3 $^3[\frac{3}{4}]$|8|8|

CO: 37-Geoffroy #243 [G]

137 | [GEOFFROY: <u>Rondeau</u> (A)]

Rondeau en amilabquar /I^r couplet ... 3

p 87^1 ¢|4|4|4|

CO: 37-Geoffroy #244 [G]

138 | [GEOFFROY: Rondeau (A)]

Rondeau en amila♮ /I[r] Couplet /Vous trouueréz encor des rondeaux page 89 et 9i. [#141-143]
p 87[2]   ₵|4|4|8|

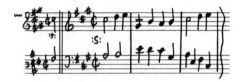

CO: 37-Geoffroy #245 [G]

---

139 | [GEOFFROY: Bourrée (A)]

Bourée /en amilabquar
p 87[2-3]   ₵|8|8|

CO: 37-Geoffroy #248 [G]

---

140 | p 88[1]-89[2]   Gigue pour 3 violes En Amila♮ |Reprise
[score on 2 staves].
CO: 37-Geoffroy #249 [G]

---

141 | [GEOFFROY: Rondeau (A)]

I[r]. couplet /Rondeau En Amilabquar ... 3
p 89[2-3] $\frac{6}{4}$|4|4|4|

CO: 37-Geoffroy #246 [G]

142 | [GEOFFROY: Chaconne (A)]

Chaconne En Amilabquar /I.^r couplet ... 4

  p 90¹⁻³   ³[³/₄] |8|6|10|13|

CO: 37-Geoffroy #250 [G]

143 | [GEOFFROY: Rondeau (A)]

Rondeau En Amilabquar /I.^r couplet ... 3

  p 91¹⁻³   ³[³/₄] |8|8|19|

CO: 37-Geoffroy #247 [G]

144 | [GEOFFROY: Gavotte (E)]

Gauotte En Esimibquar |Reprise |vous trouuerez vn

Rondeau En Esimibquar page 94 [#149]

  p 91³   ¢|8|8|

CO: 37-Geoffroy #162 (variant) [F]

p 92   Suitte Sur le Bmol de bfasi [#145-148, 150-152]

145 | [GEOFFROY: <u>Allemande</u> (Bb)]

Allemande |Reprise

  p 92^1-93^1 ^{C}|12|17|

146 | [GEOFFROY: <u>Courante</u> (Bb)]

Courante Sur le bmol de Bfasi |Reprise

  p 93$^{2-3}$ $^3[^6_4]$|10|12|

147 | [GEOFFROY: <u>Sarabande</u> (Bb)]

Sarabande Sur le bmol de la bfaSi |Reprise

  p 94$^{1-2}$ $^3[^3_4]$|8|16|

148 [GEOFFROY: <u>Gavotte en rondeau</u> (B♭)]

Gauotte En Rondeau /sur le bmol de BfaSi /La mesme
gauotte est Escrite /En CSolut page 123.

p 94$^{2-3}$ ¢|4|8|

CO: 37-Geoffroy #190 [C]

---

149 [GEOFFROY: <u>Rondeau</u> (E)]

I^r couplet /Rondeau En Esimibquar, vous trouueréz La
/Suitte page 96.

p 94$^{2-3}$, 96^3, 97^3 3[$\frac{3}{4}$]|8|8|8|

CO: 37-Geoffroy #164 [F]

---

150 [GEOFFROY: <u>Menuet</u> (B♭)]

Menuet Sur le bmol de BfaSi |Reprise

p 95^1 3[$\frac{3}{4}$]|8|8|

151 [GEOFFROY: Rondeau (B♭)]

Rondeau Sur le bmol de bfasi

p 95$^{2-3}$ $^{3}[^{3}_{4}]|8|16|$

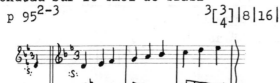

152 [GEOFFROY: Gigue (B♭)]

Gigue Sur lebmol de bfasi |Reprise

p 96^{1} $^{6}_{4}|11|16|$

CO: 37-Geoffroy #41 (variant) [D]

p 96^{3} 3e Couplet du rondeau En Esimibquar page
                    94 [#149]

p 97   Suitte sur le BfaSi [#153-158]. Vous
                    trouueréz la mesme suitte /mise En Amila
                    page ii4 [#177-183]

153 [GEOFFROY: Allemande (b)]

Allemande |Reprise

p 97$^{1-3}$ $^{C}|8|11|$

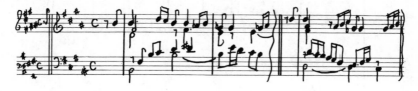

CO: 37-Geoffroy #177 [a]
    37-Geoffroy #178 [d]

p 97³   fin du rondeau /En ESimibquar /Retournez
le feuillet /pour le commencement [#149]

---

154 | [GEOFFROY: Courante (b)]

Courante Sur le BfaSi |Reprise

p 98¹⁻²   ³[₄⁶]|8|10|

CO: 37-Geoffroy #179 [a]

---

155 | [GEOFFROY: Sarabande (b)]

Sarabande, sur le BfaSi |Reprise

p 98³-99¹   ³[₄³]|8|16|

CO: 37-Geoffroy #180 [a]

---

156 | [GEOFFROY: Menuet (b)]

Menuet Sur BfaSi |Reprise

p 99¹   ³[₄³]|8|8|

CO: 37-Geoffroy #182 [a]

157 | [GEOFFROY: <u>Gavotte</u> (b)]
Gauotte Sur BfaSi |Reprise
   p 99[2]   ¢|4|8|

CO: 37-Geoffroy #181 [a]

158 | [GEOFFROY: <u>Chaconne</u> (b)]
Chaconne /En BfaSi /I[r] Couplet |vous trouueréz la
Suitte page.i09
   p 99[3], 109[3], 107[3], 101[3]   3[$\frac{3}{4}$]|8|18|26|

CO: 37-Geoffroy #183 [a]

p 100	Suitte En futfa [#159-168] qui Estoit En ESimi bquar page 38 [#58-60; also #144 and 149]
159	p 100[1-3]	Allemande |Reprise [F] CO: 37-Geoffroy #58 (qv) [E]
160	p 101[1-3]	Courante En futfa qui estoit En Esimibquar |Reprise [F] CO: 37-Geoffroy #59 (qv) [E]
	p 101[3]	4e couplet de la chaconne En BfaSi. Vous trouueréz le.commence. /dela chaconne En BfaSi page 99 [#158]

161 | p 102$^{1-2}$ Sarabande En futfa qui estoit En ESimib-
quar |Reprise [F]
CO: 37-Geoffroy #60 (qv) [E]

162 | p 102$^{2-3}$ Gauotte en futfa qui /estoit En Esimi♮ [F]
CO: 37-Geoffroy #144 (qv) [E]

---

163 | [GEOFFROY: Menuet (F)]
Menuet. Tournéz le fueillet pour vn autre petit
menuet page i05 [#167]. |Menuet En futfa qui estoit
En Esimibquar [the Menuet is not in E in 37-Geoffroy]
|Reprise
p 103$^{1-2}$ ^{3}[$\frac{3}{4}$]|8|16|

---

164 | p 103$^{2-3}$ I^{r} Couplet /Rondeau En futfa qui estoit
En ESimibquar ... 3.[F]
CO: 37-Geoffroy #149 (qv) [E]

---

165 | [GEOFFROY: Gigue (F)]
Gigue En fut fa ([removed, but visible:] qui estoit
en ...) |I^{r} couplet ... 3
p 104$^{1-2}$ ^{3}[$\frac{3}{4}$]|8|12|8|

166 | [GEOFFROY: <u>Chaconne</u> (F)]

Chaconne /En futfa ([removed, but visible:] qui estoit
...) /I.^{r} couplet ... 3
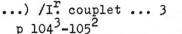
p 104^{3}-105^{2} $^{3}[\frac{3}{4}]$ |8|16|20|

---

167 | [GEOFFROY: <u>Menuet</u> (F)]

petit menuet En futfa ([removed, but visible:] qui
estoit ...) |Reprise
p 105$^{2-3}$ $^{3}[\frac{3}{4}]$ |6|6|

CO: 37-Geoffroy #223 [G]

---

168 | [GEOFFROY: <u>Gavotte</u> (F)]

Gauotte |Reprise. |Ce petit menuet et cette gauotte
Sont /Escrites en greSolbquar page i39
p 105^{3} ¢|4|8|

CO: 37-Geoffroy #221 [G]

---

p 106   Suitte En greSolbmol [#169-176] qui Estoit
En futfabmol page 40 [#61-68, qv]

169 p 106$^{1-3}$ Allemande |Reprise [g]
                      CO: 37-Geoffroy #61 (qv) [f]

170 p 107$^{1-3}$ Courante En greSolbmol qui estoit en
                      futfabmol |Reprise [g]
                      CO: 37-Geoffroy #62 (qv) [f]

    p 107^3 Suitte du 3.couplet /dela chaconne en
                      bfaSi page i09./Le commencement dela
                      chaconne /En BfaSi est page 99 [#158] et
                      vous trouueréz le 4e couplet de la cha-
                      conne page i0i.

171 p 108$^{1-2}$ Sarabande En greSolbmol qui estoit En fut-
                      fabmol |Reprise [g]
                      CO: 37-Geoffroy #63 (qv) [f]

172 p 108^3 Gauotte qui est Escrit encor page i39
                      |Reprise [g]
                      CO: 37-Geoffroy #64 (qv) [f]
                         37-Geoffroy #214 [g]

173 p 109^1 Menuet En greSolbmol qui estoit En futfa-
                      bmol |Reprise [g]
                      CO: 37-Geoffroy #65 (qv) [f]

174 p 109^2 I^r couplet /Rondeau En greSolbmol qui
                      estoit En futfabmol ... 3 [g]
                      CO: 37-Geoffroy #66 (qv) [f]

    p 109^3 Vous trouuerez le /commencement dela cha-
                      conne page 99 [#158] /3e. couplet /re-
                      tournéz le fueillet pour la Suitte [p 107^3].

175 p 110^{1}-111^3 Gigue /Gigue EngreSolbmol qui estoit en
                      futfabmol |Reprise [g]
                      CO: 37-Geoffroy #67 (qv) [f]

176 | p 112^{1}-113^{3} Chaconne En greSolbmol qui estoit En fut-
fabmol /I^{r}. couplet ... 5
CO: 37-Geoffroy #68 (qv) [f]
ED: cf Haas app B.

    p 114   Suitte En Amila [#177-183] qui Estoit
En BfaSi page 97 [#153-158, qv]

177 | p 114^{1-3} Allemande |Reprise [a]
CO: 37-Geoffroy #153 (qv) [b]
      37-Geoffroy #178 [d]

178 | p 115^{1-3} La mesme Allemande qui est en Amila mise
En Dlare |Reprise [d]
CO: 37-Geoffroy #153 (qv) [b]
      37-Geoffroy #177 [a]

179 | p 116^{1-2} Courante En Amila qui estoit En BfaSi
|Reprise [a]
CO: 37-Geoffroy #154 (qv) [b]

180 | p 116^{3}-117^{1} Sarabande en amila qui estoit en BfaSi
|Reprise [a]
CO: 37-Geoffroy #155 (qv) [b]

181 | p 117^{2} Gauotte en amila qui estoit en bfaSi
|Reprise
CO: 37-Geoffroy #157 (qv) [b]

182 | p 117^{3} Menuet en Amila qui estoit en BfaSi
|Reprise [a]
CO: 37-Geoffroy #156 (qv) (b)

183 | p 118^{1}-119^{3} Chaconne En Amila qui estoit En BfaSi
|I^{r} couplet ... 4 [a]
CO: 37-Geoffroy #158 (qv) [b]

184 | [GEOFFROY: <u>Entrée</u> (C)]

Entrée En CSolut. Vous trouueréz vne autre Entrée En amila page i25 [#195] |Reprise

p 120$^{1-3}$ $\mathbb{C}$|13|17|

185 | [GEOFFROY: <u>Courante</u> (C)]

Courante En CSolut |Reprise

p 121$^{1-2}$ $^{3}[{6 \atop 4}]$|7|8|

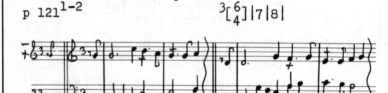

186 | [GEOFFROY: <u>Courante</u> (C)]

Autre Courante En CSolut |Reprise

p 121$^{2-3}$ $^{3}[{6 \atop 4}]$|6|8|

187 | [GEOFFROY: <u>Sarabande</u> (C)]

Sarabande En CSolut |Reprise

p 122$^{1-2}$ $^{3}[{3 \atop 4}]$|8|16|

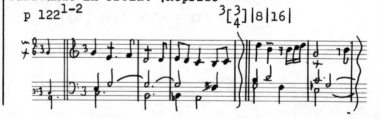

188 | [GEOFFROY: Sarabande (C)]

autre /Sarabande En CSolut |Reprise

p 122²⁻³   ³[³/₄]|8|16|

189 | [GEOFFROY: Sarabande (C)]

Autre Sarabande En CSolut |Reprise

p 123¹⁻²   ³[³/₄]|8|16|

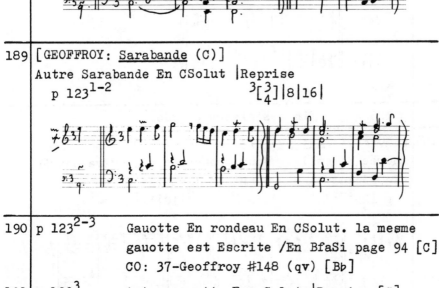

190 | p 123²⁻³   Gauotte En rondeau En CSolut. la mesme
        gauotte est Escrite /En BfaSi page 94 [C]
        CO: 37-Geoffroy #148 (qv) [B♭]

191 | p 123³   Autre gauotte En cSolut |Reprise [C]
        CO: 37-Geoffroy #74 (qv) [F]

192 | [GEOFFROY: Gavotte (C)]

Autre gauotte En CSolut |Reprise

p 124¹   ¢|4|8|

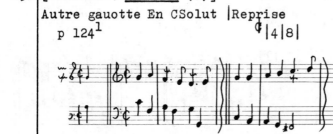

193 | p 124^2 Menuet En CSolut qui est Escrit encor page
i2 |Reprise [C]
CO: 37-Geoffroy #17 (qv) [G]

194 | [GEOFFROY: <u>Rondeau</u> (C)]
I^r couplet /Rondeau /En /CSolut ... 4 |fin
p 124^3-125^1 ¢|8|4|8|8|

p 125   fin des pieces en CSolut

195 | [GEOFFROY: <u>Entrée</u> (a)]
Entrée En Amila. Vous trouueréz vne autre entrée
/En CSolut page i20.[#184] |Reprise
p 125$^{2-3}$ ¢|10|17|

196 | [GEOFFROY: <u>Allemande</u> (d)]
petite Allemande EnDlare /grauement |Reprise
p 126$^{1-2}$ C|6|7|

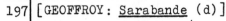

197 | [GEOFFROY: <u>Sarabande</u> (d)]
Sarabande /En dlare |Reprise
   p 126²⁻³   ³[³/₄]|8|16|

198 | [GEOFFROY: <u>Gavotte</u> (d)]
Gauotte En Dlare |Reprise
   p 127¹   ¢|4|8|

199 | [GEOFFROY: <u>Menuet</u> (d)]
Menuet En dlare |Reprise
   p 127²⁻³   ³[³/₄]|8|16|

200 | [GEOFFROY: <u>Menuet</u> (d)]
Autre menuet En dlare |Reprise
   p 127³   ³[³/₄]|8|8|

201 [GEOFFROY: <u>Rondeau</u> (d)]

Rondeau En dlare

   p 128[1]   ³[¾] |8|8|

202 [GEOFFROY: <u>Rondeau</u> (d)]

Autre Rondeau En dlare

   p 128[2]   ¢ |8|4|

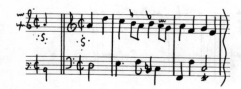

203 [GEOFFROY: <u>Gigue</u> (d)]

Gigue En Dlare |Reprise

   p 128[3]-129[2]   ³[⁶₄] |14|20|

204 [GEOFFROY: <u>Rondeau</u> (d)]

Autre rondeau /En dlare

   p 129[2-3]   ³[¾] |8|8|

205 | [GEOFFROY: Allemande grave (F)]

Allemande graue /Il faut couler les nottes |Reprise
        p 130$^{1-2}$ ^{C}|7|8|

206 | [GEOFFROY: Courante (F)]

Courante /En fut fa |Reprise
        p 130^{3}-131^{1} $^3[^6_4]$|6|9|

207 | [GEOFFROY: Sarabande (F)]

Sarabande En fut fa |Reprise
        p 131$^{1-2}$ $^3[^3_4]$|8|16|

208 [GEOFFROY: <u>Gavotte</u> (F)]

gauotte En fut fa |Reprise

   p 131³   ¢ |4|8|

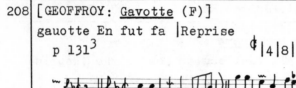

209 [GEOFFROY: <u>Menuet</u> (F)]

Menuet En fut fa |Reprise

   p 132¹⁻²   ³[¾]|8|16|

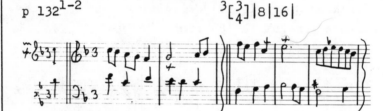

210 [GEOFFROY: <u>Menuet</u> (F)]

Autre /Menuet En fut fa |Reprise

   p 132²⁻³   ³[¾]|8|16|

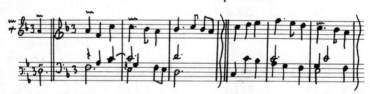

211 [GEOFFROY: <u>Rondeau</u> (F)]

Rondeau En fut fa /Iʳ couplet ... 4

   p 133¹⁻³   ⁶₄|8|4|10|10|

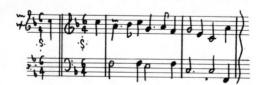

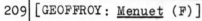

212 | [GEOFFROY: <u>Gigue</u> (F)]

Gigue En fut fa |Reprise

   p 134

213 | [GEOFFROY: <u>Courante</u> (g)]

Courante En greSolbmol |Reprise

   p 135[1-3]   2[$\frac{6}{4}$]|8|14|

214 | p 135[3]   Gauotte En greSolbmol |Reprise |La mesme

                     gauotte Est Escrite En futfabmol page

                     42 et i08.

                     CO: 37-Geoffroy #64 (qv) [f]
                            37-Geoffroy #172 [g]

215 | [GEOFFROY: <u>Rondeau</u> (g)]

Rondeau En greSolbmol /I[r]. couplet ... 4

   p 136[1-2]   ¢|8|4|4|6|

216 | [GEOFFROY: <u>Rondeau petite niaizerie</u> (g)]

I.^r couplet /Rondeau petite niaizerie /tiré de son

opera ... 3

    p 136²⁻³   ³[$\frac{3}{4}$]|8|8|8|

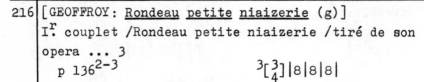

217 | [GEOFFROY: <u>Gigue</u> (g)]

Gigue En greSolbmol |Reprise

    p 137¹⁻²   ³[$\frac{3}{4}$]|14|21|.

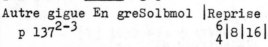
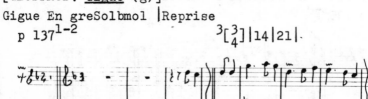

218 | [GEOFFROY: <u>Gigue</u> (g)]

Autre gigue En greSolbmol |Reprise

    p 137²⁻³ $\frac{6}{4}$|8|16|

219 | [GEOFFROY: <u>Canarie</u> (g)]

Canaries En greSolbmol /I.^{r} couplet ... 3

    p 138$^{1-2}$ $^3[{}^3_4]|8|8|8|$

---

220 | [GEOFFROY: <u>Allemande</u> <u>la</u> <u>sans</u> <u>pareille</u> (G)]

Allemande la sans pareille En greSolbquar qui estoit

en Amilabquar /de son opera [not in A in 37-Geoffroy]

|Reprise /vous trouuerez la suitte page 30

    p 138$^{2-3}$, 30^3, 61^3 ¢|20|31|

---

221 | p 139^1 Gauotte En greSolbquar. Cette mesme

                  gauotte Est Escrite En fut fa page 105

                  |Reprise [G]

                  CO: 37-Geoffroy #168 (qv) [F]

---

222 | [GEOFFROY: <u>Menuet</u> (G)]

Menuet En greSolbquar de Son opera |Reprise

    p 139$^{2-3}$ $^3[{}^3_4]|8|16|$

223 | p 139³   petit menuet en greSolbquar |Reprise.
ce mesme petit menuet /Est Escrit En fut
fa page 105. [G]
CO: 37-Geoffroy #167 (qv) [F]

---

224 | [GEOFFROY: <u>Rondeau fantaisie</u> (G)]
Rondeau fantaisie En greSolbquar, Tiré de son opera
/I.ͬ couplet ... 4
     p 140¹⁻²   ³[³/₄]|8|8|8|8|

---

225 | [GEOFFROY: <u>Danse paysanne</u> (G)]
Danse paysanne En greSolbquar, Tiré de Son Opera
|Reprise
     p 140³   ¢|8|8|

---

226 | [GEOFFROY: <u>Gavotte</u> (a)]
Gauotte En Amila |Reprise
     p 141¹   ¢|4|8|

227 | [GEOFFROY: Rondeau (a)]
Rondeau En Amila /I^r couplet ... 6
p 141$^{1-3}$ ^{3}|8|8|[etc] [$\frac{3}{4}$|48|]

228 | [GEOFFROY: Canarie (a)]
Canaries En Amila /I^r couplet ... 4
p 142^1 ¢|4|4|4|4|

229 | [GEOFFROY: Passacaille (a)]
Passacaille En Amila
p 142^2-143^3 ^{3}[$\frac{3}{4}$]|74|

230 | [GEOFFROY: <u>Tombeau</u> <u>en</u> <u>forme</u> <u>d'allemande</u> (c)]

Tombeau En CSolut/bmol En forme d'allemande /Il faut
couler les nottes |Reprise |Carillon
p 144^1-145^3 C|27|11|¢16|9|

231 | [GEOFFROY: <u>Chaconne</u> (C)]

Chaconne En CSolut Sur 4. nottes
p 146^1-147^3 ¢|149|

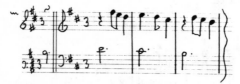

232 | [GEOFFROY: <u>Chaconne</u> (D)]

Chaconne En Dlarebquar sur 4. nottes
p 148^1-149^3 3[3/4]|85|

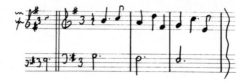

233 | [GEOFFROY: <u>Chaconne</u> (G)]

Chaconne En greSolbquar sur 4 nottes
p 150^1-152^3 3[3/4]|137|

234 | [GEOFFROY: Chaconne (G)]

Chaconne En greSolbquar qui Estoit En Amilabquar
[not in A in 37-Geoffroy] Sur 4 nottes
   p 153^1-160^3 $^3[^6_4]$ |241|

---

p 161   Suitte En greSolbquar [#235-250] qui es-
               toit En Amilabquar [#130-143, qv]

235 | p 161^{1-2} Allemande |Reprise [G]
               CO: 37-Geoffroy #130 (qv) [A]

---

236 | [GEOFFROY: Menuet (G)]

petit menuet en /greSolbquar |Reprise
   p 161^3 $^3[^3_4]$ |6|6|

---

237 | [GEOFFROY: Menuet (G)]

Autre petit menuet |Reprise
   p 161^3 $^3[^3_4]$ |8|8|

238	p 162$^{1-2}$	Courante En greSolbquar qui estoit En Ami-labquar |Reprise [G] CO: 37-Geoffroy #131 (qv) [A]
239	p 162$^{2-3}$	Sarabande en greSol♮ qui estoit En Amila-bquar |Reprise [G] CO: 37-Geoffroy #132 (qv) [A]
240	p 163^{1}	Gauotte En greSol♮ qui Estoit En Amila-bquar |Reprise [G] CO: 37-Geoffroy #133 (qv) [A]
241	p 163$^{1-2}$	Autre petite gauotte |Reprise [G] CO: 37-Geoffroy #134 (qv) [A]
242	p 163$^{2-3}$	Menuet en greSolbquar /qui estoit en A-milabquar |Reprise CO: 37-Geoffroy #135 (qv) [A]
243	p 163^{3}	Autre menuet |Reprise [G] CO: 37-Geoffroy #136 (qv) [A]
244	p 164^{1}	Rondeau En greSolbquar qui estoit En Amilabquar /I^{r} couplet ... 3 [G] CO: 37-Geoffroy #137 (qv) [A]
245	p 164^{2}	Autre rondeau [G] CO: 37-Geoffroy #138 (qv) [A]
246	p 164^{3}	Autre Rondeau [G] CO: 37-Geoffroy #141 (qv) [A]
247	p 165$^{1-2}$	Autre Rondeau En gresol♮ qui estoit en Amilabquar /I^{r} couplet ... 3 CO: 37-Geoffroy #143 (qv) [A]
248	p 165$^{2-3}$	Bourée [G] CO: 37-Geoffroy #139 (qv) [A]

249 | p 166^1-167^1 | Gigue En greSolbquar pour 3. violes qui estoit En Amilabquar |Reprise [G]
CO: 37-Geoffroy #140 [A]

250 | p 167^{1-3} | Chaconne En greSolbquar /I^r couplet /qui estoit en Amilabquar ... 4
CO: 37-Geoffroy #142 (qv) [A]

251 | p 168^1-171^3 | Dialogue En Esimi pour le claussin et des violes. Tiré de Son opera de pieces de claussin |claussin ou pour l'orgue |violes |C. |v. [etc] ... point d'orgue /pedales |p. jeu ... violes auec le claussin ... [E]

252 | p 172^1-175^3 | Dialogue En greSolbquar qui estoit En Amilabquar [not in A in 37-Geoffroy] pour le claussin et des violes, Tiré /de son opera de pieces de claussin.|ClauSSin ou pour l'orgue |2e dessus /de viole |C. |v. [etc] [G]

253 | p 176^1-177^3 | Rabat Joye charmant qui est la Suitte dela grande piece de Joye de l'opera du Geoffroy [for organ] [g]

254 | p 178^1-180^1 | Détachement de la grande piece de Joye Tiré de Son Opera de pieces de claussin /vif g.p. |g.p. |Eco |g. lente ... pedale ... [g]

255 | p 180^{1-3} | Symphonie En gresol♮ /pour 3 violes qui estoit En Amilabquar [not in A in 37-Geoffroy] [G]

     | p 181 | Table des pieces de claussin contenues /en ce liure ...

     | p 182 | [blank, unruled]

Provenance: Paris, post ca. 1658?

Location: Paris; Bibliothèque Sainte Geneviève, MS 2348
and MS 2353.

Description: 2 v. V. 1 (MS 2348): 2 p.ℓ., 24 ℓ. (plus
modern end papers); 3 quires (A^8, B^{10}, C^8); oblong
quarto format, 19.3 x 25.3 cm. (trimmed). Watermark #60. Modern full cloth binding, 19.8 x 26 cm.
V. 2 (MS 2353): 4 ℓ.; 1 quire; oblong quarto format,
19.5 x 25.8 cm. Same paper, matching binding.

Notation: Keyboard score (two 5-line staves, 3-4 systems
per page, written page by page). Clefs: G^2, F^3,
$C^{1,2,3,4}$; usually F^3, G^2.

Scribes: 4 unidentifed hands:
A: #1-32
B: 33-35
C: 36-39
D: 40-53

Marginalia: Modern numeration by ℓ. in ink. Many ℓ.
have cross mark at top (copyist's mark?); perhaps
all ℓ. had such marks, some now trimmed off. Ex-
planatory corrections in original hand on ℓ. 16r,
"d," "e."

Summary:
Composers:
CHAMBONNIERES: #1, 3-6, 9-10, 12-14, 16-18, 20-22,
25-29, 31-33, 36-39.
COUPERIN (Louis): #2, 23-24.
MONNARD: #34.
Contents: #1-39, harpsichord pieces grouped by key:
#1-2 (g)
3-8 (a)

9-21 (F)
22   (C)
23-25 (G)
26-32 (D)
33,34 (G, C)
35-38 (G)
39   (d)
40-53 Organ pieces

Inventory:

1	[CHAMBONNIÈRES: Courante (g)]

Courante. |Suitte
ℓ 1r$^{1-3}$ $^3[{}^6_4]$ |8|10|

CO: 35-Bauyn-I #103, Courante du mesme Auteur
    63-Chamb-II #22, Courante
ED: Brunold-Tessier #52, Dart-Ch #52.

2	[COUPERIN (L): Sarabande (g)]

Sarabande. |Reprise |fin
ℓ 1r^4-v^2 $^3[{}^3_4]$ |8|16|

CO: 35-Bauyn-II #94, Sarabande du même Auteur
ED: Brunold/Dart-Co #94, Curtis-Co #95.

3 | [CHAMBONNIÈRES: <u>Courante</u> (a)]

Courante. |Suitte. |Reprise |Suitte |$\overset{r}{p}$ La reprise |fin.

ℓ 1v^3-2r^1 $^3[^6_4]|7|8|$

CO: 32-Oldham #27, Aultre Courante
    35-Bauyn-I #116, Courante du meme Auteur
    62-Chamb-I #3, Courante

ED: Brunold-Tessier #3, Dart-Ch #3.

4 | [CHAMBONNIÈRES: <u>Sarabande</u> (a)]

Sarabande. |fin

ℓ 2r$^{2-3}$ $^3|5|9|$ $[^6_4|4|8|]$

CO: 35-Bauyn-I #119, Sarabande de Mr. de Chambonnieres
ED: Brunold-Tessier #134.

5 | [CHAMBONNIÈRES: <u>Courante</u> (a)]

Courante. |Reprise. |fin.

ℓ 2r^4-v^2 $^3[^6_4]|6|8|$

CO: 2-Witzendorff #94, Curant Gombonier
    62-Chamb-I #4, Courante
ED: Brunold-Tessier #4, Dart-Ch #4.

6 | [CHAMBONNIERES: <u>Sarabande</u> (a)]

Sarabande. |Reprise. |fin.

ℓ 2v^3-4 $^3[^6_4]|4|8|$

CO: 35-Bauyn-I #120, Sarabande du même Auteur
ED: Brunold-Tessier #135.

---

7 | [<u>Courante</u> (a)]

Courante. |Reprise. |fin.

ℓ 3r^1-3 $^3|7|11|$ $[^6_4|7|9|]$

---

8 | [<u>Sarabande</u> (a)]

Sarabande. |Reprise. |fin.

ℓ 3r^4-v^2 $^3[^6_4]|4|8|2|$

9 | [CHAMBONNIERES: Courante (F)]

Courante. |Reprise. |fin.

ℓ 3v$^{2-4}$ $^3[^6_4]$ |8|9|

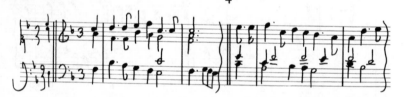

CO: 35-Bauyn-I #63, Courante du meme Auteur
    35-Bauyn-I #64, Courante de Mr de Chambonnieres
    35-Bauyn-I #73, Courante du meme Auteur

ED: Brunold-Tessier #100.

10 | [CHAMBONNIERES: Courante (F)]

Courante. |Reprise. |fin.

ℓ 4r$^{1-3}$ $^3[^6_4]$ |7|8|

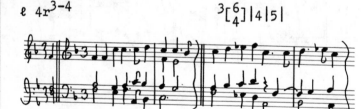

CO: 35-Bauyn-I #76, Courante de Mr de Chambonnieres
    63-Chamb-II #17, Courante

ED: Brunold-Tessier #47, Dart-Ch #47.

11 | [Sarabande (F)]

Sarabande. |fin.

ℓ 4r$^{3-4}$ $^3[^6_4]$ |4|5|

12 | [CHAMBONNIÈRES: <u>Brusque</u> (F)]

Brusque. |i Fois. |2 fois.

ℓ 4v$^{1-4}$ $^3[^6_4]$ |4|14|

CO: 35-Bauyn-I #84, Brusque de Mr. de Chambonnieres
ED: Brunold-Tessier #114.

---

13 | [CHAMBONNIÈRES: <u>Brusque</u> (F)]

Brusque. |fin.

ℓ 5r$^{1-4}$ $^3[^6_4]$ |12|16|

CO: 35-Bauyn-I #85, Autre brusque du même Auteur
ED: Brunold-Tessier #115.

---

14 | [CHAMBONNIÈRES: <u>Courante</u> (F)]

Courante. |fin.

ℓ 5v$^{1-3}$ $^3[^6_4]$ |7|9|

CO: 35-Bauyn-I #69, Courante du meme Auteur
ED: Brunold-Tessier #104.

15 | [Courante (F)]

Courante. |fin

ℓ 5v^4-6r^2

^{3}[$^6_4$] |9|10|

16 | [CHAMBONNIÈRES: Sarabande (F)]

Sarabande. |fin

ℓ 6r$^{3-4}$

^{3}|7|6| [$^6_4$|4|6|]

CO: 35-Bauyn-I #81, Sarabande du même Auteur
ED: Brunold-Tessier #111.

17 | [CHAMBONNIÈRES: Sarabande (F)]

Sarabande. |fin

ℓ 6v$^{1-3}$

^{3}|5|9| [$^3_4$|8|15|]

CO: 63-Chamb-II #19, Sarabande
ED: Brunold-Tessier #49, Dart-Ch #49.

18 | [CHAMBONNIERES: <u>Courante</u> (F)]

Courante. |Reprise
 ℓ 6v^4-7r^1 ^{3}[$^6_4$]|6|7|

CO: 35-Bauyn-I #62, Courante de Mr. de Chambonnieres
  62-Chamb-I #22, Courante

ED: Brunold-T$_e$ssier #22, Dart-Ch #22.

---

19 | [<u>Sarabande</u> (F)]

Sarabande |fin.
 ℓ 7r$^{2-3}$ ^{3}[$^6_4$]|4|6|

---

20 | [CHAMBONNIERES: <u>Courante</u> (F)]

Courante. |Reprise. |fin.
 ℓ 7v$^{1-2}$ ^{3}[$^6_4$]|6|7|

CO: 35-Bauyn-I #72, Courante de Mr. de Chambonnieres
  63-Chamb-II #18, Courante

ED: Brunold-Tessier #48, Dart-Ch #48.

21 | [CHAMBONNIERES: <u>Rondeau</u> (F)]

Rondeau. |fin.

    ℓ $7v^3-8r^2$ ^{C}|4|6|11| [$^4_4$|4|10|12|]

CO: 35-Bauyn-I #74, Rondeau de Mr. de Chambonnieres

ED: Brunold-Tessier #106.

---

22 | [CHAMBONNIERES: <u>Chaconne</u> (F)]

Chaconne. |fin

    ℓ $8r^3-9r^2$ ^{3}|6|5|10|5| [$^3_4$|8|10|12|8|]

CO: 35-Bauyn-I #86, Chaconne de Mr de Chambonnieres

ED: Brunold-Tessier #116, Curtis-Co #75 (as "Louis
    Couperin?").

---

23 | [COUPERIN (L): <u>Courante</u> (G)]

Courante. |fin.

    ℓ $9r^2-v^1$ ^{3}|5|8| [$^6_4$|8|8|]

CO: 35-Bauyn-II #90, Courante du même Auteur

ED: Dart-Co #90; Brunold-Co #90 (1st strain only,
    with 35-Bauyn-II #90a).

24 | [COUPERIN (L): <u>Courante</u> (G)]

Courante |Fin.

ℓ 9v$^{2-3}$ ^{3}[$^{6}_{4}$] |6|7|

CO: 35-Bauyn-II #90a, [untitled]

ED: Dart-Co #90bis, Curtis-Co #88; Brunold-Co #90
    (after 1st strain of 38-Gen-2348/53 #23).

25 | [CHAMBONNIÈRES: <u>Canarie</u> (G)]

Canaries |fin.

ℓ 10r$^{1-3}$ ^{3}[$^{6}_{4}$] |8|12|

CO: 35-Bauyn-I #99, Canaries de Mr de Chambonnieres
    36-Parville #96, Canaries Chanbonniere
    62-Chamb-I #30, Canaris

ED: Brunold-Tessier #30, Dart-Ch #30.

26 | [CHAMBONNIÈRES: <u>Sarabande</u> (D)]

Sarabande.

ℓ 10v$^{1-2}$ ^{3}[$^{6}_{4}$] |6|8|

CO: 35-Bauyn-I #52, Sarabande du même Auteur

ED: Brunold-Tessier #96.

27 | [CHAMBONNIÈRES: <u>Courante</u> (D)]

Courante. |Reprise.

ℓ 10v³-11r¹   ³[⁶₄] |6|8|

CO: 35-Bauyn-I #45, Courante de Mr. de Chambonnieres
ED: Brunold-Tessier #90.

---

28 | [CHAMBONNIÈRES: <u>Courante</u> (D)]

Courante. |Reprise. |fin.

ℓ 11r²⁻³   ³[⁶₄] |8|8|

CO: 63-Chamb-II #12, Courante
ED: Brunold-Tessier #42, Dart-Ch #42.

---

29 | [CHAMBONNIÈRES: <u>Courante</u> (D)]

Courante: |Reprise. |fin.

ℓ 11v¹⁻³   ³[⁶₄] |7|8|

CO: 35-Bauyn-I #55, Courante de Mr de Chambonnieres
     63-Chamb-II #13, Courante
ED: Brunold-Tessier #43, Dart-Ch #43.

30 | [Courante (D)]
Courante. |Reprise. fin.
ℓ 12r[1-3]   3[$^6_4$] |7|9|

31 | [CHAMBONNIÈRES: Courante (D)]
Courante. |fin
ℓ 12v[1-3]   3[$^6_4$] |6|10|

CO: 35-Bauyn-I #49, Courante de Mr de Chambonnieres
ED: Brunold-Tessier #94.

32 | [CHAMBONNIÈRES: Courante (D)]
Courante. |1re fois |2 fois |fin.
ℓ 13v[1]-14r[1]   3[$^6_4$] |6|8|

CO: 35-Bauyn-I #47, Courante de Mr. de Chambonnieres
ED: Brunold-Tessier #92.

33 | [CHAMBONNIERES: <u>Courante</u> (G)]

Courante.

    ℓ 13v^1-14r^1 $^3[^6_4]$ |7|10|

CO: 32-Oldham #7, Courante de Monsieur de chambon-
    nieres
    33-Rés-89ter #35, Courante Chambonnieres ...
    Double
    35-Bauyn-I #91, Courante de Mr. de Chambonnieres
    36-Parville #91, Courante Chanbonniere
    63-Chamb-II #28, Courante

ED: Brunold-Tessier #58, Dart-Ch #58, Gilbert p 192.

---

34 | [MONNARD: <u>Sarabande</u> (C)]

Sarabande.

    ℓ 14r^2-3 $^3[^3_4]$ |4|8|

CO: 6-Munich-1511e #11, Sarrabande
    23-Tenbury #4, Sarabande
    24-Babell #56, Sarabande
    30-Cecilia ℓ 48r, Sarabande ... redoublè
    31-Madrid-1360 #23/6, Sexta (Zarabanda)
    35-Bauyn-III #60, Sarabande De Mr. Monnard
    44-LaPierre p 2, [Sarabande]

ED: cf Bonfils-18 p 6, Ex 7 above.

35 | [Untitled (G)]
    ℓ 14v$^{1-3}$ $^3[{3\atop4}]$ |6|12|

36 | [CHAMBONNIÈRES: <u>Courante</u> (G)]
Courante |fin
    ℓ 15r$^{1-3}$ $^3[{6\atop4}]$ |8|8|

CO: 32-Oldham #9, Courante De Monsieur de Chambonnieres
    35-Bauyn-I #88, Courante de Mr de Chambonnieres
    36-Parville #90, Courante Chanbonniere
    63-Chamb-II #27, Courante
ED: Brunold-Tessier #57, Dart-Ch #57.

37 | [CHAMBONNIÈRES: <u>Sarabande</u> (G)]
Sarabande |fin
    ℓ 15r^{4}-v^{2} $^3[{3\atop4}]$ |10|12|

CO: 35-Bauyn-I #93, Sarabande du même Auteur
ED: Brunold-Tessier #120.

38	[CHAMBONNIÈRES: <u>Gigue</u> <u>la</u> <u>villageoise</u> (G)] Gigue La Villageoise De M^r. Chambonniere ℓ 15v$^{2-4}$ $^3[^6_4]$|8|15|

CO: 35-Bauyn-I #98, Gigue La villageoise dudit Auteur
    62-Chamb-I #29, Gigue la Vilageoise
ED: Brunold-Tessier #29, Dart-Ch #29.

39	[CHAMBONNIÈRES: <u>Allemande</u> (d)] [untitled] ℓ 16r$^{1-4}$ ¢ |14|9|

CO: 35-Bauyn-I #29, Allemande de Mr. de Chambonnieres
    63-Chamb-II #6, Allemande
ED: Brunold-Tessier #36, Dart-Ch #36.

	ℓ 16v	[blank, ruled]
40	ℓ 17r^1-v^1	Duo du 5me en C Sol ut fa.
41	ℓ 17v^2-18r^1	Duo du i^{er} ton.
42	ℓ 18r$^{2-3}$	Duo du 2 ton
43	ℓ 18v$^{1-3}$	Duo du 2. ton |fin.
44	ℓ 19r^1-20r^2	Aue Maris Stella. Plainchant en Taille du i^{er} ton ... ED: Bonfils-18 p 30.

44a	ℓ 20v^1-21v^2	Aue Maris Stella. a 3 Jeux differents ... ED: Bonfils-18 p 32.
45	ℓ 21v^2-22v^3	Autre plainchant pour Le /petit plain jeu & La pedale /de fluste.du i^{er} ton ... ED: Bonfils-18 p 33.
46	ℓ 23r^1-v^2	fugue graue pour La Trompette & le Clarion du i^{er} ton ED: Bonfils-18 p 35.
47	ℓ 23v^3-24v^2	autre fugue. a 3. du i^{er} ton ED: Bonfils-18 p 36.
48	ℓ 24v^2	prelude du 2 ton
49	ℓ 24v^3	prelude du i^{er} ton. |fin
		[MS 2348 ends here; the following 4 ℓ were detatched from the same original ms and are now bound separately as MS 2353:]
	ℓ i^{r-v}	[blank, ruled]
50 a-ℓ	ℓ 1r^1-v^3	[12 intonations for Pange lingua:] C du 5 en C Sol ut fa |C du i^{er} en de la re sol | [etc]
	ℓ 2r^1	[see #53]
51	ℓ 2r$^{2-3}$	Trio du 2. ton
52	ℓ 2v$^{1-3}$	Recit du du [sic] 2. ton
53	ℓ 3r^1-v^3, 2r^1	Plain jeu du positif /avec La pédal de fluste |Pange Lingua du 4me ton ED: Bonfils-18 p 38.

Provenance: France, post 1678 (transcription from Psyché).

Location: Paris; Bibliothèque nationale, département de la musique Vm^7 6307$^{(1)}$ (olim Vm 2750).

Description: 32 p.; 4 quires (A-D^4); oblong quarto format, 17.6 x 23 cm. (trimmed). Modern (1976) cloth binding, with former modern paper front cover bound in, 19.5 x 26 cm. Bound with an unrelated ms, 42-Vm7-6307-2 (q. v.). Watermark #104.

Notation: Mixed; harpsichord pieces in keyboard score (two 5-line staves, 3 systems per page, written page by page). Clefs: $F^{3,4}$, G^2, C^1.

Scribes: 4-6 hands; one (B) probably the teacher of the others:
A: #1
B: p 4-5, #2-3, 10
C: #4-8, 11-15
D: #9 (same as C?)
E: #12, except p 22-23
F: #13-14

Marginalia: Numeration by pages in modern pencil.

Summary:
Composers:
LULLY: #10, 12.
Contents:

#1, 4-6, 8, 14	Viol pieces
7, 13	Vocal melodies
2, 3, 10	Harpsichord pieces (hand B)
9, 11, 15	Harpsichord pieces in other hands

<u>Inventory</u>:

1	p 1-3	Préludes /pour /la Viole ... [simple preludes and a gavotte for viol, with fingerings and solfege names of notes indicated]

[ℓ lacking between p 2 and 3]

p 4-5   Tablature /pour Le /clavessin ... [solfege names of notes written on lines demonstrating C^1, G^2 and F^3 clefs; followed by explanation of other rudiments of notation.]

---

2   [<u>Prélude</u> (incomplete) (C)]

prelude
   p 6^{1-3} |-|

[ℓ lacking]

3   [<u>Canarie</u> (C)]

Canaris |fin
   p 7^{1-3} $^3[^3_4]|8|8|$

CO: 44-LaPierre p 13, 29A, Canaris

4 5 6	p 8	menuet ǀautre ǁ[untitled] [fragmentary pieces for viol]
	p 9	[blank, ruled; 2 c^3 clefs & smudged piece begun with 3 notes only]
7	p 10	[text between staves:] Ma plus chere brebis [?] /Basse continue [fragment]
	p 11	[blank, ruled]
8	p 12-13	[fragments, untitled viol pieces]
		[ℓ lacking; p 13 does not form half a sheet with p 11-12]

9 [Untitled (F)]
    p 14^1-15^3 ^{2}ǀ11ǀ$^3_2$15ǀ   [$^4_4$ǀ11ǀ$^3_4$18ǀ]

10 [LULLY, arr: <u>La beauté la plus sevère</u> from <u>Atys</u> (1676) IV-5 (C)]

La beaute la plus seuere ǀsuitte
    p 16^1-17^3 ¢ǀ4ǀ12ǀ

CO: cf 47-Gen-2356 #17, Gauotte

p 18   [blank, ruled]

11 | [Untitled (a)]
     p 19$^{1-2}$ ¢ |4|8|

---

12 | [LULLY, arr: <u>Premier air pour les suivants de Mars</u>
from <u>Psyché</u> (1678) V-4 (C)]
Les grandes Trompettes a Deux choeurs en Rondeau ...
p 20: [fragment of melody only]

[ℓ lacking; pp 19-20 do not form a sheet with 21-22]

p 21: [title repeated]
p 22^{1}-23^{2}: [complete piece in keyboard score in hand
          C]

p 24: [blank, ruled]
p 26: [title repeated; part of another copy of the
       keyboard transcription (see p 22)]
p 27: [blank, ruled]
                              ¢ |8|8|8|

CO: 36-Parville #123, Les fanfares de Psiché
    36-Parville #147, Les trompettes de Psiché

---

	p 28	[4 note fragment]
13	p 29	[melody with text:] petis oyseaus vas sure
	p 30	[blank, ruled]

14	p 31	bransle de vilage [Air ancien, for viol]
		CO: cf 27-Gresse #7
		cf 55-Redon #10
		cf Terburg
		cf Celle p 140
		cf Add-16889 ℓ 99r [lute]
15	p 32	[untitled unmeasured melody (intended as r h of harpsichord piece?)]

40-RÉS-476

<u>Provenance</u>: France (Paris?), post 1679 (transcription from <u>Bellerophon</u>).

<u>Location</u>: Paris; Bibliothèque nationale, département de la musique, fonds conservatoire, Réserve 476 (<u>olim</u> Conservatoire de musique, 24827).

<u>Description</u>: 1 p.ℓ., 88ℓ.; oblong quarto format, 17.6 x 23 cm. Watermark #68. Contemporary full sprinkled calf binding, gilt-tooled spine, sprinkled edges; on cover in ink (barely legible): CONT [CONTINUO], 18.2 x 24 cm.

<u>Notation</u>: Keyboard score (two 5-line staves, 3 systems per page, written page by page). Clefs: $C^{1,3}$, $F^{3,4}$, $G^{1,2}$; usually F^3, G^2.

<u>Scribe</u>: One professional hand, the same as in Thiéry.

<u>Marginalia</u>: Modern library notes on ℓ. i^{r-v}. Inside back cover, the same notation as in 37-Geoffroy, largely scratched out, "a la maître /De ...." Modern numeration by ℓ. in blue ink.

<u>Summary</u>:

Composers:

COUPERIN (Louis): #29.

LULLY : #26, 35-42.

NIVERS : #8, 30.

Contents:

#1-5, 27-28	Noëls (for organ)
16-25, 30-34	Liturgical pieces (for organ)
29	Allemande by COUPERIN
25, 35-42	LULLY transcriptions

Inventory:

	ℓ i^{r-v}	[blank, unruled; see "Marginalia"]
1	ℓ 1r^1-2r^3	Allons nous en-/promptement aupres /de la crèche /Prelude |Recit |Double |Duo |Dialogue /pos. |gr [etc] [G] ED: Bonfils-LP p 1.
2	ℓ 2v^1-4r^3	Nöel /Nous sommes en uoie ... [d] ED: Bonfils-LP p 4.
3	ℓ 4v^1-6r^3	Enfin le iour /est aduenu ... [d] ED: Bonfils-LP p 7.
4	ℓ 6v^1-8r^3	ha uoisin /quelle nouuelle ... [d] ED: Bonfils-LP p 10.
5	ℓ 8v^1-10r^3	Noël /Graces soient rendües ... [F] ED: Bonfils-LP p 13.
6	ℓ 10v^1-12r	Prelude |Stabat mater dolorosa ... [C] ED: Bonfils-LP facs II.
7	ℓ 12v^1-13r^3	Prelude |hic uir despiciens ... mundum ... [d] ED: Bonfils-LP facs IV
8	ℓ 13v^1-14r^3	Prelude |Récit [arr of motet **Veni de libano** by NIVERS (G)] CO: cf 40-Rés-476 #30 ED: Bonfils.LP p 16.
9	ℓ 14v^1-15r^3	Prelude |O Sacrum conuiuium ... [F] ED: Bonfils-LP facs V.
10	ℓ 15v^1-18r^3	Offerte. /Grand Jeu ... [C] ED: Bonfils-LP p 18.
11	ℓ 18v^1-19r^3	Aue /regina ... [a] ED: Bonfils-LP p 21.

12 | ℓ 19v¹-25r³ Prelude |Memento domine Dauid ... [G]
ED: Bonfils-LP p 22.

13 | ℓ 25v¹-27r² Regina. ... [G]
ED: Bonfils-LP p 31.

14 | ℓ 27v¹-34r³ Prelude [and 6 versets (c)]
ED: Bonfils-LP p 34.

15 | ℓ 34v¹-36r³ Lucis creator ... [e]
ED: Bonfils-LP p 41.

16 | ℓ 36v¹-39r³ Offerte /en fanfare ... [C]
ED: Bonfils-LP p 44.

17 | ℓ 39v¹-42r³ Offerte /en Dialogue [d]
ED: Bonfils-LP p 48.

18 | ℓ 42v¹-50r³ Kyrie ... Et in terra ... Sanctus ...
Agnus [g]
ED: Bonfils-LP p 52.

19 | ℓ 50v¹-57r² Prelude [and 6 versets (a)]
ED: Bonfils-LP p 61.

20 | ℓ 57v¹-61r³ offerte graue [g]
ED: Bonfils-LP p 68.

21 | ℓ 61v¹-63r³ hymne [4 versets (G)]
ED: Bonfils-LP p 72.

22 | ℓ 63v¹-70r³ Prelude ... Et exultauuit Spiritus meus
... [d]
ED: Bonfils-LP p 75.

23 | ℓ 70v¹-72r³ Laudibus ciues ... [g]
ED: Bonfils-LP p 84.

24 | ℓ 72v¹⁻³ Prelude [fragment (F)]
ED: Bonfils-LP facs VI.

[ℓ lacking]

25 | ℓ 72Ar$^{1-3}$ [end of continuo fragment with Latin text]
                       ED: Bonfils-LP facs VI

---

26 | [LULLY, arr: <u>Ouverture</u> from <u>Bellérophon</u> (1679) (C)]
Louuerture de Bellerophone |i^{ere} fois |2re fois
|Reprise
       ℓ 72Av^1-73r^3 ¢|14|26|

CO: cf 14-Schwerin-619 #83, Ouverture de Bellerophon
    cf 24-Babell #199, Ouverture de Bellerophone
    cf 27-Gresse #53, [untitled]
    cf 46-Menetou #87, Entree de Bellerophon
    cf Bod-576 p 54, Ouverture de Bellerofon
ED: Bonfils-LP p 86, Howell #1

---

27 | ℓ 73v^1-75r^3 Noël /Il fallut une mere ... [g]
                       ED: Bonfils-LP p 88.

28 | ℓ 75v^1-77r^3 Noël nouueles ...[g]
                       ED: Bonfils-LP p 91

---

29 | [COUPERIN (L): <u>Allemande</u> (a)]
Allemande
       ℓ 77v^1-78r^3 C|9|9|

CO: 35-Bauyn-II #102, Allemande de Mr. Couperin
    36-Parville #47, ALLemande Couprin
    47-Gen-2356 #3, L'aimable allemande de Mr Couperin
ED: Bonfils-LP p 94; cf Brunold/Dart-Co #102, Curtis-
    Co #2.

30 | ℓ 78v[1]-79r[3] Prelude |Veni de Libano ... [with con-
tinuo part for motet, NIVERS (G)]
CO: cf 40-Rés-476 #8
ED: Bonfils-LP p 95.

31 | ℓ 79v[1]-80r[2] Dialogue [G]
ED: Bonfils-LP p 98.

32 | ℓ 80r[2-3] Amen [G]
ED: Bonfils-LP p 99.

33 | ℓ 80r[1]-81r[2] Dialogue /de Verbum &c ... [G]
ED: Bonfils-LP p 100.

34 | ℓ 81r[3] Amen [G]
ED: Bonfils-LP p 101.

35 | [LULLY, arr: Ouverture from Isis (1677) (g)]
Louuerture /d'Isis
ℓ 81v[1]-82v[3] $^2[\frac{4}{4}]|14|^3[\frac{6}{4}]29|$

CO: cf 14-Schwerin-619 #51, Ouverture Disis
cf 24-Babell #128, Ouverture D'Isis
cf 33-Rés-89ter #42c, Ouuertuor d'Isis
cf 36-Parville #42, Ouuerture disis
cf 42-Vm7-6307-2 #5, Ouuerture de Lopera disis
cf 46-Menetou #85, Ouuerture de lopera Disis
cf 49-RésF-933 #24, Ouuerture d isis
cf Stoss ℓ 24v

ED: Bonfils-LP p 101, Howell #2; cf Gilbert p 199.

36 | [LULLY, arr: <u>Air</u> (<u>trompettes</u>) from <u>Isis</u> (1677) Pro-
logue-3 (C)]

Trompette .de l'opera
ℓ 83r$^{1-3}$ $^2[^4_4]|4|8|$

CO: cf 14-Schwerin-619 #74, Trompet Disis
    cf 22a-Roper #28 [untitled]
ED: Bonfils-LP p 103, Howell #3.

---

37 | [LULLY, arr: <u>Troisieme Air</u> from <u>Isis</u> (1677) III-6 (C)]

menuet
ℓ 83v$^{1-2}$ $^3[^6_4]|4|4|$

ED: Bonfils-LP p 104, Howell #4.

37a | [<u>Double</u> (C)]

Double
ℓ 83v$^{2-3}$ $^3[^6_4]|4|4|$

ED: Bonfils-LP p 104, Howell #3[a]

38   [LULLY, arr: <u>Deuxieme</u> <u>Air</u> <u>pour</u> <u>les</u> <u>muses</u> from <u>Isis</u>
(1677) Prologue-3 (g)]

Menüet

   ℓ 84r$^{1-3}$ $^3[\frac{3}{4}]$|8|16|

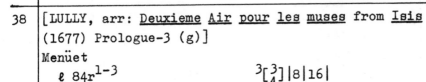

CO: 36-Parville #127, Menuet
ED: Bonfils-LP p 104, Howell #5.

39   [LULLY, arr: <u>Ouverture</u> from <u>Alceste</u> (1674) (a)]

Louuerture de /l'opera d'alceste.

   p 84v^{1}-85r^{3} $^2[\frac{4}{4}]$|12|$^3[\frac{6}{4}]$20|^{2}8|

CO: 46-Menetou #113, Ouuerture d Alceste
ED: Bonfils-LP p 105, Howell #6.

40   [LULLY, arr: <u>Rondeau</u>, <u>la</u> <u>gloire</u> from <u>Alceste</u> (1674)
Prologue (C)]

Marche /de lopera

   ℓ 85v^{1}-86r^{2} ₵|10|6|7|

ED: Bonfils-LP p 107, Howell #7.

41 [LULLY, arr: <u>Les Plaisirs à ses yeux</u> from <u>Atys</u> (1676)
Prologue (a)]
pièce de /l'opera
ℓ 86v[1]-87r[3] ^{3}|9|30| [$\frac{3}{4}$|9|31|]

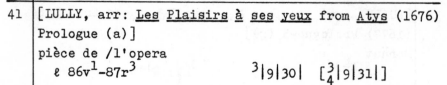

ED: Bonfils-LP p 108, Howell #8.

42 [LULLY, arr: <u>Marche</u> from <u>Thésée</u> (1675) I-8 (C)]
La marche
ℓ 87r[1-3]   ¢|9|8|8|

CO: cf 14-Schwerin-619 #72, Sacrifiee de Thesee
    cf 36-Parville #133, Marche de Thesée
    cf 44-LaPierre p 23A, Marche
ED: Bonfils-LP p 109, Howell #9.

ℓ 88r-v   [blank, unruled]

41-THOMELIN

Provenance: France (Paris?), ca. 1680-1700?

Location: Paris; Bibliothèque nationale, département de la musique, Vm^7 1817 bis.

Description: 2 ℓ.; 1 quire; oblong quarto format, 19.3 x 24.9 cm. Watermark #29. Modern half leather binding, paper boards.

Notation: Keyboard score (two 5-line staves, 3 systems per page, written originally as one unfolded sheet: original recto, p.1 and 2 beside each other; original verso, p. 3 and 4 beside each other; now folded, creating the page order: 2, 3, 4, 1). Clefs: F^3, G^2.

Scribe: One unidentified hand.
Marginalia: "Trouvé dans les sonates de Fabio (Vm^7 1178) en février 1939," pencil note.

Inventory:

1   [THOMELIN, Jacques-Denis (ca. 1640-1693): Allemande (g)]
Allemande de M Thomelin /P^{re} partie |P^{re} fois |2e fois |Reprise |P^{re} fois
    ℓ 1r-2v ^{C}|10|9|

ED: Bonfils-18 p 3.

Provenance: France (Paris?), post 1684 (transcription from Amadis).

Location: Paris; Bibliothèque nationale, département de la musique Vm^7 6307$^{(2)}$ (olim Vm 2750).

Description: 22 p. (stubbed, much repaired); oblong quarto format, 18.8 x 25.2 cm. (trimmed). Modern (1976) cloth binding, with former modern paper front cover bound in, 19.5 x 26 cm. Bound with an unrelated ms, 39-Vm7-6307-1 (q.v.). Watermark #69.

Notation: Keyboard score (two 5-line staves, 3 systems per page, written page by page). Clefs: F^3, G^2, C^1.

Scribe: One unidentifed hand (not the same as any in 39-Vm7-6307-1).

Marginalia: Numeration by pages in modern pencil.

Summary:
Composer:
LULLY: #5-11.
Contents: Miscellaneous harpsichord pieces, mostly opera transcriptions:
#1-10 (G/g)
11-12 (D)

Inventory:

1 [Gigue d'Angleterre (G)]
   gigue d'angleterre |1 couplet ... 3me couplet
   p 1^1-2^2 $^3_2[^3_4]|6|10|14$

2 | [La Furstenburg (Air ancien) (g)]

La fustanbert

p 2³-3³   ₵ |8|19|

CO: cf 24-Babell #79, Air en Bourée
    cf 49-RésF-933 #16, Air Anglois

2a | [Double (g)]

double

p 4¹-5³   [₵] |8|19|

---

3 | [Rigaudon (G)]

Rigaudon

p 6¹-7¹   ²[4/4] |8|12|

---

p 8   [blank, ruled]

4   [<u>Marche</u> (G)]

Marche de Jannissaires

p 9^1-12^3 ¢|68|

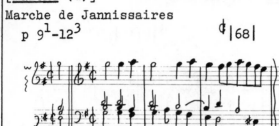

CO: cf 24-Babell #282, Marche des Janissaires
    cf 49-RésF-933 #20, Marche des janissaires

---

5   [LULLY, arr: <u>Ouverture</u> from <u>Isis</u> (1677) (g)]

Ouuerture de Lopera d isis |premiere /fois |2me fois
|fin

p 13^1-15^2 2[$\frac{4}{4}$]|15|[$\frac{3}{4}$]59|

CO: cf 14-Schwerin-619 #51, Ouverture Disis
    cf 24-Babell #128, Ouverture D'Isis
    cf 33-Rés-89ter #42c, Ouuertuor d'Isis
    cf 36-Parville #42, Ouuerture disis
    cf 40-Rés-476 #35, Louuerture d'Isis
    cf 46-Menetou #85, Ouuerture de lopera Disis
    cf 49-RésF-933 #24, Ouuerture d isis
    cf Stoss ℓ 24v

ED: cf Bonfils-LP p 101, Howell #2, Gilbert p 199.

6 | [LULLY, arr: <u>Premier</u> <u>Air</u> <u>pour</u> <u>les</u> <u>muses</u> from <u>Isis</u>
Prologue-3 (g)]
air du mesme opera
p 15³-16²   ²[4/4] |8|10|

CO: cf 24-Babell #130, Entrée des muses
cf 45-Dart #52, Entrée des muses
cf 46-Menetou #61, vn berger charmant

7 | [LULLY, arr: <u>Deuxieme</u> <u>Air</u> from <u>Isis</u> (1677) II-7 (g)]
bourée |Reprise
p 16³-17³   ²[4/4] |8|20|

8 | [LULLY, arr: <u>Vous</u> <u>ne</u> <u>devez</u> <u>plus</u> <u>attendre</u> from <u>Amadis</u>
(1684) II-7 (g)]
Menuet de Lopera d'amadis
p 18¹-19²   ³[3/4] |6|30|

CO: cf 36-Parville #110, Trio d'Amadis ...
cf 46-Menetou #20, vous ne devez ... [a]
cf 46-Menetou #39, vous nedeuez ...
cf 49-RésF-933 #23, vous ne devés ...
cf 10-Schwerin-617 #19, Menuet

9 | [LULLY, arr: <u>Suivons</u> <u>l'amour</u> from <u>Amadis</u> (1684) Pro-
logue (G)]

menuet du mesme opera

p 19$^{2-3}$ $^3[{}^3_4]|8|8|$

CO: cf 44-LaPierre p 23, 57A, Menuet D'amadis
    cf 46-Menetou #14, Menuet
    cf Copenhagen-396, Menuet Intavolat di Joh Laurent
ED: cf Lundgren #8.

---

10 | [LULLY, arr: <u>Que</u> <u>ces</u> <u>lieux</u> from <u>Isis</u> (1677) II-7 (g)]

gauotte /ensuitte de /la bourée [cf #7]

p 20$^{1-3}$ ₵|12|13|

CO: cf 27-Gresse #40, Que ces lieux
ED: cf Curtis-MMN #82.

---

11 | [LULLY, arr: <u>Allemande</u> (D)]

L'allemande

p 21$^{1-3}$ ₵|8|12|

CO: cf 14-Schwerin-619 #48, Allemande des fragments

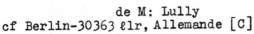

de M: Lully

cf Berlin-30363 ℓ1r, Allemande [C]

12 | [<u>Menuet</u> (D)]

Menuet

p 22¹⁻³ $^3[\frac{3}{4}]|8|8|$

Provenance: Paris (?), post 1685 (transcription from Roland).

Location: Paris; Bibliothèque Sainte Geneviève, MS 2354.

Description: 11 ℓ. (plus modern end papers), 17 x 22.3 cm.; oblong quarto format (no watermarks), Modern full cloth binding, 17.7 x 23 cm.

Notation: Keyboard score (two 5-line staves, 3 systems per page, written page by page). Clefs: F^3, G^2.

Scribes: 2 unidentifed hands:
A: #1-2
B: 3-5

Marginalia: Modern numeration by ℓ. in ink; miscellaneous library marks.

Summary:
Composer:
LULLY: #1, 2.
Contents: 5 miscellaneous harpsichord pieces.

Inventory:

[ℓ 1-4 are written upside-down on staff paper; ℓ 5-11 are written right-side-up; the latter ℓ were probably originally facing the back of the volume.]

1 | [LULLY, arr: <u>Chaconne</u> from <u>Phaéton</u> (1683) II-5 (G)]
Chaconne /de phaEton |Suitte dela /chaconne [etc]
|fin

   ℓ 1r^1-3v^3 $^3[\frac{3}{4}]$|153|

CO: cf 14-Schwerin-619 #61, Chaconne de Phäeton
    cf 24-Babell #263, Chaconne de Phaéton
    cf 44-LaPierre p 24, 45A, Chaconne de Phaëton
    cf 46-Menetou #9, chaconne
    cf 68-d'Anglebert #15, Chaconne de Phaeton Mr de
                   Lully

ED: cf Gilbert p 100, Roesgen-Champion p 30.

2 | [LULLY, arr: <u>Menuet</u> from <u>Roland</u> (1685) IV-3 (C)]
[untitled] |fin

   ℓ 4r$^{1-3}$ $^3[\frac{3}{4}]$|8|12|

CO: cf 46-Menetou #37, menuet

[ℓ lacking]

3 | [Ballet du Basque (incomplete; 1st strain lacking) (G)]
Reprise
ℓ 5r$^{1-3}$ [$^4_4$]|12|

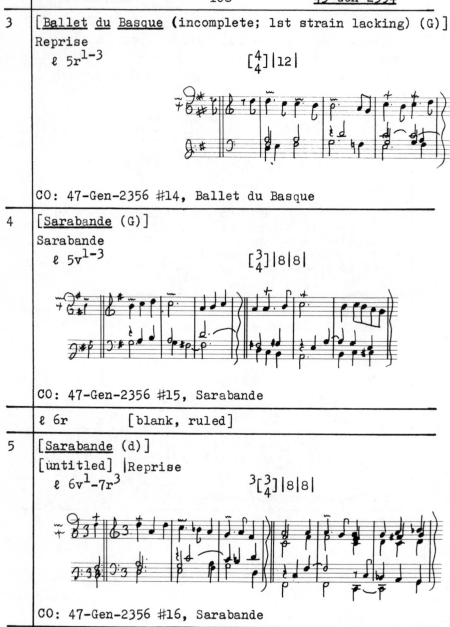

CO: 47-Gen-2356 #14, Ballet du Basque

4 | [Sarabande (G)]
Sarabande
ℓ 5v$^{1-3}$ [$^3_4$]|8|8|

CO: 47-Gen-2356 #15, Sarabande

ℓ 6r   [blank, ruled]

5 | [Sarabande (d)]
[untitled] |Reprise
ℓ 6v^1-7r^3 ^{3}[$^3_4$]|8|8|

CO: 47-Gen-2356 #16, Sarabande

ℓ 7v-11v   [blank, ruled]

<u>Provenance</u>: France, post 1687 (dated, *l*. i, "Mademoiselle
de La pierre a commencé a Joüer du Clavessin le
sixiesme jour du mois de septembre----1687").

<u>Location</u>: Currently (1975-1978) in the unsettled estate
of Madame la comtesse de Chambure (Geneviève Thi-
bault).

<u>Description</u>: at least 152 p.; leather binding.

<u>Notation</u>: Keyboard score (two 5-line staves). Clefs: F^3,
G^2, C^1.

<u>Marginalia</u>: Final *l*., "1730." On *l*. 62, "Fin de touttes
les leçons de Mad^e Le Noble." See also "Provenance."

<u>Summary</u>:

  Composers:

    CHAMBONNIÈRES: p 18, 42, 34A.

    FAVIER: p 16, 27A.

    HARDEL: p 52, 54.

    LULLY: p 14, 23, 24, 40, 44, 46, 48, 20A, 22A, 25A,
       33A, 45A, 57A.

    MONNARD: p 2.

    MONTELAN: p 58A.

  Contents:

    p. 1-72   31 miscellaneous harpsichord pieces and
                opera transcriptions.

    p. 1A-62A Copies (written from the other end of the
              book forward) of the same pieces,
              with a few other pieces intermixed.

<u>Inventory</u>:

p 1 | Prelude [unmeasured, in mixed note values (C)]
     | CO: 44-LaPierre p 18A, Prelude

p 2 | Sarabande [MONNARD (C)]
     | CO: 6-Munich-1511e #11, Sarrabande
     | 23-Tenbury #4, Sarabande
     | 24-Babell #56, Sarabande
     | 30-Cecilia *l* 48r, Sarabande ... redoublé

31-Madrid-1360 #23/6, Sexta (Zarabanda)
35-Bauyn-III #60, Sarabande De Mr. Monnard
38-Gen-2348/53 #34, Sarabande

ED: cf Bonfils-18 p 6, Ex 7 above.

p 3   Menuet [C]

CO: 44-LaPierre p 28A

p 4   Folies d'espagne [6 couplets (d)]

CO: 44-LaPierre p 2A, folies d'espagne

p 10 Gigue d'angleterre [d]

CO: 44-LaPierre p 16A, Gigue
    48-LaBarre-6 #38, Gigue

p 12 Courante en de la re [d]

CO: 5-Munich-1503ℓ #10, Courante
    7-Munich-1511f #12, Courante
    22a-Roper #55, Courante

p 13 Canaris [C]

CO: 39-Vm7-6307-1 #3, Canaris
    44-LaPierre p 29A

p 14 [LULLY, arr: Air from Acis et Galathée (1686) Prologue (

CO: 36-Parville #67, Rigaudon
    44-LaPierre p 25A, Rigaudon
    cf 22a-Roper #51, 53, La Rigaudoe, Le Rigodon
    cf 45-Dart #37, Rigodon de Galateé
    cf 36-Parville #67a, Double ... fait par Mr. Coupra:
ED: cf Curtis-Co #32.

p 15 Second Rigaudon [C]

CO: 44-LaPierre p 26A

p 16 Rigaudon du Sr Favier [C]
CO: 44-LaPierre p 27A
    Vm7-3555 p 28, Rigaudon

p 17 noel [A la venue de noël (d)]

CO: cf 7-Munich-1511f #25, alavenue de noel
    cf 67-Gigault p I-10, A la uenu de noel

p 18 Courante [Iris] Chamboniere [C]
CO: 8-Hintze, Courante
    22a-Roper #58, Courante Chambonniere
    23-Tenbury #3, (courante chambonii)
    24-Babell #58, Courante de Mr. de Chambonniere

33-Rés-89ter #2, Courante. Chambonnieres.
35-Bauyn-I #9, Courante de Mr De Chambonnieres
36-Parville #61, Courante Chanbonniere
44-LaPierre p 34A [Courante]
47-Gen-2356 #12, Courante
53-Oldham-2 p 107, Courante de Chambonniere
55-Redon #23, Courante de Monsieur de Chamboniere
62-Chamb-I #8, Courante Iris

ED: cf Brunold-Tessier #8, Dart-Ch #8, Gilbert p 148.

p 20 | Double de la courante [C]
CO: 44-LaPierre p 36A
cf 22a-Roper #58a, double
cf? 32-Oldham #17, Double de La Courante Iris
cf 33-Rés-89ter #2, Double

ED: cf Gilbert p 149, Brunold-Tessier p 116.

p 22 | Menuet [G]

CO: 44-LaPierre p 55A, menuet

p 23 | Menuet D'amadis [LULLY, arr: Suivons l'amour from

Amadis (1684) Prologue (G)]

CO: 44-LaPierre p 57A, Menuet
cf 42-Vm7-6307-2 #9, menuet du mesme opera
cf 46-Menetou #14, Menuet
cf Copenhagen-396, Menuet Intavolat di Joh
Laurent

ED: cf Lundgren #8.

p 24 | Chaconne de Phaëton [LULLY (1683) II-5 (G)]

CO: 44-LaPierre p 45A, Chaconne de Phaeton
cf 14-Schwerin-619 #61, Chaconne de Phaeton
cf 24-Babell #263, Chaconne de Phaeton
cf 43-Gen-2354 #1, Chaconne de phaEton
cf 46-Menetou #9, chaconne
cf 68-d'Anglebert #15, Chaconne de Phaeton Mr Lully

ED: cf Gilbert p 100, Roesgen-Champion p 30.

p 33 | Menuet en Suitte [G]
CO: 44-LaPierre p 56A, 2me menuet

p 34 | Prelude en C sol ut [unmeasured in mixed note
values (C)]
CO: 44-LaPierre p 30A

p 37 | Bouré la Siamoise [C]
CO: 44-LaPierre p 41A, Bourrée Siamoise

p 38 | Menuet [C]
CO: 44-LaPierre p 38A, Menuet

p 39 | Douple [C]
CO: 44-LaPierre p 39A

p 40 | menuet en Trio [LULLY, arr: J'entens un bruit from Roland (1685) IV-2 (C)]
CO: cf 46-Menetou #33, Menuet pour les hautbois

p 41 | Gavotte ma merre mariez moy [a]

p 42 | Les Zephirs de Mr de Chanboniere [Sarabande jeunes zéphirs (G)]
CO: 5-Munich-1503ℓ #1, Sarrabande de Mons: Chambon-
                              nier
      32-Oldham #8, Sarabande de Monsieur de Chambon-
                              nieres
      33-Rés-89ter #36, Sarabande Chambonnieres ...
                              Double
      35-Bauyn-I #96, Sarabande de Mr de Chambonnieres
      36-Parville #93, Sarabande Chanbonniere
      45-Dart #55, Sarabande de Chambonniere
      63-Chamb-II #29, Sarabande Jeunes Zephirs
      cf Philidor p 22, Jeunes Zephirs (de Mr de chan-
                              boniere) [for instruments]
ED: cf Brunold-Tessier #59, Dart-Ch #59, Gilbert p
    194.

p 44 | Descente de Mars [LULLY, arr: Trompettes (Mars) from Thésée (1675) Prologue (C)]
CO: 44-LaPierre p 20A, Descente de Mars
      cf 14-Schwerin-619 #69, Descente De Mars De
                              Thesee
      cf 36-Parville #131, La descente de Mars

p 46 | Marche des Trompettes de l'opera Thesée [LULLY]

p 48 | le Sacrifice de Mars [LULLY, arr: Marche des sacri-
ficateurs from Cadmus (1673) III-6 (C)]
CO: cf 14-Schwerin-619 #75, Sacrifice de Mars de
                              Cadmus

p 50 | flon flon flon La mandonaine ... [?] [C]

p 51 | Marguerite La Raliseuse [?] de Navets [G]

p 52 | Allemande de Mr Hardel [d]
CO: 24-Babell #219, Allemande
35-Bauyn-III #44, Allemande de Mr hardel
36-Parville #22, Allemande hardel
ED: cf Quittard-H p 3.

p 54 | Premiere Courante [HARDEL (d)]
CO: 32-Oldham #31, Courante de Mr hardel
35-Bauyn-III #45, Courante de Mr hardel
ED: cf Quittard-H p 4.

p 56 | [unmeasured prelude in mixed note values (d)]

p 58 | folies d'espagnes ... in variatio ... il faut
harpeger tous les accords [d]

p 73 | [Here follow miscellaneous copies of the pieces
listed above; then the remainder of the book is
written from the other end:]

p 1A | [unmeasured prelude in mixed note values (d)]

p 2A | folies d'espagne [d]
CO: 44-LaPierre p 4, Folies d'espagne

p 16A | Gigue [d]
CO: 44-LaPierre p 10, Gigue d'angleterre
48-LaBarre-6 #38, Gigue

p 18A | Prelude [unmeasured, in mixed note valutes (C)]
CO: 44-LaPierre p 1, Prelude

p 20A | Descente de Mars [LULLY, arr: Trompettes (Mars)
from Thésée (1675) Prologue (C)]
CO: 44-LaPierre p 44, Descente de Mars
cf 14-Schwerin-619 #69, Descente De Mars De
Thesee
cf 36-Parville #131, La descente de Mars

p 22A | menuet [LULLY, arr: Hautbois from Thésée (1675) Pro-
logue (C)]
CO: cf 14-Schwerin-619 #71, Menuet

cf 25-Bod-426 #7,   Menuet
cf 36-Parville #132, Menuet

p 23A Marche [LULLY, arr: Marche from Thésée (1675) I-8 (C)]

CO: cf 14-Schwerin-619 #72, Sacrifiee de Thesee
    cf 36-Parville #133, Marche de Thésée
    cf 40-Rés-476 #42, La marche

ED: cf Bonfils-LP p 109, Howell #9.

p 25A Rigaudon [LULLY, arr: Air from Acis et Galathée
             (1686) Prologue (C)]

CO: 36-Parville #67, Rigaudon
    44-LaPierre p 14, Rigaudon
    cf 22a-Roper #51, 53, La Rigaudoe, Le Rigodon
    cf 45-Dart #37, Rigodon de Galateé
    cf 36-Parville #67a, Double...fait par Mr. Couprain

ED: cf Curtis-Co #32.

p 26A [Second Rigaudon (C)]

CO: 44-LaPierre p 15, Second Rigaudon

p 27A [Rigaudon du Sr Favier (C)]

CO: 44-LaPierre p 16, Rigaudon du Sr Favier
    Vm7-3555 p 28, Rigaudon

p 28A [Menuet (C)]

CO: 44-LaPierre p 3, Menuet

p 29A [Canarie (C)]

CO: 39-Vm7-6307-1 #3, Canaris
    44-LaPierre p 13, Canaris

p 30A Prelude [unmeasured, in mixed note values (C)]

CO: 44-LaPierre p 34, Prelude en C sol ut

p 34A [CHAMBONNIÈRES: Courante Iris (C)]

CO: 8-Hintze #15, Courante
    22a-Roper #58, Courante Chambonniere
    23-Tenbury #3, (ŏourante chambonii)
    24-Babell #58, Courante de Mr. de Chambonniere
    33-Rés-89ter #2, Courante. Chambonnieres
    35-Bauyn-I #9, Courante de Mr De Chambonnieres
    36-Parville #61, Courante Chanbonniere
    44-LaPierre p 18, Courante Chamboniere
    47-Gen-2356 #12, Courante
    53-Oldham-2 p 107, Courante de Chamboniere
    55-Redon #23, Courante de Monsieur de Chamboniere
    62-Chamb-I #8, Courante Iris

ED: cf Brunold-Tessier #8, Dart-Ch #8, Gilbert p 148.

p 36A | [Double (C)]
CO: 44-LaPierre p 20, Double de la courante
        cf 22a-Roper #58a, double
        cf? 32-Oldham #17, Double de La Courante Iris
        cf 33-Rés-89ter #2, Double
ED: cf Gilbert p 149, Brunold-Tessier p 116.

p 38A | Menuet [C]
CO: 44-LaPierre p 38, Menuet

p 39A | Double [C]
CO: 44-LaPierre p 39, Douple

p 40A | Marche des mosquetaires [C]

p 41A | Bourée Siamoise
CO: 44-LaPierre p 37, Bouré la Siamoise

p 42A | Menuet [C]

p 43A | Prelude [unmeasured (e)]

p 45A | Chaconne de Phaeton [LULLY (1683) II-5 (G)]
CO: 44-LaPierre p 24, Chaconne de Phaëton
        cf 14-Schwerin-619 #61, Chaconne de Phaëton
        cf 24-Babell #263, Chaconne de Phaëton
        cf 43-Gen-2354 #1, Chaconne de phaEton
        cf 46-Menetou #9, chaconne
        cf 68-d'Anglebert #15, Chaconne de Phaeton Mr de Lully
ED: cf Gilbert p 100, Roesgen-Champion p 30.

p 55A | menuet [G]
CO: 44-LaPierre p 22, Menuet

p 56A | 2me menuet [G]
CO: 44-LaPierre p 33, Menuet en Suitte

p 57A | menuet [LULLY, arr: Suivons l'amour from Amadis
(1684) Prologue (G)]
CO: 44-LaPierre p 23, Menuet D'amadis
        cf 42-Vm7-6307-2 #9, menuet du mesme opera
        cf 46-Menetou #14, Menuet
        cf Copenhagen-396, Menuet Intavolat di Joh
                                    Laurent
ED: cf Lundgren #8.

p 58A | Rigaudon de Montalain [MONTELAN, arr? (G)]

p 59A | Rigaudon des Veissaux [g]
CO: cf 22a-Roper #30, Rigaudon [d]
cf 36-Parville #113, Rigaudon
cf 45-Dart #67, Rigaudon de la marine
cf 48-LaBarre-6 #27, Rigaudon [d]

p 61A | Second Rigaudon [g]

CO: cf 36-Parville #114, 2e. Rigaudon
cf 48-LaBarre-6 #28, 2e Rigaudon [d]

Provenance: France, post 1687 (hand A; copies from 65-
Lebègue-II), post 1697 (hand C; transcriptions from
l'Europe galante).

Location: Currently (1978) in the estate of Thurston Dart,
on permanent loan to the Faculty of Music, King's College,
London; item #2 on the unpublished "Handlist of
Manuscripts, Books and Printed Music from the Dart
Collection in Room 303 152/3 Strand [London] W.C.1."

Description: 2 p.ℓ., 45 ℓ. (originally 52: 9 ℓ. lacking);
14 quires (A^2, B-C^4, E-G^4, H-I^3, J-K^4, L^3, M^4, N^2);
oblong quarto format, 17.5 x 25.1 cm. Watermark #61.
Contemporary vellum binding, sprinkled edges, 18 x
25.5 cm.

Notation: Keyboard score (two 5-line staves, 3 systems
per page, written page by page). Clefs: F^3, G^2, C^1.

Scribes: 2-4 unidentified hands, interspersed:
A (post 1687): #2, 4-15, 17-20, 22-23, 25-30, 42-43,
55, 58-64.
B (same as A?): 16a, 33-40.
B^1(same as B?): 31.
C (post 1697): 1, 3, 16b, 21, 24, 32, 41, 41a, 44-54,
56-57, 63b, 65-67.

Marginalia: Writing on front cover, illegible, "Joseph
...." On front paste-down: scribbles and several
words, "Monsieur /Largeur /de touche /et Longeur
|Longeur /de tout." On ℓ. ii^r: scribbles in pencil
and ink, colored ink design; ℓ. ii^v and throughout
the book: pencil notes in the hand of Thurston Dart.
Irregular pagination in hand A, corresponding to
64-Lebègue-I, with a few discrepancies. On back

pastedown: miscellaneous numerals.

Summary:

Composers:

d'ANGLEBERT: #39.

CAMPRA: #3, 49, 50, 53, 66.

CHAMBONNIÈRES: #55, 61-62.

COUPERIN: #31.

FARINEL: #16, 35, 38.

GAULTIER (Ennemond): #40.

GAULTIER (Pierre): #44.

HARDEL: #60.

LEBEGUE: #2, 4-15, 17-20, 22-23, 25-29.

LULLY: #34, 37, 52, 65.

MARCHAND: #1.

VERDIER: #42.

Contents:

#1-28   Copies from 64-Lebègue-I and 65-Lebègue-
             II, with spaces filled-in with miscel-
             laneous harpsichord pieces by hands B-C.

29-66   Miscellaneous harpsichord pieces, largely
             opera transcriptions.

Inventory (letters in parentheses indicate scribe):

	ℓ i-ii	[blank, unruled; see "Marginalia"]
1 (C)	ℓ 1r$^{1-3}$	Gauotte /M^r. Marchand [Louis? (g)]
2 (A)	ℓ 1v^1-2r^3	Courante /graue |Reprise [LEBEGUE (d)] CO: 13-Möllersche 64-Lebègue-I #3 [copy thereof] ED: cf Dufourcq-L p 3.
3 (C)	ℓ 2v^1-3r^2	Air des Masques [CAMPRA, arr: l'Europe galante (1697) IV-2 (d)]

4   ℓ $3v^1$-$4r^2$ Courante /gaye |R. [LEBEGUE (d)]
(A)   CO: 13-Möllersche
                       48-LaBarre-6 #26
                       64-Lebègue-I #4 [copy thereof]
              ED: cf Dufourcq-L p 3.

5   ℓ $4v^1$-$5r^3$ Sarabande |R [LEBEGUE (d)]
(A)   CO: 13-Möllersche
                       64-Lebègue-I #5 [copy thereof]
              ED: cf Dufourcq-L p 5.

6   ℓ $5v^{1-3}$ [LEBEGUE: <u>Gavotte</u> (d)]
(A)   CO: 13-Möllersche
                       64-Lebègue-I #6 [copy thereof]
              ED: cf Dufourcq-L p 6.

7   ℓ $6r^{1-3}$ Menuet [LEBEGUE (d)]
(A)   CO: 13-Möllersche
                       64-Lebègue-I #7 [copy thereof]
              ED: cf Dufourcq-L p 6.

8   ℓ $6v^1$-$7r^3$ Courante |Reprise [LEBEGUE (g)]
(A)   CO: 12-Walther
                       13-Möllersche
                       64-Lebègue-I #19
              ED: cf Dufourcq-L p 15.

9   ℓ $7v^{1-3}$ Gauotte |R. [LEBEGUE (D)]
(A)   CO: 13-Möllersche
                       64-Lebègue-I #14 [copy thereof]
              ED: cf Dufourcq-L p 11.

10   ℓ $8r^{1-3}$ Gavotte |R [LEBEGUE (g)]
(A)   CO: 12-Walther
                       13-Möllersche
                       64-Lebègue-I #21
              ED: cf Dufourcq-L p 16.

11   ℓ $8v^1$-$9r^3$ Sarabande /graue [LEBEGUE (a)]
(A)   CO: 13-Möllersche
                       22a-Roper #12
                       64-Lebègue-I #32 [copy tnereof]
              ED: cf Dufourcq-L p 25.

12
 (A)
	ℓ 9v$^{1-3}$	Menuet |R [LEBEGUE (g)]
		 CO: 12-Walther
		     13-Möllersche
		     64-Lebègue-I #22 [copy thereof]
		 ED: cf Dufourcq-L p 17
		
		 [2 ℓ lacking (originally?)]

13
 (A)
	ℓ 10r$^{1-3}$	Menuet |R |1 fois. |2 fois [LEBEGUE (G)]
		 CO: 12-Walther
		     13-Möllersche
		     64-Lebègue-I #27 [copy thereof]
		 ED: cf Dufourcq-L p 21.

14 (A)	ℓ 10v^{1}-12r^{1}	Passacaille /du 2me, [LEBEGUE (g)] CO: 14-Schwerin-619 #7 65-Lebègue-II #12 [copy thereof] ED: cf Dufourcq-L p 58.
15 (A)	ℓ 11v^{1}	Courante [LEBEGUE; beginning only (a)] CO: 13-Möllersche 64-Lebègue-I #31 [copy thereof] ED: cf Dufourcq-L p 25.

16 (B) (C)	[FARINEL, arr: Menuet (D)] Menuet /Monsr farinel ℓ 12r$^{2-3}$ $^{3}[\frac{3}{4}]$|8|16|

17 (A)	ℓ 12v$^{1-3}$	Menuet /du 2 |R [LEBEGUE (g)] CO: 14-Schwerin-619 #8 65-Lebègue-II #13 [copy thereof] ED: cf Dufourcq-L p 60.
18 (A)	ℓ 13r$^{1-3}$	Gavotte /du 2 |R [LEBEGUE (g)] CO: 14-Schwerin-619 #9 65-Lebègue-II #14 [copy thereof] ED: cf Dufourcq-L p 60.

19　ℓ 13v^1-3　Menuet /du 2me [LEBÈGUE (B♭)]
(A)
　　　　　　CO: 14-Schwerin-619 #11
　　　　　　　　65-Lebègue-II #16 [copy thereof]
　　　　　　ED: cf Dufourcq-L p 61.

20　ℓ 14r^1-3　Gavotte /du 2 |R [LEBÈGUE (a)]
(A)
　　　　　　CO: 14-Schwerin-619 #14
　　　　　　　　65-Lebègue-II #20 [copy thereof]
　　　　　　ED: cf Dufourcq-L p 64.

21　[Canarie (C)]
(C)　Canarie
　　　ℓ 14v^1-3　　　　　　　　C^6_4 |4|12|

22　ℓ 15r^1-3　Gauotte |R [LEBÈGUE (C)]
(A)
　　　　　　CO: 10-Schwerin-617 #10
　　　　　　　　13-Möllersche
　　　　　　　　14-Schwerin-619 #91
　　　　　　　　21-Rés-1186bis #12
　　　　　　　　23-Tenbury #6
　　　　　　　　24-Babell #60
　　　　　　　　30-Cecilia ℓ 47r
　　　　　　　　35-Bauyn-III #54
　　　　　　　　36-Parville #68
　　　　　　　　46-Menetou #102
　　　　　　　　50-Paignon #11
　　　　　　　　64-Lebègue-I #43 [copy thereof]
　　　　　　ED: cf Dufourcq-L p 38, Brunold/Dart-Co
　　　　　　　　#132.

23　ℓ 15v^1-16r^1　Sarabande /for grave /de 2me [LEBÈGUE (A)]
(A)
　　　　　　CO: 14-Schwerin-619 #18
　　　　　　　　65-Lebègue-II #24 [copy thereof]
　　　　　　ED: cf Dufourcq-L p 68.

24
(C)
[Menuet (d)]
Menuet
ℓ 16r$^{2-3}$ C$\frac{3}{4}$|8|8|

25
(A)
ℓ 16v$^{1-3}$ Menuet /du 2me ([hand C:] /de M^r Le Begue)
                     [F]
                     CO: 14-Schwerin-619 #23
                         24-Babell #8
                         65-Lebègue-II #33 [copy thereof]
                     ED: cf Dufourcq-L p 75.

26
(A)
ℓ 17r$^{1-3}$ Bourrée /du i |R [LEBEGUE (C)]
                     CO: 13-Möllersche
                         22a-Roper #5
                         64-Lebègue-I #41 [copy thereof]
                     ED: cf Dufourcq-L p 35.

27
(A)
ℓ 17v^1-18r^2 Air de /haubois [LEBEGUE (G)]
                     CO: 14-Schwerin-618 #26
                         65-Lebègue-II #42 [copy thereof]
                     ED: cf Dufourcq-L p 88.

28
(A)
ℓ 18v$^{1-3}$ Bourrée |R [LEBEGUE (G)]
                     CO: 12-Walther
                         13-Möllersche
                         22a-Roper #21
                         23-Tenbury #41
                         24-Babell #85
                         64-Lebègue-I #25 [copy thereof]
                     ED: cf Dufourcq-L p 19.

29
(A)
ℓ 18v^3-19v^1 Menuet |tournée |2me fois [LEBEGUE (G)]
                     CO: 12-Walther
                         13-Möllersche
                         23-Tenbury #42
                         24-Babell #86
                         64-Lebègue-I #26 [copy thereof]
                     ED: Dufourcq-L p 20.

30
(A)

[Prélude (d)]
[untitled]
ℓ 19v[2-3]

|-|

31
(B[1])

[COUPERIN: Chaconne (G)]
Chacone de /Monsr Couperin
ℓ 20r[1]-21v[1]

$\frac{3}{4}$|5|5|[etc]   [$\frac{3}{4}$|5| x 12]

CO: cf 46-Menetou #95, chaconne [same theme]
ED: Dart-Co App III.

32
(C)

[Menuet (D)]
Menuet |Rep
ℓ 21v[2-3]

C$\frac{3}{4}$|8|8|

33 [<u>Menuet</u> (F)]

(B) Menuet

ℓ 22r$^{1-3}$ ^{3}[$\frac{3}{3}$] |8|12|

34 [<u>LULLY</u>, arr: <u>La Mariée</u> from <u>Roland</u> (1685) (unlocated)

(B) (G)]

La /Mariée

ℓ 22v^1-23r^2 ^{2}[$\frac{4}{4}$] |14|12|

CO: cf 14-Schwerin-619 #62, La Mariee De Roland
    cf 22a-Roper #19, Air de l'opera
    cf 36-Parville #122, La Mariée
    cf 45-Dart #65, la marie de rolant

35 [<u>FARINEL</u>, arr: <u>Menuet</u> (G)]

(B) Menuet de farinelly

ℓ 23v^2-24r^1 ^{3}[$\frac{3}{4}$] |8|16|

36   [<u>Menuet</u> (C)]
(B)   [untitled]
     ℓ 24r$^{2-3}$ $^3[^3_4]$ |8|8|

37   [LULLY, arr: <u>Air</u> from <u>Acis</u> <u>et</u> <u>Galathée</u> (1686) Prologue
     (C)]

Rigodon de /Galateé
     ℓ 24v^1-25r^1 ^{C}|4|6|2|4|

CO: cf 22a-Roper #51, 53, La Rigaudoe, Le Rigodon
     cf 36-Parville #67, Rigaudon
     cf 44-LaPierre p 14, 25A, Rigaudon

ED: cf Curtis-Co #32.

38   [FARINEL: <u>Menuet</u> <u>on</u> <u>va</u> <u>mourir</u> (d)]
(B) Menuet /on va [?] mourir /de farinelly
     ℓ 25r$^{2-3}$ $^3_4$|8|8|

39 [d'ANGLEBERT: <u>Chaconne</u> (incomplete) (C)]
(B) Chacone
       ℓ 25v¹⁻³   ³|4|4|[etc] [³/₄|4| x 6]

CO: 24-Babell #204, Chaconne
     33-Rés-89ter #7, Chaconne. D'Anglebert
     36-Parville #65, Chaconne Danglebert
     51-LaBarre-11 p 212, Chaconne de Mr D'anglebert
     51-LaBarre-11 p 229, Chaconne D'Anglebert
ED: cf Gilbert p 160, Roesgen-Champion p 148.

[2 ℓ lacking]

40 [GAULTIER (E), **arr:** <u>Courante</u> l'immortelle (g)]
(B) L'imorte/lé
       ℓ 26r¹-v¹   ³[³/₄] |11|15|

CO: cf 24-Babell #226, Courante L'immortelle
     cf 33-Rés-89ter #29, Courante du Vieux Gautier.
                          L'Immortelle.
     cf 66-Perrine #1, l'jmmortelle du vieux Gaultier
     cf Stockholm-176 ℓ 4v, L'Immortelle Courante du V.
                          Gautier
     cf Skara #20,   Courant Monsr Gautier
     cf Stockholm-2 p 32, Courant immortele de Mons:
                          Gautie
     cf Ottobeuren p 142, L'Immortelle Courrante de
                          Suitte du mesme
ED: cf Gilbert p 182, Souris-G #81, Souris-G #66.

41
(C)

[<u>Menuet</u> (C)]

Menuet | segue

ℓ 26v²⁻³   C 3/4 | 8 | 8 |

41a
(C)

[<u>Double</u> (C)]

Double

ℓ 27r¹⁻²   C 3/4 | 8 | 8 |

42
(A)

[VERDIER (?): <u>Chaconne</u> (C)]

Chaconne / de Mʳ Verdre | 2 | Suitte | fin

ℓ 27v¹-30r¹   3 | 8 | 8 | [etc] [3/4 | 8 | x 9]

ED: Dart-HII #27

43
(A)

[Menuet (C)]

Menuet

ℓ 29r^2-3

^{3}[$\frac{3}{4}$] |8|8|

44
(C)

[GAULTIER (P), arr: Les Plaisirs (g)]

les plaisirs de Gautier |fin

ℓ 29v^1-30r^1

C$\frac{3}{4}$ |9|22|

CO: cf 14-Schwerin-619 #54, Les plaisirs de Gautier
cf 14-Schwerin-619 #57, Les plaisirs de Gautier
cf 36-Parville #138, Les plesirs de Gautier
cf Gaultiér p 35, Les Plaisirs [for instruments]

45
(C)

[Gavotte (g)]

Gauotte

ℓ 30r^2-v^1

¢ |4|12|

46 [Menuet (a)]
(C) Menuet
      ℓ 30v¹-31r¹   C$\frac{3}{4}$|8|16|

47 [Menuet (a)]
(C) Menuet
      ℓ 31r²-v¹   C$\frac{3}{4}$|8|16|

48 [La Savoye (g)]
(C) La Sauoye
      ℓ 31v²-33r²   ¢|8|16|

49 [CAMPRA arr: Menuet from Europe galante (1697) I-1 (g)]
(C) Menuet
      ℓ 32r³-v¹   C$\frac{3}{4}$|8|8|

50
(C)

[CAMPRA, arr: <u>Menuet</u> from <u>Europe galante</u> (1697) I-1 (G)
Menuet

ℓ 32v[2-3]   C$\frac{3}{4}$|8|8|

51
(C)

[<u>Gigue</u> (a)]
Gigue

ℓ 33r[1]-v[3]   C$\frac{3}{4}$|17|30|

52
(C)

[LULLY, arr: <u>Premier</u> <u>Air</u> <u>pour</u> <u>les</u> <u>muses</u> from <u>Isis</u>
(1677) Prologue-3 (g)]
Entreè des muses

ℓ 34r[1-3]   ¢|8|10|

CO: cf 24-Babell #130, Entrée des muses
    cf 42-Vm7-6307-2 #6, Air du mesme opera
    cf 46-Menetou #61, vn berger charmant

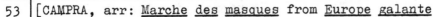

53
(C)
[CAMPRA, arr: <u>Marche</u> <u>des</u> <u>masques</u> from <u>Europe</u> <u>galante</u> (1697) IV-2 (D)]

Marche des Masques |1^r fois |2e fois
ℓ 34v^1-35r^1 ¢|8|16|

54
[<u>Prélude</u> (d)]

Prelude |fin
ℓ 35r$^{2-3}$ ¢|12|

55
(A)
[CHAMBONNIÈRES: <u>Sarabande</u> <u>jeunes</u> <u>zéphirs</u> (G)]

Sarabande /de chamboniere
ℓ 35v^1-36r^1 $^3[\frac{3}{4}]$|8|16|

CO: 5-Munich-1503ℓ #1, Sarrabande de Mons: Chambonnier
    32-Oldham #8, Sarabande de Monsieur de Chambon-
                  nieres
    33-Rés-89ter #36, Sarabande Chambonnieres ...
                  Double
    35-Bauyn-I #96, Sarabande de Mr de Chambonnieres
    36-Parville #93, Sarabande Chanbonniere
    44-LaPierre p 42, Les Zephirs de Mr de Chanboniere
    63-Chamb-II #29, Sarabande Jeunes Zephirs
    cf Philidor p 22, Jeunes Zephirs (de Mr de chan-

boniere) [for instruments]
ED: cf Brunold-Tessier #59, Dart-Ch #59, Gilbert p 194.

56	[Gavotte (c)]
(C)	Gauotte

ℓ 36r²-v¹   ¢ |4|8|

57	[Bourrée (c)]
(C)	vite /Bourée

ℓ 36v²⁻³   ¢ |8|8|

[1 ℓ lacking since before hand C wrote in book]

58	[Prélude (d)]
(A)	prelude

ℓ 37r¹⁻³ |-|

59
(A) [Les Folies d'Espagne (d)]
folies des/pagne |2me ... 5me
ℓ 37v^1-39v^3 ^{3}|16|16|[etc] [$\frac{3}{4}$|16| x 5]

60
(A) [HARDEL: Gavotte (a)]
Gauotte de /Monsr /Ardel
ℓ 40r$^{1-3}$ ¢|4|8|

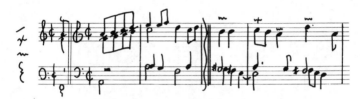

CO: 23-Tenbury #12, Gavotte Mr. Hardel
    24-Babell #159, Gavotte
    25-Bod-426 #20, Gavotte d'Ardelle
    31-Madrid-1360 #41, Jabouste de Ardel
    35-Bauyn-III #50, (Gauotte) de Mr Hardel
    36-Parville #52, Gauotte de Mr Hardel
    49-RésF-933 #13, gavotte d ardelle
    St-Georges ℓ 51, Gavotte
    cf Saizenay-I p 61, Gavotte Ardelle [lute]
    cf Saizenay-II p 17, Gavotte d'hardelle [lute]
    cf Vm7-4867 p 52, Gavotte d'ardelle [violin]
ED: cf Brunold/Dart-Co #131, Curtis-Co #11, Quittard-H p 1.

61
(A) [CHAMBONNIÈRES: Sarabande (d)]
Sabande de /Mon.^{r} Chambo/niere |R
ℓ 40v$^{1-3}$ ^{3}[$\frac{3}{4}$]|8|8|

62
(A)

[CHAMBONNIÈRES: Courante (d)]

Courante de |Chanboniere |R

    ℓ 41r$^{1-4}$ ^{3}[$\frac{3}{4}$]|6|7|

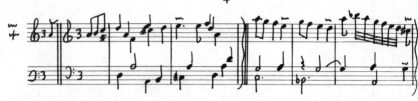

63
(A)
(C)

[Les Folies d'Espagne (d)]

([hand A:] folie de/pagne |1 |2) ([hand C:] 3 ... 6

|fin)

    ℓ 41v^{1}-43r^{3} ^{3}|16|16|[etc] [$\frac{3}{4}$|16| x 6]

64
(A)

[Rondeau (C)]

Rondeau

    ℓ 43v$^{1-3}$ ^{3}[$\frac{3}{4}$]|8|5|4|

65   [LULLY, arr: <u>La Mariée</u> from <u>Roland</u> (1685) (unlocated)
(C) (G)]

la mariè de rolant |fin
  ℓ 44r$^{1-3}$ ¢|14|12|

CO: cf 14-Schwerin-619 #62, La Mariee De Roland
    cf 22a-Roper #19, Air de L'opera
    cf 36-Parville #122, La Mariée
    cf 45-Dart #34, La Mariée

66   [CAMPRA, arr: <u>Air en rondeau</u> from <u>Europe galante</u> (1697)
(C) II-3 (g)]

Air |Rondeau |fin
  ℓ 44v$^{1-3}$ ¢|7|6|6|

67   [Anon, arr: <u>Rigaudon</u> (g)]
(C) Rigaudon de la marine
  ℓ 45r$^{1-3}$ ¢|8|12|

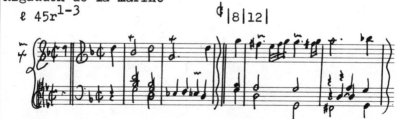

CO: cf 22a-Roper #30, Rigaudon [d]
    cf 36-Parville #113, Riguaudon
    cf 44-LaPierre p 59A, Rigaudon des Veissaux
    cf 48-LaBarre-6 #27, Rigaudon [d]

ℓ 45v   [chart of fingerings:] A corso pour La
               Basse de violle

               [1 ℓ lacking]

Provenance: Paris, post ca. 1689 (<u>Airs</u> <u>de</u> <u>mademoiselle</u>
Menetou).

Location: Berkeley, California; University of California,
Music Library, MS 777.

Description: 86 ℓ. (ℓ. 52v-86v duplicated with reverse
numeration: 1A-35A); 22 quires in 4 (except L^2);
oblong quarto format, 18.5 x 26 cm. Full leather
contemporary binding, gilt-tooled spine, 19.2 x 28.3
cm.

Notation: Keyboard score (two 5-line staves, 3 systems
per page, written page by page). Clefs: F^3, G^2, C^1.

Scribes: 2-3 hands:

A: #1-4

A^1: 5-113 (same as A?)

B: 114-118 (hand of La Barre?; the same as hand A
of 48-LaBarre-6 and 51-LaBarre-11; and
hand I of 36-Parville)

Marginalia: Modern pencil numeration by ℓ.; originally,
the modern back of the volume (#83-118) was considered
the front (notation in original ink inside that cover,
"Livre 4e."). Also inside that cover, red crayon
number, 1206. Inside modern front cover: miscellaneous
writing in contemporary hands, "Jay 6I coquille [re-
peated]... Jay ché m' de goit 435# ... [another hand:]
qu il me fete la grasse de me garder /Bertet." Some
pieces marked with "x" marks (copyist's marks?).

Summary:

Composers:

d'ANGLEBERT: #117.

LAMBERT: #71.

LEBÈGUE: #102.

137

LULLY: #1-6, 8-10, 13-18, 20-24, 27-33, 35-40, 42-53,
        56-61, 64-65, 69, 70, 73-74, 83, 85, 87, 89-
        94, 96, 101, 104, 107, 112-118.

MENETOU: #77-82.

Contents:

#1-11   Transcriptions, largely from Phaéton.

13-24   Transcriptions, largely from Amadis.

27-38   Transcriptions, largely from Roland.

40-56   Transcriptions, largely from Temple de la
          paix, Idylle sur la paix.

57-60   Transcriptions from Armide.

63-82   Vocal music.

83-118   Miscellaneous transcriptions and 1 piece
          by LEBEGUE.

(omitted numbers indicate miscellaneous pieces.)

Inventory:

1   [LULLY, arr: Ouverture from Phaéton (1683) (C)]
    Ouuerture /de phaeton |Reprise /2 fois /Lenetement
    | 2 fois
      ℓ 1r^1-2r^3 ^{2}[$^4_4$]|17|33|

    CO: cf 14-Schwerin-619 #77, Ouverture De Phaëton

2 | [LULLY, arr: <u>Rondeau</u> from <u>Phaéton</u> (1683) I-7 (C)]
Gauotte |Reprise |2e Reprise |Double |Premiere Reprise
|seconde Reprise |fin

ℓ $2v^1$-$3r^3$ $^2|4|4|$[etc] $[\frac{4}{4}|44|]$

3 | [LULLY, arr: <u>Le Plaisir est necessaire</u> from <u>Phaéton</u>
(1683) I-7 (C)]
Gauotte [text, between staves:] Le plaisir est nece-
ssaire ... |Reprise ... |Double |Reprise

ℓ $3v^{1-3}$ $^2[\frac{4}{4}]|5|5|5|5|$

4 | [LULLY, arr: <u>Dans ce palais</u> from <u>Phaéton</u> (1683) IV-1
(g)]
[text between staves:] Dans Ce palais brauez l'enuie...

ℓ $4r^{1-3}$ $^3[\frac{3}{4}]|8|16|$

5 | [LULLY, arr: <u>Cherchons</u> <u>la</u> <u>paix</u> from <u>Phaéton</u> (1683)
Prologue (C)]
[text between staves:] Cherhons la paix dans cet
azille ...
    ℓ 4v$^{1-3}$ ^{3}|8|15| [$^3_4$|8|16|]

6 | [LULLY, arr: <u>Troupe</u> d'<u>Astrée</u> <u>danante</u> from <u>Phaéton</u>
(1683) Prologue (C)]
[untitled]
    ℓ 5r$^{1-3}$ ^{3}[$^3_4$]|8|16|

7 | [<u>J'ay</u> <u>pour</u> <u>tous</u> <u>bien</u> <u>une</u> <u>musette</u> (C)]
[text between staves:] Jay pour tous bien vne musette
...
    ℓ 5v$^{1-2}$ ^{3}[$^3_4$]|8|8|

8 [LULLY, arr: <u>Dans ces lieux</u> from <u>Phaéton</u> (1683) Prologue (a)]
[text between staves:] Dans ces Lieux tout rit sans
cesse ...
    ℓ 6r$^{1-2}$ ^{3}[$\frac{3}{4}$] |8|8|

9 [LULLY, arr: <u>Chaconne</u> from <u>Phaéton</u> (1683) II-5 (G)]
chaconne,
    ℓ 6v^1-9r^2 ^{3}[$\frac{3}{4}$] |153|

CO: cf 14-Schwerin-619 #61, Chaconne de Phäeton
    cf 24-Babell #263, Chaconne de Phaéton
    cf 43-Gen-2354 #1, Chaconne de phaEton
    cf 44-LaPierre p 24, 45A, Chaconne de Phaéton
    cf 68-d'Anglebert #15, Chaconne de Phaeton Mr de
                          Lully
ED: cf Gilbert p 100, Roesgen-Champion p 30.

10 [LULLY, arr: <u>Plaisirs venez sans crainte</u> from <u>Phaéton</u>
(1683) Prologue (C)]
Bourrée[text between staves:] Plaisir venez ...
    ℓ 9v$^{1-3}$ ^{2}[$\frac{4}{4}$] |8|8|

11 | [Menuet (c)]
Menuet /en c /sol vt /bemol
  ℓ 10r$^{1-3}$ ^{3}[$^3_4$]|8|8|8|

12 | [Chaconne (C)]
Chaconne en c sol vt 1683 [i e Phaéton?] |suitte
  ℓ 10v^1-11v^2 ^{3}|6|6|[etc] [$^3_4$|181|]]

13 | [LULLY, arr: Ouverture from Amadis (1684) (g)]
Ouuerture /d'amadis 1684
  ℓ 11v^2-12r^3 ^{2}[$^4_4$]|31|

CO: cf Stoss ℓ 47v

14 | [LULLY, arr: <u>Suivons l'amour</u> from <u>Amadis</u> (1684) Pro-
logue (G)]

Menuet [text between staves:] Suiuons L'amour ...
ℓ 12v$^{1-2}$ ^{3}[$\frac{3}{4}$]|8|8|

CO: cf 42-Vm7-6307-2 #9, Menuet du mesme opera
cf 44-LaPierre p 23, 59A, Menuet D'Amadis
cf Copenhagen-396, Menuet Intavolat di Joh Laurent
ED: cf Lundgren #8.

15 | [LULLY, arr: <u>Coeurs accablez</u> from <u>Amadis</u> (1684) IV-6
(C)]

Menüet [text between staves:] Coeurs accablez ...
ℓ 13r$^{1-3}$ ^{3}[$\frac{3}{4}$]|8|13|

16 | [LULLY, arr: <u>Second Air, Les trompettes</u> from <u>Amadis</u>
(1684) II-4 (C)]

Les trompette
ℓ 13v^1-14r^1 ^{3}[$\frac{3}{4}$]|8|22|

17 [LULLY, arr: <u>Menuet</u> <u>pour</u> <u>les</u> <u>suivants</u> <u>d'Ugande</u> from <u>Amadis</u> (1684) IV-6 (G)]

Menuet

ℓ 14r¹⁻³   ³[¾]|7|17|

18 [LULLY, arr: <u>Prelude</u>, <u>Arcabonne</u> from <u>Amadis</u> (1684) II-1 (F)]

amour que veutu demoy

ℓ 14v¹⁻³   ¢|17|

19 [<u>De</u> <u>toutes</u> <u>les</u> <u>heures</u> (a)]

[text between staves:] De touttes les heures du jour il n'en est qu'vne pour ...

ℓ 15r¹⁻³   ³[¾]|15|14|

20 | [LULLY, arr: <u>Vous</u> <u>ne</u> <u>devez</u> <u>plus</u> <u>attendre</u> from <u>Amadis</u> (1684) II-7 (a)]

[text between staves:] vous ne deuez pas attendre...
ℓ 15v^{1}-16r^{1} $^{3}[\frac{3}{4}]$|6|30|

CO: cf 10-Schwerin-617 #19, Menuet
    cf 36-Parville #110, Trio d'Amadis vous ne devez...
    cf 46-Menetou #39, vous ne devez ...
    cf 42-Vm7-6307-2 #8, Menuet de Lopera d'amadis
    cf 49-RésF-933 #23, vous ne devés plus attendre

21 | [LULLY, arr: <u>Bois</u> <u>épais</u> from <u>Amadis</u> (1684) II-4 (F)]

[text between staves:] bois espais redouble ...
ℓ 16r$^{1-3}$ $^{2}[\frac{4}{4}]$|7|$[\frac{3}{4}]$2|^{2}1|10|

22 | [LULLY, arr: <u>Que</u> <u>l'incertitude</u> from <u>Phaéton</u> (1683) II-3 (C)]

[text between staves:] que lencertitude est vn ...
ℓ 16v$^{1-3}$ $^{3}[\frac{3}{4}]$|22|

23 | [LULLY, arr: <u>Marche</u> <u>pour</u> <u>le</u> <u>combat</u> <u>de</u> <u>la</u> <u>barrière</u> from
<u>Amadis</u> (1684) I-4 (C)]

Marche d'amadis en rondeau
ℓ 17r$^{1-3}$ $^2[^4_4]|8|8|10|$

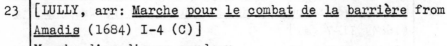

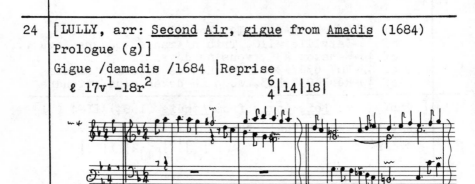

24 | [LULLY, arr: <u>Second</u> <u>Air</u>, <u>gigue</u> from <u>Amadis</u> (1684)
Prologue (g)]

Gigue /damadis /1684 |Reprise
ℓ 17v^1-18r^2 $^6_4|14|18|$

25 | [<u>Menuet</u> (d)]

menuet
ℓ 18r$^{2-3}$ $^3[^3_4]|8|12|$

26 | [Gavotte (a)]

Gauotte

ℓ 18v[1-2] $^2[\frac{4}{4}]$ |5|5|

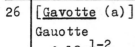

---

27 | [LULLY, arr: Ouverture from Roland (1685) (d)]

Ouuerture De Rolande furieux

ℓ 18v[2]-20r[3] $^2[\frac{4}{4}]$ |23| $^3[\frac{6}{4}]$ |21| $^2[\frac{4}{4}]$ |20|

CO: cf 14-Schwerin-619 #49, Ouverture de Roland
    cf 24-Babell #182, Ouuerture de Roland

---

28 | [LULLY, arr: C'est l'amour from Roland (1685) Prologue-2 (d)]

Gauotte [text between staves:] c'est lamour ...

ℓ 20v[1-3] $^2[\frac{4}{4}]$ |4|14|

CO: cf 24-Babell #183, Gavotte
    cf Stockholm-228 ℓ 9v, Aria 1 Francoise galand
    cf Lüneburg-1198 p 64, Air Rolande

29 | [LULLY, arr: <u>Gavotte</u> from <u>Roland</u> (1685) Prologue-2 (d)]

Gauotte

ℓ 21r¹⁻³ $^2[{}^4_4]|6|14|$

30 | [LULLY, arr: <u>Gigue</u> from <u>Roland</u> (1685) Prologue-2 (d)]

Gigue |premiere reprise |reprise |pr reprise |2 re-

prise

ℓ 21v¹-22r¹ ${}^6_4|11|13|$

31 | [LULLY, arr: <u>Entrée</u>, <u>gavotte</u> from <u>Roland</u> (1685) II-5

(a)]

Gauotte

ℓ 22r²⁻³ $^2[{}^4_4]|4|8|$

32 | [LULLY, arr: Le Marié, marche from Roland (1685) IV-3 (C)]

Marche /rondeau [text between staves:] quand on vient dans ce boccage ...

ℓ 22v^1-23r^1 $^3[^3_4]|6|30|$

33 | [LULLY, arr: J'entens un bruit, menuet from Roland (1685) IV-2,3 (C)]

Menuet /pour /les /hautbois

ℓ 23r^2-3 $[^3_4]|6|8|$

CO: cf 44-LaPierre p 40, menuet en Trio

34 | [Menuet (F)]

[untitled]

ℓ 23v^1-3 $^3[^3_4]|7|15|$

35 | [LULLY, arr: <u>Menuet</u> [2] from <u>Roland</u> (1685) Prologue-1 (F)]

Menuet

   ℓ 23v³-24r²   ³[¾]|6|6|8|

36 | [LULLY, arr: <u>Menuet</u> [1] from <u>Roland</u> (1685) Prologue-1 (F)]

menuet

   ℓ 24r²⁻³   [¾]|10|10|

37 | [LULLY, arr: <u>Menuet</u> from <u>Roland</u> (1685) IV-3 (C)]

menuet

   ℓ 24v¹⁻²   [¾]|8|12|

CO: cf 43-Gen-2354 #2, [untitled]

38 [LULLY, arr: <u>Qui gouste de ces eaux</u> from <u>Roland</u> (1685)
II-5 (a)]

trio

   ℓ 25r$^{1-3}$ $^2[^4_4]$|7|10|

39 [LULLY, arr: <u>Vous ne devez plus attendre</u> from <u>Amadis</u>
(1684) II-7 (g)]

vous nedeuez plus atandre

   ℓ 25v^1-26r^2 $^3[^3_4]$|6|30|

CO: cf 10-Schwerin-617 #19, Menuet
    cf 36-Parville #110, Trio d'Amadis vous ne devez...
    cf 42-Vm7-6307-2 #8, Menuet de Lopera d'amadis
    cf 46-Menetou #20, vous ne deuez pas attendre ...
    cf 49-RésF-933 #23, vous ne devés plus attendre

40 [LULLY, arr: <u>Preparons nous</u> from <u>Temple de la paix</u>
(1685) Prologue (a)]

premier air du tample delapaix [text between staves:]
preparons nous pour la feste nouuelle ...

   ℓ 26v$^{1-2}$ $^2[^4_4]$|14|

CO: cf 24-Babell #123, Preparons nous ... [g]

41 | [Aymez desormais (d)]
[text between staves:] aymez desormais sans crainte...
ℓ 27r$^{1-3}$ $^3[\frac{3}{4}]|6|12|$

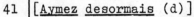

42 | [LULLY, arr: La Gloire luy suffit from Temple de la paix Prologue (a)]
[text between staves:] la gloire luy suffit ...
ℓ 27v$^{1-3}$ $^2[\frac{4}{4}]|9|_{[\frac{3}{4}]}12|$

43 | [LULLY, arr: Menuet from Temple de la paix (1685) Prologue (a)]
menuet
ℓ 28r$^{1-2}$ $^3[\frac{3}{4}]|8|8|$

44 | [LULLY, arr: <u>Gigue</u> from <u>Temple</u> <u>de</u> <u>la</u> <u>paix</u> (1685) Pro-
logue (a)]
Gigue
ℓ 28v^1-29r^2 $\frac{6}{8}$|11|16|

45 | [LULLY, arr: <u>Entrée</u> <u>de</u> <u>bergers</u> <u>et</u> <u>bergères</u> from <u>Temple</u>
<u>de</u> <u>la</u> <u>paix</u> (1685) Prologue (a)]
Entree des bergers Et bergerres
ℓ 29v$^{1-3}$ $^2[\frac{4}{4}]$|12|13|

46 | [LULLY, arr: <u>La</u> <u>Paix</u> <u>revient</u> from <u>Temple</u> <u>de</u> <u>la</u> <u>paix</u>
(1685) (C)]
[text between staves:] la paix reuient dans cet a-
zille ...
ℓ 30r$^{1-3}$ $^3[\frac{3}{4}]$|8|8|8|8|

47 | [LULLY, arr: <u>On conteroit plus tost</u> from <u>Temple de la paix</u> (1685) Prologue (C)]
[text between staves:] on conteroit plus tost ...
  ℓ 30v^{1}-31r^{1} $^{3}[\frac{3}{4}]$ |12|16|

48 | [LULLY, arr: <u>Canarie</u> from <u>Temple de la paix</u> (1685) (C)]
canaris
  ℓ 31r$^{1-3}$ $\frac{6}{8}$ |4|8|

49 | [LULLY, arr: <u>Passepied</u> from <u>Temple de la paix</u> (1685) (C)]
passepied
  ℓ 31v$^{1-2}$ $\frac{3}{8}$ |4|12|

50 | [LULLY, arr: <u>Menuet</u> from <u>Temple</u> <u>de</u> <u>la</u> <u>paix</u> (1685) (C)]

Menuet

ℓ 32¹⁻³ $^3[\frac{3}{4}]$|12|12|

---

51 | [LULLY, arr: <u>Suivons</u> <u>l'aimable</u> <u>paix</u> from <u>Temple</u> <u>de</u> <u>la</u>

<u>paix</u> (1685) (C)]

[text between staves:] Suiuons laimable paix ...

ℓ 32v¹⁻³ $\frac{4}{8}$|6|10|

---

52 | [LULLY, arr: <u>Suivons</u> <u>l'aimable</u> <u>paix</u> (2nd verse) from

<u>Temple</u> <u>de</u> <u>la</u> <u>paix</u> (1685) (C)]

trio [text between staves:] nous fuyons la beaute ...

ℓ 33r¹⁻³ $\frac{4}{8}$|6|10|

53 | [LULLY, arr: <u>Chantons</u> <u>bergers</u> from <u>Idylle</u> <u>sur</u> <u>la</u> <u>paix</u>
(1685) (d)]
lidil de seaux [text between staves:] chantons bergers
et nous resjouissons ...

ℓ 33v$^{1-3}$ ^{3}[$\frac{3}{4}$] |24|

54 | [<u>Sans</u> <u>crainte</u> <u>dans</u> <u>nos</u> <u>prairies</u> (a)]
[text between staves:] sans crainte ...

ℓ 34r$^{1-3}$ [$\frac{3}{4}$] |6|12|

55 | [<u>Charmant</u> <u>repos</u> (a)]
[text between staves:] charmant repos dune vie ... |fin

ℓ 34v$^{1-3}$ [$\frac{3}{4}$] |8|13|10|

56 | [LULLY, arr: <u>Ouverture</u> from <u>Temple</u> <u>de</u> <u>la</u> <u>paix</u> (1685) (a)]

Ouuertue Du Tample dela paix

   ℓ 35r^1-36r^2 ^{2}[$\frac{4}{4}$] |14|$\frac{6}{8}$27|^{2}6|

CO: cf 14-Schwerin-619 #68, Ouverture du Temple de La
                                paix
    cf 28-Brussels-926 ℓ 63v, Ouuerture

57 | [LULLY, arr: <u>Ouverture</u> from <u>Armide</u> (1686) (C)]

ouuerture darmide

   ℓ 36v^1-37r^3 ¢|10|$\frac{6}{4}$15|^2[$\frac{4}{4}$]10|

58 | [LULLY, arr: <u>Entrée</u> from <u>Armide</u> (1686) Prologue (C)]

Entree |pre fois |2 fois

   ℓ 37v$^{1-3}$ ^{2}[$\frac{4}{4}$] |10|10|

59 | [LULLY, arr: <u>Menuet</u> from <u>Armide</u> (1686) Prologue (C)]
menuet

ℓ 38r[1-2]   3[¾] |6|16|

---

60 | [LULLY, arr: <u>Gavotte, rondeau</u> from <u>Armide</u> (1686) Pro-
logue (C)]
Gauotte /rondeau |fin

ℓ 38v[1-3]   2[⁴₄] |16|

---

61 | [LULLY, arr: <u>Premier Air pour les muses</u> from <u>Isis</u>
(1677) Prologue-3 (g)]
vn berger /charmant

ℓ 39r[1-3]   ¢ |4|10|

CO: cf 24-Babell #130, Entrée des muses
    cf 42-Vm7-6307-2 #6, Air d'Isis
    cf 45-Dart #52, Entrée des muses

62 | [Les Plaisirs ont choisy pour azile (g)]
[text between staves:] les plaisirs ont choisy pour
azille ... |flutte |violons |flutte |violons
ℓ 39v^1-40r^3 $^3[{3 \atop 4}]$|13|8|25|16|16|

[#63-82: vocal pieces, some notated as
merely vocal melodies, some with figured
bass; all titles are texts between staves:]

63 | ℓ 40v^1-41r^2 Les oyseaux de ce bocage ...

64 | ℓ 41v$^{1-6}$ Prologue du /Triomph /de Lamour |vn heros
que le ciel ...

65 | ℓ 42r^1-42v^3 de phäeton /prothée |puis que vous my
forcés ...

66 | ℓ 42v^4-43r^3 çonsolés vous ...

67 | ℓ 43r^4-43v^3 Ses constantes rigeurs mont apris ...

68 | ℓ 43v^4-44r^2 cet heureuxJour doit nous charmer ...

69 | ℓ 44r^3-v^6 de cadmus |Quoy cadmus fils d'un roy ...
[1 ℓ lacking]

69a| ℓ 45r^1 Lentreprens en vain ... [end of scene
from Cadmus]

70 | ℓ 45r$^{2-4}$ airs |on a beau fuir ... [from Cadmus]

71 | ℓ 45r^5-v^3 Lambert |aimables bois

72 | ℓ 45v^4-46r^2 Lors que mon Iris me chagrine ...

73 | ℓ 46r^3-v^3 helas vne chaine si belle [LULLY, from
Phaéton V-7]

[1 ℓ lacking]

74   ℓ 47r^1-v^2 La Saison des frimats ... [LULLY, from <u>Atys</u> (1676) Prologue]

75   ℓ 47v^3-48r^2 Tristes honeurs gloire

76   ℓ 48r^3-v^2 gardés touts vn Silence ...

      ℓ 48v   airs Serieux de mademoiselle de menetou [#77-82]

77   ℓ 48v^3-49r^2 pour le /Roy |Je ne suis q'une bergere...

78   ℓ 49r^3-50r^1 pour le /Roy |Louis seul attaque par cent peuples divers ...

79   ℓ 50r^2-51r^1 Pour monseigneur |plus jeune qu'alexandre

80   ℓ 51r^2-v^1 ah Si vous sçauiez mes compagnes ...

81   ℓ 51v^2-52r^1 auprés de vous je Souffrois chaque jour...

82   ℓ 52r$^{2-3}$ quoy déja petite bergere ... [continued on piece of paper attached]

      ℓ 52r   fin des airs de mademoiselle /de menetou

                     [ℓ 52v-86v are written from the back of the volume towards the middle:]

83   [LULLY, arr: <u>Ouverture</u> from <u>Les</u> <u>Fêtes</u> <u>de</u> <u>l'Amour</u> <u>et</u> <u>de</u> <u>Bacchus</u> (1672) (g)]
Ouuerture Des festes /debaccus /et de /lamour |2 fois |Repris |fin
      ℓ 1Ar^1-2Ar^3 $^2[{}^4_4]|13|{}^6_435|$

CO: cf 14-Schwerin-619 #52, Ouverture Des Festes ...

84 | [Jupiter (g)]
Jupiter |fin
   ℓ 2Av¹-3Ar¹   ²[4/4] |28|

85 | [LULLY, arr: Ouverture from Isis (1677) (g)]
Ouuerture de lopera Disis |Repris |fin
   ℓ 3Ar¹-4Ar³   ²[4/4]15|[3/4]60|

CO: cf 14-Schwerin-619 #51, Ouverture Disis
    cf 24-Babell #128, Ouverture D'Isis
    cf 33-Rés-89ter #42c, Ouuertuor d'Isis
    cf 36-Parville #42, Ouuerture disis
    cf 40-Rés-476 #35, Louuerture /d'Isis
    cf 42-Vm7-6307-2 #5, Ouuerture de Lopera disis
    cf 49-RésF-933 #24, Ouuerture d isis
    cf Stoss ℓ 24v

ED: cf Bonfils-LP p 101, Howell #2, Gilbert p 199.

86 | [Menuet (g)]
[untitled]
   ℓ 4Av¹⁻³   ³[3/4] |12|16|

87 [LULLY, arr: <u>Ouverture</u> from <u>Bellérophon</u> (1679) (C)]

Entree /de Bellerophon |Repris

ℓ 5Ar¹-6Ar²   ¢|14|26|

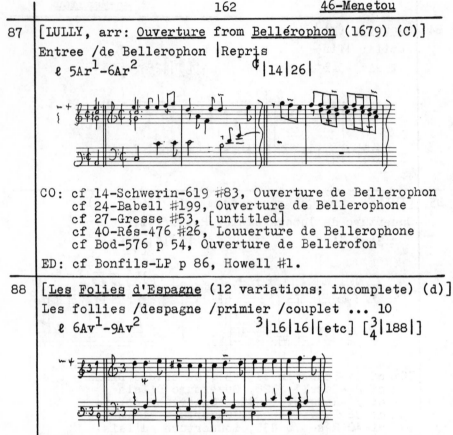

CO: cf 14-Schwerin-619 #83, Ouverture de Bellerophon
    cf 24-Babell #199, Ouverture de Bellerophone
    cf 27-Gresse #53, [untitled]
    cf 40-Rés-476 #26, Louuerture de Bellerophone
    cf Bod-576 p 54, Ouverture de Bellerofon

ED: cf Bonfils-LP p 86, Howell #1.

88 [<u>Les</u> <u>Folies</u> <u>d'Espagne</u> (12 variations; incomplete) (d)]

Les follies /despagne /primier /couplet ... 10

ℓ 6Av¹-9Av²   ³|16|16|[etc] [³/₄|188|]

ℓ 10Ar   [blank, ruled]

89 [LULLY, arr: <u>Trompettes</u> from <u>Bellérophon</u> (1679) V-3
    (C)]

trompette de bellerophon /rondeau

ℓ 10Av¹⁻³   ³[³/₄]|10|12|12|

90 | [LULLY, arr: <u>Marche</u> <u>des</u> <u>Amazones</u> from <u>Bellérophon</u>
(1679) I-5 (C)]

trompette debellerrophon /rondeau |fin

ℓ 11Ar$^{1-3}$ $^{3}[\frac{3}{4}]|8|9|8|$

CO: cf 14-Schwerin-619 #122, Marche

91 | [LULLY, arr: <u>Le</u> <u>Malheur</u> from <u>Bellérophon</u> (1679) III-5
(G)]

Gauotte

ℓ 11Av$^{1-3}$ $^{2}[\frac{4}{4}]|4|10|$

92 | [LULLY, arr: <u>Ouverture</u> from <u>Proserpine</u> (1680) (d)]

entree Deprosperine |fin

ℓ 12Ar^{1}-13Ar^{2} $\mathvarphi|11|^{6}_{4}22|^{C}13|$

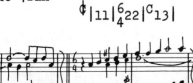

CO: cf 68-d'Anglebert #48, Ouuerture de Proserpine
ED: cf Gilbert p 92, Roesgen-Champion p 90.

93 | [LULLY, Second Air from Proserpine (1680) II-8 (a)]
bellefleur charmante onbrage gauotte |entrio
   ℓ 13Av¹⁻³   ²|4|4|[etc] [⁴₄|4| x 8]

94 | [LULLY, arr: Ouverture from Le Triomphe de l'amour
(1681) (F)]
Ouuerture /delopera /dutrion/phe delamour
   ℓ 14Ar¹-15Ar³   ²[⁴₄]|14|⁶₄30|²13|

CO: cf 14-Schwerin-619 #84, Ouverture du Triomp de
                                      Lamour
     cf 24-Babell #231, Ouverture du Triomphe de L'A-
                                      mour

95 | [Chaconne (G)]
chaconne
   ℓ 15Av¹-16r¹   ³|5|5|[etc] [³₄|5| x 12]

CO: cf 45-Dart #31, Chaconne de Monsʳ Couperin [same
                                      theme]
ED: cf Dart-Co app III.

96 | [LULLY, arr: <u>Passacaille</u> from <u>Persée</u> (1682) V-8 (a)]
passacaille /de persee
ℓ 16Av[1]-18Ar[2] $^3[\frac{3}{4}]$ |99|

CO: cf 14-Schwerin-619 #67, Passacaille de persee

---

97 | [LULLY, arr: <u>Haubois</u> from <u>Persée</u> (1682) Prologue (a)]
passepied
ℓ 18Av[1-3] $^6_8[\frac{3}{8}]$ |10|22|

CO: cf 36-Parville #120, Passepied de Persée

---

98 | [LULLY, arr: <u>Ouverture</u> from <u>Persée</u> (1682) (a)]
Ouuerture /D Andromede |Reprise |fin
ℓ 19Ar[1]-20Ar[3] $^2[\frac{4}{4}]$ |18|26|

CO: cf 14-Schwerin-619 #66, Ouverture De Persëe
cf 24-Babell #152, Ouverture de Persée

99 | [LULLY, arr: Gigue from Persée (1682) IV-6 (D)]

Gigue /entrio

   ℓ 20Av^1-21Ar^2 $\frac{6}{8}$|9|15|

CO: cf 31-Madrid-1360 #38, Obra de Pensier [C]

---

100 | [LULLY, arr: Entrée d'Apollon from Le Triomphe de l'amour (g)]

entree /dappollon

   ℓ 21Av^1-22Ar^2 ¢|9|19|

CO: cf 14-Schwerin-619 #56, Ouverture dapollon du
                             Triomphe de Lamour
    cf 24-Babell #129, Entrée d'Apollon
    cf 30-Cecilia ℓ 52r, Dessante dopollon
    cf 36-Parville #43, Entree dapollon
    cf 68-d'Anglebert #35, Air d'Apollon du Triomphe
                           de l'Amour de Mr de Lully
    cf Stockholm-176 ℓ 14v, Entreé d'Apollon
    cf Saizenay-I p 222, Entrée d'Apollon [lute]

ED: cf Gilbert p 118, Roesgen-Champion p 64.

101 | [LULLY, arr: <u>Second</u> <u>Air</u>, <u>le</u> <u>printemps</u> from <u>Phaéton</u> (1683) IV-1 (g)]

menuet /dephaeton

ℓ 22Av[1-3]   ³[¾] |8|20|

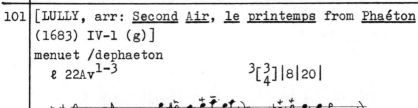

102 | [LEBÈGUE: <u>Gavotte</u> (C)]

[untitled] |fin

ℓ 23Ar[1-3]   ¢ |5|8|

CO: 10-Schwerin-617 #10, Gavotte
13-Möllersche, [copy of 64-Lebègue-I #43]
14-Schwerin-619 #91, Gavotte
21-Rés-1186bis #12, Gavott
23-Tenbury #6, Gavotte Mr Le Begue
24-Babell #60, Gavotte de Mr. le Begue
30-Cecilia ℓ 47r, Gavotte
35-Bauyn-III #54, (Gavotte) de Mr Lebegue
36-Parville #68, Gauotte Mr le Begue
45-Dart #22, [copy of 64-Lebègue-I #43]
50-Paignon #11, Balet de Mr lebegue
64-Lebègue-I #43, Gauotte

ED: cf Dufourcq-L p 38, Brunold/Dart-Co #132.

103 | [Tranquil Coeur (F)]
tranquil /coeur
ℓ 23Av$^{1-3}$

$^{3}[\frac{3}{4}]$|13|14|

104 | [LULLY, arr: Deuxiesme Menuet pour les graces from
Le Triomphe de l'amour (1681) (F)]
menuet du tronphe delamour
ℓ 24Ar$^{1-3}$

$^{3}[\frac{3}{4}]$|8|16|

105 | [Gavotte (g)]
gauotte |1re fois |2 fois
ℓ 24Av$^{1-3}$

¢|4|8|

106 | [Gavotte (A)]
[untitled]
  ℓ 25Ar¹⁻³

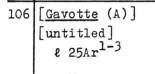

---

107 | [LULLY, arr: Premier Air, le printemps from Phaéton
(1683) IV-1 (g)]
le praintemps /dephaeton |1 fois |2 fois |derniere
fois
  ℓ 25Av^1-26Ar^3 $^2[{4 \atop 4}]$|11|19|

CO: cf 24-Babell #120, Air pr Le Printemps

---

108 | [La Guerre, les fiffres, les tambours en rondeau (C)]
la guerre |2 fois |3 fois |3 fois |3 fois |les fiffres
|reprise |les tambours rondeau |reprise |autre re-
prise |R
  ℓ 26Av^1-27Ar^2 ^{2}|4|1|1|[etc] $[{4 \atop 4}$|45|]

109 [Menuet (d)]

menuet
ℓ 27Ar²⁻³

³[3/4]|8|12|

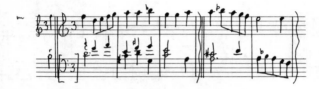

110 [Les Olivettes (F)]

les olliuette
ℓ 27Av¹⁻³

¢|8|11|

111 [Menuet (d)]

menuet
ℓ 28Ar¹⁻³

³[3/4]|8|16|

112 [LULLY, arr: <u>Gavotte</u> <u>pour</u> <u>Orithie</u> <u>et</u> <u>ses</u> <u>nymphes</u> from
<u>Le</u> <u>Triomphe</u> <u>de</u> <u>l'amour</u> (1681) (g)]

gauotte
ℓ 28Av$^{1-3}$ $^{2}[\frac{4}{4}]$|5|9|

CO: cf 24-Babell #133, Gavotte d'Orithie

113 [LULLY, arr: <u>Ouverture</u> from <u>Alceste</u> (1674) (a)]

Ouuerture d Alceste |reprise
ℓ 29Ar^{1}-30Ar^{3} ₵|12|$^{3}[\frac{6}{4}]$|21|$^{2}[\frac{4}{4}]$9|

CO: cf 40-Rés-476 #39, Louuerture de l'opera d'alceste
ED: cf Bonfils-LP p 105, Howell #6.

114 [LULLY, arr: <u>Les</u> <u>Songes</u> <u>agréables</u> from <u>Atys</u> (1676)
III-4 (g)]

Les Songes agreables d'atis |1ere fois |2e fois |Re-
prise
ℓ 30Av^{1}-31Ar^{2} $^{3}[\frac{3}{4}]$|10|20|

CO: cf 14-Schwerin-619 #53, Songes Agreables Datis

cf 24-Babell #131, Les Songes Agreables
cf 33-Rés-89ter #43, Air de Ballet, les Songes
              agreables
cf 36-Parville #117, Les Songes agreables d'Atys
cf 68-d'Anglebert #34, Les Songes agreables d'Atys...
ED: cf Gilbert p 116, Roesgen-Champion p 63.

115 | [LULLY, arr: <u>Les Songes funestes</u> from <u>Atys</u> (1676)
III-4 (B♭)]

Les Songes funeste d'atis |Suitte |1er fois |2^e fois
|Reprise

   ℓ 31Ar^3-32Ar^1 $[^6_4]$|10|13|

CO: cf 14-Schwerin-619 #86, 2 Air des Songes funestes

116 | [LULLY, arr: <u>Chaconne</u> from <u>Ballet des Muses</u> (1666)
II-2 (G)]

Pleurs d'atis |Suitte |1er fois |2^e fois |fin
   ℓ 32Ar^2-v^2 $^3[^3_4]$|29|

CO: cf 14-Schwerin-619 #111, chaconne
   cf 36-Parville #116, Air des Sorciers [B♭]
   cf 50-Paignon #12, Chaconne des magitions [C]
   cf Minorite ℓ 50r

117 [LULLY, arr d'ANGLEBERT: <u>Courante</u> (g)]
Courante de M^r de lully |1er fois |R 2e fois |Suitte
ℓ 33Ar^1-v^2 ^{3}[$^6_4$]|9|7|

CO: 33-Rés-89ter #42d, Courante
    36-Parville #41, Courante de Mr Lully
    68-d'Anglebert #21, Courante Mr de Lully
ED: cf Gilbert p 95, 96; Roesgen-Champión p 42.

118 [LULLY, arr: <u>Ouverture</u> from <u>La Grotte de Versailles</u>
(g)]
La grotte de Versaille |Reprise
ℓ 34Ar^1-35Ar^3 ₵|10|[$^3_4$]32₵5|

CO: cf 14-Schwerin-619 #121, Ouverture de La Grotte
                              de Versaille
    cf 36-Parville #121, Ouuerture de la grotte de
                          Versailles
    cf 49-RésF-933 #3, Ouuerture de la Grote de Ver-
                        saille
    cf Minorite ℓ 44r, De Mr Baptiste de Lulli Ouuer-
                        ture La Grotte de Versaille
    cf Saizenay-I p 226, La Grotte de Versailles [lute]
ED: cf Strizich p 104.

[ℓ 35A is the final page of the first
section of the ms, numbered 52r above]

Provenance: Paris, ca. 1690?

Location: Paris; Bibliothèque Sainte Geneviève, MS 2356.

Description: 20 ℓ. (plus modern end papers; originally
   22 ℓ.: 2 ℓ. torn out); 1 quire; oblong quarto format,
   17.5 x 21.5 cm. Watermark #11 (same paper as 34-Gen-
   2357[a], but not same ruling of staves). Modern full
   cloth binding, 17.8 x 23.3 cm.

Notation: Keyboard score (two 5-line staves, 3 systems
   per page, written page by page). Clefs: $C^{1,3,4}$,
   $F^{3,4}$, G^2; usually F^3, G^2 (or F^3, C^1).

Scribes: 2-5 unidentified hands:
   A: #1
   B: 2-11
   C: 12-17 (same as B?)
   D: 18   (same as C?; similar to hand of 34-Gen-2357[a])
   E: ℓ. 19 (same as C?)

Marginalia: Original numeration by ℓ. starts on modern
   number 3-8 as "1-6"; modern numeration by ℓ. (main-
   tained in Inventory below) in red ink. Miscellaneous
   modern library markings and explanations, passim.

Summary:
   Composers:
      BURETTE (Claude?): #10.
      CHAMBONNIÈRES: #2, 8, 12.
      COUPERIN (Louis): #1(?), 3-6.
      FROBERGER: #7.
      LULLY: #17.
      PINEL: #13.
      RICHARD: #9.

Contents:

Inventory:

1	ℓ 1r^1-2r^3	Morceau de Couperin [Louis?: <u>Carillon</u> (in-complete) (C)] [ℓ 1r was originally the top half of the same sheet as ℓ 2r; after the piece was written, the folio ℓ was ar-bitrarily cut in half through the music.]
	ℓ 1v, 2v	[blank; 1 ℓ lacking between them; visible on remaining stub is:] Journess

2 [CHAMBONNIÈRES: <u>Le</u> <u>Printemps</u> (a)]
Paschalia De M^r. Chambonniere |Il fault Repeter 2 fois cette fin |(Due tarde [?])qu'vne mire
  ℓ 3r$^{1-3}$ ^{3}[$^6_4$]|6|10|

CO: 32-Oldham #15, 15a, Le printemps
    36-Parville #145, Le Printems de Mr Chambonnieres
ED: Brunold-Tessier #142.

3 | [COUPERIN (L): <u>Allemande</u> (a)]

L'aimable allemande de Mr Couperin |Suitte |refrain pour La fin

    ℓ 3v^1-4r^2 ^{C}|9|9|1|

CO: 35-Bauyn-II #102, Allemande de Mr. Couperin
    36-Parville #47, ALLemande Couprin
    40-Rés-476 #29, Allemande

ED: Brunold/Dart-Co #102, Curtis-Co #2; cf Bonfils-LP
    p 94.

4 | [COUPERIN (L): <u>Courante la mignonne</u> (a)]

La mignone Du Mesme Mr Couperin

    ℓ 4v$^{1-3}$ ^{3}[$^6_4$]|6|8|1|

CO: 35-Bauyn-II #106, Courante de Mr Couperin
    36-Parville #48, Courante Couprin dit la mignonne
ED: Brunold/Dart-Co #106, Curtis-Co #3.

5 | [COUPERIN (L): <u>Allemande</u> (G)]

allemande Du mesme Mr Couperin

ℓ 5r[1-3]   C|9|9|

CO: 24-Babell #252, Allemande
    33-Rés-89ter #33, Allemande de Couperin ... Double
    35-Bauyn-II #82, Allemande du même Auteur
    36-Parville #88, Allemande Couprin

ED: Brunold/Dart-Co #82, Curtis-Co #86; cf Gilbert p 186.

6 | [COUPERIN (L): <u>Gigue</u> (d)]

Gigue de Monsr Couperin |Suitte

ℓ 5v[1]-6r[2]   2/3[6/4]|12|14|

CO: 35-Bauyn-II #123, Gigue de Monsr Couperin
    36-Parville #7, Gigue Couprain
    cf Roberday #8, Fugue ... Caprice [on this theme]

ED: Brunold/Dart-Co #123, cf 123bis; Curtis-Co #61.

	ℓ 6v	[blank, ruled]
7	ℓ 7r[1-3]	Sarabande [FROBERGER (a)]
		CO: 35-Bauyn-III #14
		ED: Adler-II p 81.
7a	ℓ 7r[3]-v[1]	Double [a]

8 | [CHAMBONNIERES: <u>Gigue la vetille (la coquette)</u> (a)]

Gigue de Mons.ʳ Chambonniere |Suitte |fin
ℓ 5v¹-6r²   ³[⁶₄]|14|10|

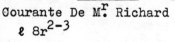

CO: 32-Oldham #28, La Vetille
    35-Bauyn-I #122, Gigue (la Coquette) de Mr de
                    Chambonnieres
ED: Brunold-Tessier #137.

9 | [RICHARD: <u>Courante</u> (a)]

Courante De M.ʳ Richard
ℓ 8r²⁻³   ³[⁶₄]|6|6|

ED: Bonfils-18 p 20.

9a | [RICHARD: <u>Double</u> (a)]

Double |Suitte |fin
ℓ 8r³-v¹   ³[⁶₄]|6|6|

ED: Bonfils-18 p 20.

10 | [BURETTE: Brusque (a)]

Brusque de M.r Bura. L aisné |fin

ℓ 8v2-3   [4/4] |8|12|8|

[1 ℓ lacking which was originally written on both sides.]

11 | ℓ 9r-10r   [plain chants in whole notes] aue maris stella |O salutaris hostia |Veni Creator |Kyrie |Et in terra pax |Sanctus |Agnus dei L'hymne de la natiuité de nostre seigneur |L'hymne des laudes A solis ortus Cardine & de l apiste des Roy /hostis herodes impie

---

12 | [CHAMBONNIÈRES: Courante Iris (C)]

Courante |Reprise

ℓ 10v1-11r1   3[6/4] |8|8|

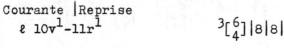

CO: 8-Hintze #15, Courante
    22a-Roper #58, Courante Chambonniere ... double
    23-Tenbury #3, (courante chambonii)
    24-Babell #58, Courante de Mr. de Chambonniere
    33-Rés-89ter #2, Courante. Chambonnieres... Double
    35-Bauyn-I #9, Courante de Mr De Chambonnieres
    36-Parville #61, Courante Chanbonniere
    44-LaPierre p 18, p 34A, Courante Chambonniere...Double
    53-Oldham-2 p 107, Courante de Chamboniere
    55-Redon #23, Courante de Monsieur de Chambonniere
    62-Chamb-I #8, Courante Iris

ED: cf Brunold-Tessier #8, Dart-Ch #8, Gilbert p 148.

13 | [PINEL, arr: <u>Sarabande</u> (C)]

Sarabande |2me. fois |Reprise

ℓ 11r²-v¹   ³[³/₄] |8|12|

CO: 35-Bauyn-III #90, Sarabande de M^r. Pinel
    36-Parville #64, Sarabande de Mr pignel
    cf 33-Rés-89ter #4, Sarabande Pinel ... Double

ED: cf Gilbert p 152.

14 | [<u>Ballet du Basque</u> (G)]

Ballet du Basque |Reprise |fin

ℓ 11v²-12r²   ¢ |8|12|

CO: 43-Gen-2354 #3 [untitled fragment]

15 | [<u>Sarabande</u> (G)]

Sarabande |Reprise |fin

ℓ 12r³-v¹   ³[³/₄] |8|8|

CO: 43-Gen-2354 #4 [untitled]

16 | [<u>Sarabande</u> (d)]
Sarabande |Reprise |fin
   ℓ 12v^2-13r^2 $^3[^3_4]$|8|8|

CO: 43-Gen-2354 #5 [untitled]

17 | [LULLY, arr: <u>Gavotte</u> from <u>Atys</u> (1676) IV-5 (C)]
Gauotte |Reprise |fin
   ℓ 13v$^{1-3}$ ¢|4|12|

CO: cf 39-Vm7-6307-1 #10, La beaute la plus seuere

18 | ℓ 14r-17r   [blank, ruled]
ℓ 17v^1-18r^2 [untitled piece for organ]
ℓ 18v   [blank, unruled]
ℓ 19r-v   pour apprendre la Composition ... [rules
                of counterpoint]
ℓ 20r-v   [blank, unruled]

<u>Provenance</u>: Paris, post 1697 (score of <u>L'Europe galante</u>).

<u>Location</u>: Berkeley, California; University of California, Music Library, MS 770.

<u>Description</u>: 424 p. (i.e., 404: 80-99 omitted in numeration); oblong quarto format, 19.5 x 25.5 cm. (trimmed), sprinkled edges. Watermark #26. Contemporary sprinkled vellum-covered binding, matching the La Barre group of mss; mutilated spine labels: "LEurop ... /Idylle sur la /Paix /Alceste /... &"; 20.7 x 27 cm.

<u>Notation</u>: Mixed vocal and keyboard scores. Keyboard score: two 5-line staves, 4 systems per page, written page by page. Clefs: C^1, G^2, F^3.

<u>Scribe</u>: One hand, probably that of the Berkeley La Barre. The same as I in 36-Parville, A in 51-LaBarre-11 and B in 46-Menetou.

<u>Marginalia</u>: Original numeration by pages.

<u>Summary</u>:
    Composers:
      BERTHET: #2-23.
      CAMPRA: #41.
      COLLASSE: #35.
      LEBÈGUE: #26, 36, 37, 39, 40.
      LULLY: #1, 23a, 32, 33, 35.
    Contents:

#1	Vocal score of <u>Idylle sur la paix</u>
2-23	Vocal score of motets by Berthlet
23a	Vocal score of <u>Alceste</u>
24-28	Suite (d)
29-34	Suite (C)
35-38	Suite (D/d)

	39-40	Harpsichord pieces (A, F)
	41	Vocal score of L'Europe galante

Inventory:

	p 1-2	[Blank, ruled]
1	p 1-48	IDYLLE: Sur La paix /avec L'egologue De Versailles /Mises en Musique /Par /Monsieur De Lully /EN /1685. [vocal score, with continuo]
	p 49	Motets de Mr Berthet [#2-23]
2	p 49^1-52^6	Motet pour le jour de Noel [text:] Cantate domino ...
3	p 52^7-54^2	Motet du J.S. Sacrement [text:] O sacramentum pietatis ...
4	p 54^3-55^4	Motet Du J.S. Sacrement [text:] O sacrum conuiuium ...
5	p 55^5-56^8	Motet Du J.S. Sacrement [text:] Bone Pastor ...
6	p 57^1-58^2	Motet Du J.S. Sacrement [text:] Tantum Ergo ...
7	p 58^3-59^8	Motet Du J.S. Sacrement [text:] Ego sum ...
8	p 60^{1-8}	Motet Du J.S. Sacrement [text:] Panis angelicus ...
9	p 61^1-63^2	Motet du J.S. Sacrement [text:] Venite populi ...
10	p 63^3-64^6	Elevation [text:] O Salutaris hostie ...
11	p 64^7-68^8	Motet a n-s-j-g [text:] Mihi adhaere domino ...
12	p 67^1-68^8	Motet du J.S. Sacrement [text:] Jesu jesu mitissime ...
13	p 69^1-70^2	Priere au St. Esprit [text:] Veni Sancte

Spiritus ...

14	p 70^4-71^2	Priere pour Le Roy [text:] Domine Saluum facregem ...
15	p 71^3-74^3	Motet po Le jour de Noel [text:] O admirabile Commercium ...
16	p 74^4-75^4	Priere po Le Roy [text:] Domine Saluum fac regem ...
17	p 75^5-76^8	Antiene a la Ste Vierge au temps de Pasque [text:] Regina coeli ...
18	p 77^{1-8}	Ant. a La Ste Vierge au temps de puis La purification jusqua pasques [text:] Ave Regina coelorum ...
19	p 78^{2-7}	Antiene a La Ste Vierge autemps de pasques [text:] Regina coeli ...
20	p 79^2-100^4	[i.e., p 79-80] Antiene a La Ste Vierge autemps de l'advent [text:] Alma Redemptoris mater ...
21	p 100^5-102^2	Motet po vne Vierge [text:] Veni, veni, veni sponsa christj ...
22	p 102^{3-8}	Ant. a St joseph [text:] Salue patriarcharum deus ...
23	p 103^1-104^2	2 Motet de St Joseph [text:] Constituit eum deus ...
	p 104	Fin des Mottets de Monsieur Berthet
23a	p 105-300	ALCESTE /Tragedie /Mise /En Musique /Par /Monsieur De Lully [vocal score, with continuo]
	p 301-329	[blank, ruled]

24 | [Prélude (d)]

Prélude En delaré
p 330[1-3]

CO: cf 64-Lebègue-I #1 [similar prelude]

ED: cf Dufourcq-L p 1.

---

25 | [Allemande (d)]

ALmande |Reprise
p 330[4]-331[4]   C|7|9|

---

26 | [LEBÈGUE: Courante (d)]

Courante |R
p 332[1-4]   3|10|9| [6/4|8|9|]

CO: 13-Möllersche [copy of 64-Lebègue-I #4]
    45-Dart #4 [copy of 64-Lebègue-I #4]
    64-Lebègue-I #4, Courante gaye

ED: cf Dufourcq-L p 3.

26a | [LEBEGUE: <u>Double</u> (d)]

Double |R
    p 333^{1-4} $^3[^6_4]$ |8|9|

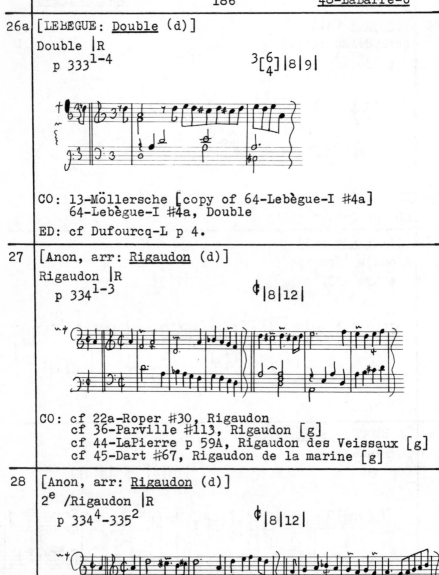

CO: 13-Möllersche [copy of 64-Lebègue-I #4a]
    64-Lebègue-I #4a, Double
ED: cf Dufourcq-L p 4.

27 | [Anon, arr: <u>Rigaudon</u> (d)]

Rigaudon |R
    p 334^{1-3}   ¢ |8|12|

CO: cf 22a-Roper #30, Rigaudon
    cf 36-Parville #113, Rigaudon [g]
    cf 44-LaPierre p 59A, Rigaudon des Veissaux [g]
    cf 45-Dart #67, Rigaudon de la marine [g]

28 | [Anon, arr: <u>Rigaudon</u> (d)]

2e /Rigaudon |R
    p 334^4-335^2   ¢ |8|12|

CO: cf 36-Parville #114, 2e Rigaudon [g]
    cf 44-LaPierre p 61A, Second Rigaudon [g]

29 | [Prélude (C)]

Prelude En C.Sol vt
   p 335³⁻⁴

30 | [Allemande (C)]

ALmande |R
   p 336¹⁻⁴

31 | [Sarabande (C)]

sarabande |R
   p 337¹⁻²

32 | [LULLY, arr: <u>Nostre Espoit alloit</u> from <u>Persée</u> (1682)
IV-6 (C)]
Menuet |R
p 337^{3-4} $[\frac{3}{4}]$ |8|10|

CO: cf Lüneburg-1198 p 69, Menuet [D]

33 | [LULLY, arr: <u>Entrée des Basques</u> from <u>Le Temple de</u>
<u>la paix</u> (1685) (C)]
Canary |R
p 338^{1-3} $[\frac{2}{2}]$ |8|14|

CO: cf 14-Schwerin-619 #76, Entree des Basques ...

34 | [<u>Menuet</u> (C)]
Menuet |R
p 338^{4}-339^{1} $^{3}[\frac{3}{4}]$ |8|8|

CO: 22a-Roper #29, Menuet

34a [Double (C)]

Double
   p 339²⁻³   ³[³/₄]|8|8|

CO: 22a-Roper #29a, double

---

35 [LULLY/COLLASSE, arr: Ouverture from Thétis et Pélée
   (1654) (D)]

Ouuerture de Thetis Et pellée |R
   p 340¹-341³   [²/₂]|12|⁶/₄15|₵11|

CO: cf 14-Schwerin-619 #42, Ouverture De Tetis Et
                              pelëe
    cf 23-Tenbury #17, Ouverture de Thetis Mr Colasse

---

36 [LEBÈGUE: Allemande (d)]

Allemande |R
   p 342¹⁻³   C|6|7|

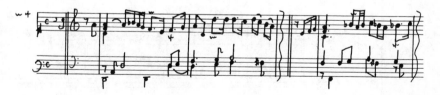

CO: 11-Ryge #10 [copy of 65-Lebègue-II #1]
    65-Lebègue-II #1, Allemande
ED: cf Dufourcq-L p 49, Bangert p 26.

37 | [LEBÈGUE: <u>Courante</u> (d)]

Courante |R
    p 343$^{1-4}$ $\frac{3}{2}$|8|11|

CO: 11-Ryge #11 [copy of 65-Lebègue-II #2]
     65-Lebègue-II #2, Courante
ED: cf Dufourcq-L p 50, Bangert p 26.

38 | [<u>Gigue</u> (d)]

Gigue |R |petitte reprise
    p 344$^{1-3}$ $^3[\frac{3}{4}]$|8|8|8|

CO: 44-LaPierre p 10, Gigue d'angleterre
     44-LaPierre p 16A, Gigue

39 | [LEBÈGUE: <u>Courante</u> (A)]

Courante En ami La ré # |R
    p 345$^{1-4}$ $^3[\frac{6}{4}]$|8|9|

CO: 14-Schwerin-619 #17 [copy of 65-Lebègue-II #23]
     65-Lebègue-II #23, Courante
ED: cf Dufourcq-L p 67.

40 | [LEBÈGUE: <u>Courante</u> (F)]

Courante |R

    p 346¹⁻⁴

CO: 65-Lebègue-II #29, Courante

ED: cf Dufourcq-L p 73.

41 | p 347-424   L'EUROPE /galante /Balet /Mis en Musique /En 1697 [CAMPRA] [vocal score with continuo]

Provenance: France (Paris?): post ca. 1715.

Location: Paris; Bibliothèque nationale, département de
la musique (fonds conservatoire), Réserve F 933
(olim Conservatoire de musique Réserve F 933).

Description: 2 p.ℓ., 40, 2 ℓ.; folio format, 38 x 24.4
cm. Watermarks: #28, 54. Contemporary full leather
binding, gilt-tooled spine, red leather label on
front cover: "PIECES /DE /CLAVECIN," 38.5 x 26.5 cm.

Notation: Keyboard score (two 5-line staves, 6 systems
per page, written page by page). Clefs: $F^{3,4}$, G^2.

Scribe: One unidentified hand.

Marginalia: Numeration by leaves in modern pencil.

Summary:
Composers:
BABELL (William): #27, 30.
CAMPRA: #8, 9, 18, 19.
COUPERIN (Louis): #13a.
DESTOUCHES: #26.
HARDEL: #13.
LULLY: #1-4, 7, 23, 24.
MARAIS (Roland): #34.
TELEMANN: #17.
Contents:
#1-26   Harpsichord pieces, largely opera
transcriptions
27-30   Harpsichord pieces by Babell
31-34   Miscellaneous harpsichord pieces

Inventory:
ℓ i-ii   [blank]

1 | ℓ 1r^1-2v^5 | Passacaille D'armide [LULLY (1686) V-2 (g)]

CO: cf 14-Schwerin-619 #63
    cf 24-Babell #138
    cf 31-Madrid-1360 #27
    cf 68-d'Anglebert #37
    cf Minorite ℓ 44v

ED: cf Gilbert p 108, Roesgen-Champion p 67.

[2 ℓ lacking]

2 | ℓ 3r$^{1-5}$ | Sourdines D'Armide [LULLY: Second air (sourdines) II-4 (1686) (g)]

CO: cf 14-Schwerin-619 #64
    cf 23-Tenbury #49
    cf 24-Babell #124
    cf 36-Parville #115, 149
    cf 68-d'Anglebert #33

ED: cf Gilbert p 115, Roesgen-Champion p 62.

3 | ℓ 3v$^{1-6}$ | Ouverture de la Grote de Versaille [LULLY (1668) (g)]

CO: cf 14-Schwerin-619 #121
    cf 36-Parville #121
    cf 46-Menetou #118
    cf Minorite ℓ 44r
    cf Saizenay-I p 226 [lute]

ED: cf Strizich p 104.

4 | ℓ 4r$^{1-6}$ | [LULLY, arr: Chaconne from Acis et Galathée (1686) II-5 (D)]

CO: cf 14-Schwerin-619 #123
    cf 23-Tenbury #75
    cf 24-Babell #97
    cf 36-Parville #29
    cf 51-LaBarre-11 p 206
    cf 68-d'Anglebert #55

ED: cf Gilbert p 106, Roesgen-Champion p 112.

5 | ℓ 4v^1-5r^2 | [untitled (A)]

ℓ 5v-6r | [blank, ruled]

6 | ℓ 6v^1-7r^4 menuet [with Double (G)]

   | ℓ 7v   [blank, ruled]

7 | ℓ 8r$^{1-6}$ Chaconne de Scaramouche [LULLY, arr:
   | Chaconne d'Arlequin from Le Carnaval
   | (1668) V (G)]

8 | ℓ 8v$^{1-2}$ 1^r menuet de l'europe galante [CAMPRA
   | (1697) Prologue (g)]

9 | ℓ 8v$^{2-4}$ 2^e menuet [CAMPRA, arr: from L'Europe
   | galante (1697) Prologue (G)]

10 | ℓ 8v$^{5-6}$ [untitled (a)]

11 | ℓ 9r$^{1-3}$ [Menuet (C)]

12 | ℓ 9r$^{3-6}$ 2^e menuet [C]

   | ℓ 9v   [blank, ruled]

13 | [HARDEL: Gavotte (a)]

gavotte d ardelle
    ℓ 10r$^{1-3}$ 2[$\frac{4}{4}$] |4|8|

CO: 23-Tenbury #12, Gavotte Mr. Hardel
    24-Babell #159, Gavotte
    25-Bod-426 #20, Gavotte d'Ardelle
    31-Madrid-1360 #41, Jabouste de Ardel
    35-Bauyn-III #50, (Gavotte) de Mr Hardel
    36-Parville #52, Gavotte de Mr Hardel
    45-Dart #60, Gauotte de Monsr Ardel
    St-Georges ℓ 51, Gavotte
    cf Saizenay-I p 61, Gavotte   Ardelle [lute]
    cf Saizenay-II p 17, Gavotte d'hardelle [lute]
    cf Vm7-4867 p 52, Gavotte d'ardelle [violin]
ED: cf Brunold/Dart-Co #131, Curtis-Co #11,
    Quittard-H p 1.

13a | [COUPERIN (L): Double (a)]

[untitled]
ℓ 10r[4-6] $^2[{}^4_4]|4|8|$

CO: 23-Tenbury #12a, Double
24-Babell #159a, Double
31-Madrid-1360 #41a [Double]
35-Bauyn-III #50a, Double (de la gauotte) cy
                  dessus Par Mr Couperin
36-Parville #52a, Double de la gauotte fait par
                  Mr Couprin
cf Vm7-4867 p 77, Double [violin]

ED: cf Brunold/Dart-Co #131[a], Curtis-Co #11a, Quittard-H p 2.

---

14 | ℓ 10v[1-3]   menuets [a]

15 | ℓ 10v[4-6]   [Menuet (a)]

16 | ℓ 11r[1-4]   Air Anglois [La Furstenburg (Air ancien)
(g)]

CO: cf 24-Babell #79
    cf 42-Vm7-6307-2 #2

ℓ 11v-12r   [blank, ruled]

17 | ℓ 12v[1]-13r[6] Telémann [f]

ℓ 13v   [blank, ruled]

18 | ℓ 14r[1-3]   Menuets des fêtes venitienes [Le Bal
(1710) CAMPRA, arr (g)]

19 | ℓ 14r[4-6]   [CAMPRA, arr: Menuet from Les Festes
venitiennes Le Bal (1710) (G)]

20 | ℓ 14v[1]-15r[6] Marche de janissaires [G]

CO: cf 24-Babell #282
    cf 42-Vm7-6307-2 #4

21 | ℓ 15v[1-3]   [Menuet (a)]

22	ℓ 15v$^{4-6}$	[Oh gué lanla (Air ancien, 1712) (a)]

CO: cf 51-LaBarre-11 p 226
    cf Rés-Vma-ms-7/2 p 409

23	ℓ 16r$^{1-5}$	wous ne devés plus attendre [LULLY, arr: from Amadis (1684) II-7 (g)]

CO: cf 10-Schwerin-617 #19
    cf 36-Parville #110
    cf 42-Vm7-6307-2 #8
    cf 46-Menetou #20, 39

24	ℓ 16v^{1}-17r^{6}	Ouverture d isis [LULLY, arr (1677) (g)]

CO: cf 14-Schwerin-619 #51
    cf 24-Babell #128
    cf 33-Rés-89ter #42c
    cf 36-Parville #42
    cf 40-Rés-476 #35
    cf 42-Vm7-6307-2 #5
    cf 46-Menetou #85
    cf Stoss ℓ 24v

ED: cf Bonfils-LP p 101, Howell #2, Gilbert p 199,

25	ℓ 17v$^{1-3}$	L'autre jour malaux promenen [?] [g]
26	ℓ 17v$^{3-6}$	sarabande d issé [DESTOUCHES, arr (1697) III-2 (g)]
	ℓ 18r-19r	[blank, ruled]
27	ℓ 19v^{4}-22r^{2}	Babel /vivace [D]
28	ℓ 22r^{3}-25r^{3}	Aria vivacé [with variations (G)]
29	ℓ 25r^{5}-28r^{2}	Aria /vivace [g]
30	ℓ 28r^{3}-36r^{3}	Caprise /De /Babel ... [G]
	ℓ 36v	[blank, ruled]
		[2 ℓ lacking; succeeding ℓ all stubbed into the volume (originally?)]
31	ℓ 37r$^{1-6}$	Menuet de la lanterne magique
32	ℓ 37v$^{1-5}$	[Gigue (F)]
33	ℓ 38r$^{1-6}$	1er air des démurs [F]
34	ℓ 38v$^{1-6}$	2e air [F]

49-RésF-933

ℓ 39r   [blank, ruled]

35 ℓ 39v^1-40r^2 marais fils [Le Golefon (g)]

CO: cf Marais-R I p 12

50-PAIGNON

Provenance: Paris, ca. 1716 (dated, ℓ. 8Ar).

Location: Paris; Bibliothèque Sainte Geneviève,
MS 2374.

Description: 27 ℓ. (i.e., 30: 3 ℓ. stubbed-in; originally 50: 20 ℓ. cut out of the middle of the book);
oblong quarto format, 18.1 x 25 cm. (stubbed ℓ.
of different paper: 19.2 x 25 cm.). Watermark
#52. Original full leather binding, gilt-tooled
spine and edges, 18.5 x 21.5 cm.

Notation: Keyboard score (two 5-line staves, 3 systems
per page, written page by page). Clefs: F^3, G^2.

Scribes: 4 hands:
A #1-14   Teacher of Mlle Paignon? (M. Deviucehauant?)
B 15-21   Mlle Paignon?
C ℓ. 16r
D #22, ℓ. 1Ar-8Ar   Clérambault?

Marginalia: Inside front cover: "M. Deviucehauant."
On ℓ. 1r: "Ce liure apartion a Mademoiselle
Pagneon," ℓ. 13r (another hand): "monsieur C Paignon ..."
(with miscellaneous marks and words). Miscellaneous
comments throughout the book, including, on ℓ. 11r:
"quel bonheur pour la france destre sou la puissance
d'un /rois si renomé." Two differing modern numerations
by ℓ., one in red ink, one in pencil.

Summary:
Composers:
CLÉRAMBAULT: ℓ 1A-8A.
COUPERIN (François): #18-20.
DANDRIEU: #16, 17.
LEBÈGUE: #11.

LULLY: #10, 12.

Contents:

#1-6	Suite (d)
7-12	Suite (C)
13-14	Miscellaneous
15-21	Pieces by Dandrieu, Couperin, Lully, anon.
22	Prélude (G)
ℓ. 1A-11A	"Regles D'accompagnement," Clérambault

<u>Inventory</u>:

	ℓ 1r-v	[blank, unruled; see "Marginalia"]
1	ℓ 2r$^{1-2}$	Suitte en delare ([almost removed:] prelude [cf #6]) /menuet [d]
2	ℓ 2v^1-3r^3	Almande la prude [d]
3	ℓ 3v^1-4r^2	Courantte de'apollon [d]
4	ℓ 4v^1-5r^1	gigue [d]
5	ℓ 5r$^{2-3}$	gauotte [d]
6	ℓ 5v$^{1-3}$	prelude [unmeasured] [d]
7	ℓ 6r^1-v^1	Suitte an C. Solut Sarabande an Chaconne
8	ℓ 6v^2	gauotte [C]
8a	ℓ 6v^3	mesme /gauotte /plus fidelle [C]
9	ℓ 7r$^{1-3}$	Chaconne [C]
10	ℓ 7v$^{1-2}$	Sarabande /espagnol [LULLY, arr: 1er <u>Air</u> <u>des</u> <u>Espagnols</u> from <u>Le</u> <u>Bourgeois</u> <u>Gentil-</u> <u>homme</u> (1670) Nations-3 (C)]

CO: cf 23-Tenbury #80
  cf 24-Babell #269
  cf 36-Parville #130
  cf Saizenay-I p 287 [lute]

11 [LEBÈGUE: Gavotte (C)]

Balet de M^r lebegue

ℓ 7v^2-8r^1 ¢|4|8|

CO: 10-Schwerin-617 #10, Gavotte
   13-Möllersche [copy of 64-Lebègue-I #43]
   14-Schwerin-619 #91, Gavotte
   21-Rés-1186bis #12, Gavott
   23-Tenbury #6, Gavotte Mr Le Begue
   24-Babell #60, Gavotte de Mr. le Begue
   30-Cecilia ℓ 47r, Gavotte
   35-Bauyn-III #54, (Gavotte) de Mr Lebegue
   36-Parville #68, Gauotte Mr le Begue
   45-Dart #22 [copy of 64-Lebègue-I #43]
   46-Menetou #102, Gavotte
   64-Lebègue-I #43, Gauotte

ED: cf Dufourcq-L p 38, Brunold/Dart-Co #132.

11a [Double (C)]

le double |Suitte

ℓ 8r^1-v^1 ¢|4|8|

CO: cf 13-Möllersche [copy of 64-Lebègue-I #43a]
   cf 23-Tenbury #6a, Double
   cf 24-Babell #60a, Double
   cf 64-Lebègue-I #43a, Double
   cf 14-Schwerin-619 #91a, [Double]
   cf 35-Bauyn-III #54a, Double par Mr Couperin
   cf 36-Parville #68a [Double]
   cf 36-Parville #146, Double de la Gavotte de Le
                        Bègue

ED: cf Dufourcq-L p 38, Brunold/Dart-Co #132[a].

12	ℓ 8v^1-9r^1	Chaconne des Magitions [LULLY, arr: from *Ballet des muses* (1666) II-2 (C)]

		CO: cf 14-Schwerin-619 #111
		     cf 36-Parville #116
		     cf 46-Menetou #116
		     cf Minorite ℓ 50r

13	ℓ 9r^2-10v^2	folie despagne [4 variations (d)]
14	ℓ 10v^3-11r^2	gigue anglayse [C]
15	ℓ 11v$^{1-3}$	menuet [d]
16	ℓ 12r$^{1-2}$	menuet [DANDRIEU (d)] ED: cf François-Sappey p 68.
17	ℓ 12r^3-v^1	autre menuet [DANDRIEU (d)] ED: cf François-Sappey p 68.
18	ℓ 12v^2-13r^3	La nanette [FR. COUPERIN, I-1]
19	ℓ 13v$^{1-3}$	Canarie [FR. COUPERIN, I-2]
	ℓ 14r	[blank, ruled]
20	ℓ 14v$^{1-3}$	Les abeille /tendrement [FR. COUPERIN, I-1]
	ℓ 15r	[blank, ruled]
21	ℓ 15v$^{1-3}$	La marche /des /mousque/taires [C]
	ℓ 16r	Regles pour laccompagnement ... [chart of "good" and "bad" chords, without musical illustrations]
22	ℓ 16v$^{1-3}$	prelude en G. re sol ♮ ... [irregularly measured]
		[20 ℓ cut out; the rest of the volume is written from the other end:]
	ℓ 1Ar-8Ar	Regles D'accompagnement ... clerambault 1716.
	ℓ 8Av-11Ar	[blank, ruled; some marginalia]
23	ℓ 11Av	Je ne veray plus ce que jaime ... [melody with text beneath]
		[3 ℓ stubbed into volume: partial copy of]

<u>50-Paignon</u>

Principes d'Accompagnement par M.[r] Cleram-
baut ... [cf ℓ 1A-8A]

51-LABARRE-11

Provenance: Paris, post 1724 (hand A), with additions
  post 1753.

Location: Berkeley, California; University of California,
  Music Library, MS 775.

Description: 357 p. (i.e., 352: pp. 7-10 lacking, 41
  bound as [356], 43 quires in 4, except A^6; oblong
  quarto format, 19 x 26.5 cm. Watermark #65. Contemporary sprinkled vellum-covered boards and spine,
  matching the La Barre group of mss; mutilated spine
  label: "Recueil /de plusieurs /airs à chanter /Et
  de plusieurs /pièces de Clavessin," 20.3 x 27 cm.

Notation: Mixed vocal and keyboard scores. Keyboard score:
  two 5-line staves, 4 systems per page, written page
  by page. Clefs: $C^{1,3}$, $G^{1,2}$, F^3 (usually G^2, F^3).

Scribes: Two hands:
  A p 1-288,   Berkeley La Barre (?); the same as I in
      356   36-Parville, B in 46-Menetou and A in
                 48-LaBarre-6.
  B 289-355, Unidentified.
      357

Marginalia: Numeration by p. to p. 284 in original ink.
  Inside front cover: "Ce Liure Appartient A Monsieur
  /De La Barre Organiste."

Summary:
  Composers:
    d'ANGLEBERT : p 205, 206, 212, 229.
    ANSELME : passim.
    BERTHET: passim.
    BLAINVILLE (Charles Henri?): passim.
    BOUSSET: passim.

COUPERIN (Francois): p 215-217, 231-258, cf 267-288.

DANDRIEU : cf p 267-268.

DESFONTAINES : passim.

DESMARETS : passim.

DESTOUCHES : passim.

DES VOYES : passim.

DUBREUIL : passim.

DU BUISSON : passim.

DUPLESSIS ("l'aîné"): passim.

GAULTIER (Pierre?): passim.

LACOSTE : passim.

LULLY : p 1, 205, 206.

MARCHAND (Louis): p 219.

MONDONVILLE : passim.

MONTELAN : p 207-211.

RAMEAU : passim.

REBEL : passim.

ROUSSEAU : passim.

SUFFRET : p 221.

Contents:

p 1-2	Chaconne, LULLY
3-204	Vocal music
205-258	Harpsichord music
259-265	Vocal music
266-288	Harpsichord pieces, COUPERIN, DANDRIEU
289-357	Vocal music

Inventory: For a more detailed inventory of the vocal music, see: Alan Curtis, "Musique française classique à Berkeley," Revue de musicologie 56:2 (1970), pp. 123-164.

Inventory of harpsichord music:

p 1^1-2^3 Chaconne d'Arlequin [LULLY, arr: Chaconne des Scaramouches from Le Bourgeois Gentil-

homme (1670) Nations-4 (bass-treble score (G))]
CO: cf 24-Babell #258
    cf Saizenay-I p 340 [lute]

p 3-204   [Vocal music]

p 205^1-4   [LULLY, arr d'ANGLEBERT: Menuet dans nos
bois from Trios pour le coucher du roi (G)]
Dans nos bois de M^r de lully |R
$^3[\frac{3}{4}]$|8|16|

CO: 36-Parville #109, Menuet dans nos bois.
              Mr de Lully.
    68-d'Anglebert #14, Menuet. dans nos
              bois Mr de Lully
    cf 27-Gresse #20, Air Dans un bois
    cf 27-Gresse #52, [untitled]
ED: cf Gilbert p 112, Roesgen-Champion
    p 29.

206^1-207^2   [LULLY, arr d'ANGLEBERT: Chaconne from
Acis et Galathée (1686) II-5 (D)]
Chaconne de Galatée de M^r de lully
$^3[\frac{3}{4}]$|41|

CO: 68-d'Anglebert #55, Chaconne de Gala-
              tée Mr de Lully
    cf 14-Schwerin-619 #123, Chaconne de
              Galothe
    cf 23-Tenbury #75, Chaconne de Galatée
    cf 24-Babell #97, Chaconne de Galatée

cf 36-Parville #29, Chaconne de galatée
cf 49-RésF-933 #4 [untitled]
ED: cf Gilbert p 106, Roesgen-Champion
p 112.

| p 207³-208⁴ | [MONTELAN: <u>Allemande</u> (C)] |

Allemande /De M^r De montalant |R
¢ |11|16|

p 209¹⁻⁴   [MONTELAN: <u>Courante</u> (C)]

Courante /du même |R
$\frac{3}{2}$|6|7|

p 210¹⁻⁴   [MONTELAN: <u>Gavotte</u> (C)]

Gauotte du mesme |R
²[$\frac{4}{4}$]|4|8|

p 211[1]-212[1]	[MONTELAN: <u>Rigaudon</u> (g)] Rigodon du mesme $^2[\frac{4}{4}]$|8|13| 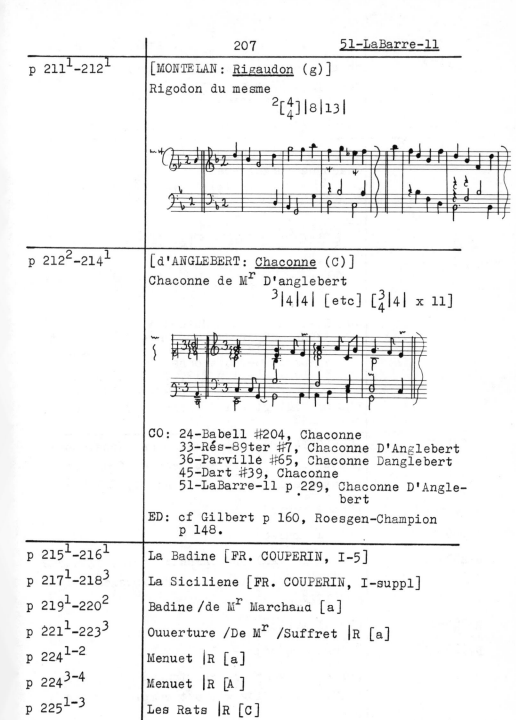

p 212[2]-214[1]	[d'ANGLEBERT: <u>Chaconne</u> (C)]
	
	Chaconne de M[r] D'anglebert
	
	^{3}|4|4| [etc] $[\frac{3}{4}$|4| x 11]
	
	CO: 24-Babell #204, Chaconne
	    33-Rés-89ter #7, Chaconne D'Anglebert
	    36-Parville #65, Chaconne Danglebert
	    45-Dart #39, Chaconne
	    51-LaBarre-11 p 229, Chaconne D'Angle-
	                  bert
	
	ED: cf Gilbert p 160, Roesgen-Champion
	    p 148.

p 215[1]-216[1]	La Badine [FR. COUPERIN, I-5]
p 217[1]-218[3]	La Siciliene [FR. COUPERIN, I-suppl]
p 219[1]-220[2]	Badine /de Mr Marchand [a]
p 221[1]-223[3]	Ouuerture /De M[r] /Suffret |R [a]
p 224[1-2]	Menuet |R [a]
p 224[3-4]	Menuet |R [A]
p 225[1-3]	Les Rats |R [C]

p 226[1-3]	oh gué Lanla |R [Air ancien (a)] CO: cf 49-RésF-933 #22 cf Rés-Vma-ms-7/2 p 409
p 227[1]-228[3]	Badine /Couprin [Fr] /Les vendengeuses

[d'ANGLEBERT: Chaconne (C)]

p 229[1]-230[3]	[d'ANGLEBERT: Chaconne (C)] Chaconne /D'Anglebert ^{3}|4|4|[etc] [$\frac{3}{4}$|4| x 12]

CO: 24-Babell #204, Chaconne
    33-Rés-89ter #7, Chaconne D'Anglebert
    36-Parville #65, Chaconne Danglebert
    45-Dart #39, Chaconne
    51-LaBarre-11 p 212, Chaconne de Mr
                       D'anglebert
ED: cf Gilbert p 160, Roesgen-Champion
    p 148.

p 231-258	[COUPERIN (FR): Miscellaneous harpsichord pieces from Ordres 1-6, copied from the printed editions of 1713 and 1716-1717]
p 259-269	[Vocal music]
p 266	[blank, ruled]
p 267-288	[COUPERIN (FR) and DANDRIEU: Miscellaneous pieces, copied from the editions of 1713 and 1724]
p 289-254	[Vocal music]
p 355	[blank, ruled]
p 356	[originally, p 41, continuing music from p 40, but ending without completing the music]

p 357

paste-down

[Vocal music]

Table des pieces de Clavessin contenües
dans ce luire ... [hand A, with two
additions in a later hand for pieces not
found in the ms:] 1. Air hongrois et
Tyrolien en duo /2. Air hongrois avec
lair Tyrolienne

Provenance: France, post 1742 (watermark dated).

Location: Paris; Bibliothèque nationale, département de la
musique, fonds conservatoire, Réserve 2671 (olim
Conservatoire de musique, Réserve 2671).

Description: 1 p.ℓ., 89, 1 ℓ.; oblong quarto format, 19 x
24.8 cm. Watermark 56; cf 83 (binding end papers). Original green vellum-covered boards, post 1742; paper
label on front: "Pieces /de /Clavecin," 19.8 x 25.2
cm.

Notation: Keyboard score (two 5-line staves, 3 systems
per page, written page by page). Clefs: F^4, G^2.

Scribes: 3-4 unidentified hands:
A #1-12, 16, 20-21
B 14-15, 17-19 (same as A?)
C 13
D 22

Marginalia: On ℓ. i^v: pencil library note stating that
not all of the compositions are by (François) Couperin. The same hand identified many of the Couperin
pieces throughout the book. In modern ink on ℓ. 1r:
"M.i. iii. 6 en la."

Summary:
Composers:
CHAMBONNIÈRES: #14.
COUPERIN (François): #5-7, 9-12, 15-18, 20-21.
MARCHAND: #21.
RAMEAU: #23, 24.
SCARLATTI (Domenico): #22.
Contents: Harpsichord pieces grouped by key:

#1-8 (a)   16-19 (F)
 9-10 (G)   20-24 (miscellaneous)
11-15 (d)

<u>Inventory</u>:

	ℓ i^{r-v}	[blank, unruled; see "Marginalia"]
1	ℓ 1r$^{1-3}$	prelude [a]
2	ℓ 1v^1-2r^3	Tambourin /Rondeau ... [a]
	ℓ 2v	[blank, ruled]
3	ℓ 3r$^{1-3}$	Menuet [a]
4	ℓ 3v^1-4v^3	La Lisette /Rondeau [Air ancien: <u>Ne</u> <u>revenez</u> <u>plus</u>. <u>Lisette</u> (a)]
	ℓ 5r-7r	[blank, ruled]
5	ℓ 7v^1-8r^3	Les /Vendangeuses /Rondeau ... [COUPERIN (FR), I-5 (a)]
6	ℓ 8v^1-9r^2	La Badine /Legerement et flaté /Rondeau ... [COUPERIN (FR), I-5 (a)]
7	ℓ 9v^1-11r^3	Les Ondes /gracieusement sans lenteur /Rondeau ... [COUPERIN (FR), I-5 (a)]
8	ℓ 11v^1-12r^3	Menuet [a]
	ℓ 12v-14v	[blank, ruled]
	ℓ 15r	en sol
9	ℓ 15v^1-17r^3	Les Silvains /Majesteüsement sans lenteur /Rondeau ... [COUPERIN (FR), I-1 (G)]
10	ℓ 17v^1-18r^3	Les Delices de Couperin /Rondeau [COUPERIN (FR), II-7 (G)] [ℓ 17v is pasted over another page]
	ℓ 18v-20v	[blank, ruled]
	ℓ 21r	en Re

11 | ℓ 21v[1]-22r[3] La Voluptueuse /Tendrement &c. /Rondeau
... [COUPERIN (FR), I-2 (d)]

12 | ℓ 22v[1]-23r[3] Canaries ... Doubles ... [COUPERIN (FR),
I-2 (d)]

13 | ℓ 23v[1]-28r[3] Les pantins ... [modern pencil notation:]
Chanson Que pantin serait content [d]

14 | [CHAMBONNIÈRES: Les Barricades (d)]
Les Baricades
ℓ 28v[1]-29r[3] ^{3}[$^6_4$] |12|15|

CO: 35-Bauyn-I #36, Courante de Mr de Chambonnieres
dit les barricades
62-Chamb-I #16, les Baricades
cf 59-Dumont-1657 ℓ 31v, Allemande [by Dumont]
ED: cf Brunold-Tessier #16, Dart-Ch #16; cf Bonfils-13
p 6, Cohen p 16.

[1 ℓ removed between ℓ 28 and 29 before
#14 was written]

15 | ℓ 29v[1]-30r[3] La Blonde et la Brune de Couprin ...
[COUPERIN (FR): La Babet (I-2) (d)]

ℓ 30v-31v   [blank, ruled]

ℓ 32r   en fa

16 | ℓ 32v[1]-33r[1] Soeur Monique. tendrem[t.] Sans lenteur.
/Rondeau [COUPERIN (FR),III-18 (F)]

17 | ℓ 34v[1]-36r[3] Le /Reveil-matin ... [COUPERIN (FR), I-4
(F)]

18 | ℓ 36v[1]-37r[3] La Marche /des Gris vêtus /Pesament, Sans
lenteur. [COUPERIN (FR), I-4 (F)]

19	ℓ 37v^1-38r^2	Air [modern pencil:] Marchand [F] CO: 14-Schwerin-619 #108, Venitienne de Mr Marchand
	ℓ 38v-42v	[blank, ruled]
	ℓ 43r	en Si Bemol
20	ℓ 43v^1-45r^3	Les /Bergeries /Rondeau /naivement ... [COUPERIN (FR), II-6 (B♭)]
	ℓ 45v-54v	[blank, ruled]
	ℓ 55r	en vt
21	ℓ 55v^1-61r^3	Les Fastes De la grande, et ancienne /Mxnxstrxndxsx ... [COUPERIN (FR), II-11 (C)]
23	ℓ 62v^1-68r^3	[La Furstenburg (Air ancien) with 7 Variations (g)]
22	ℓ 61v^1-62r^3	[smudged:] La boutique [?] [SCARLATTI: Sonata, K. 95 (C)]
24	ℓ 68v^1-72r^3	[RAMEAU: Les Tricotets (G)] CO: Rameau-1728
25	ℓ 72v^1-73v^3	Variations des sauvages [RAMEAU (g)] CO: Rameau-1728
	ℓ 74r-89v	[blank, ruled]
		[1 ℓ, blank, unruled]

Provenance: France, post 1752 (transcription from Le De-
   vin du village)

Location: London; private collection of Guy Oldham.

Description: 190 written p. Contemporary leather binding.

Notation: Keyboard score (two 5-line staves).

Scribe: One careful hand, with a few additions at the
   end of the ms.

Summary:
   Composers (incomplete list):
     AUBERT, Jacques "le vieux" (ca. 1689-1753)
     CHAMBONNIÈRES, Jacques Champion (1601/2-1672)
     COUPERIN, François (1668-1733)
     DANDRIEU, Jean-François (ca. 1682-1738)
     LOEILLET, Jean-Baptiste (b. 1688)
     LULLY, Jean-Baptiste (1632-1687)
     ROUSSEAU, Jean-Jacques (1712-1778)
   Contents:
     Harpsichord pieces, including transcriptions from
     operas by Lully (Phaéton and Isis) and Rousseau
     (Le Devin du village).
Inventory of 17th-century French harpsichord music:

p 107 | [CHAMBONNIÈRES: Courante Iris (C)]
      | Courante /de /Chamboniere

      | CO: 8-Hintze #15, Courante
      | 22a-Roper #3, (courante chambonii)
      | 23-Tenbury #3, (courante chambonii)

24-Babell #58, Courante de Mr. de Chambonniere
33-Rés-89ter #2, Courante. Chambonnieres...Double
35-Bauyn-I #9, Courante de Mr De Chambonnieres
36-Parville #61, Courante Chanbonniere
44-LaPierre p 18, p 34A, Courante Chambonniere,..Double
47-Gen-2356 #12, Courante
55-Redon #23, Courante de Monsieur de Chambon-
          niere
62-Chamb-I #8, Courante Iris
cf 32-Oldham #17, Double de La Courante Iris

ED: cf Brunold-Tessier #8, Dart-Ch #8, Gilbert p 148.

Provenance: France (Paris?), ca. 1630-1670.

Location: Paris; Bibliothèque Sainte Geneviève, MS 2350
and ℓ. 5-12 of MS 2357.

Description: 2 vols. Vol. 1 (MS 2350): 17 ℓ.; oblong
quarto format (trimmed), 17 x 21.7 cm. Watermark
#12. Modern full cloth binding, 17.5 x 23.5 cm.
Vol. 2 (MS 2357): ℓ. 5-12 (i.e., 8 ℓ.); same paper,
format, matching binding. Bound after 4 ℓ. from
another ms (see 34-Gen-2357[a]).

Notation: Keyboard score (two 5-line staves, 3 systems
per page, written page by page). Clefs: F^3, G^2,
$C^{1,4}$; usually F^3, G^2. Keyboard score sometimes
supplemented with letter names of notes written
below the staves.

Scribes: 1-3 inexperienced hands (not the same as
34-Gen-2357[a]).

Marginalia: Modern numeration by ℓ. in red ink. In
modern pencil on ℓ. 4v: "(vignonne?)" and on ℓ.
6r: identification of Boccan as Jacques Cordier.

Summary:
  Composers:
    CHANCY, François de (d. 1656): #26.
    CORDIER, Jacques "Bocan" (ca. 1580-post 1621): #9, 35.
    GUEDRON, Pierre (d. 1620/21): #15, 21.
  Contents:
    #1-15   Harpsichord pieces
    16-20   Organ pieces
    21-36   Harpsichord pieces

Inventory:

1　[Bergamasco (G)]
　[untitled]
　　ℓ 1r$^{1-3}$　　　C|8|8|　[$\frac{2}{4}$|9|9|]

2　[Pièce (G/C)]
　[untitled]
　　ℓ 1v$^{1-3}$　　　C|11|

3　[Pièce (G)]
　[untitled]
　　ℓ 2r^{1}-3r^{2}　　　C|20|15|

4　[Pièce (G)]
　[untitled]
　　ℓ 3v$^{1-2}$　　　C3[$\frac{3}{4}$]|4|4|

5 | [Gavotte (g)]

gauotte /Suite de la gauotte

ℓ 3v³-4r³   C |4|4|4|4|

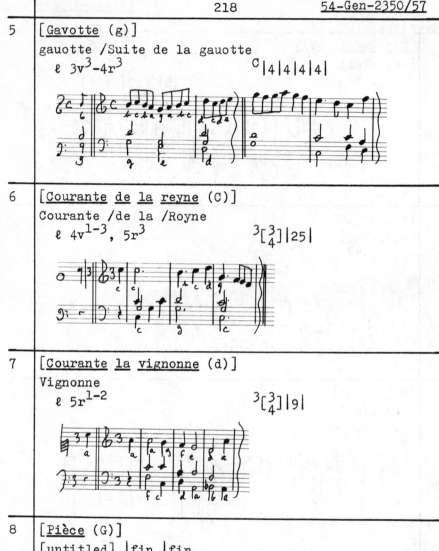

6 | [Courante de la reyne (C)]

Courante /de la /Royne

ℓ 4v¹⁻³, 5r³   ³[³/₄] |25|

7 | [Courante la vignonne (d)]

Vignonne

ℓ 5r¹⁻²   ³[³/₄] |9|

8 | [Pièce (G)]

[untitled] |fin |fin

ℓ 5v¹⁻³   [⁴/₄] |12|

9 | [CORDIER, arr: <u>Branle</u> (d)]

Bransles /de boccan |Tournez |Suitte

ℓ 6r[1]-v[2] |11|11| [$\frac{4}{4}$|12|12|]

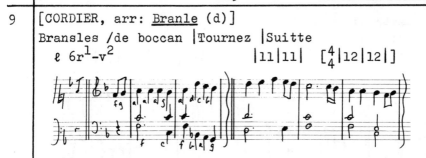

CO: cf 54-Gen-2350/57 #35, premier branle De bocan

10 | [<u>Air italien</u> (G)]

air italien

ℓ 7r[1-3]   C|12|

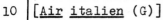

11 | [<u>Que dis-tu Jehan de ...elle</u> (C)]

Que /dis tu /Jehan /(depuis elle? [illegible])

ℓ 7v[1-3]   C|7|6| [$\frac{4}{4}$|6|6|]

12 | [<u>Ballet</u> (C)]

ballet

ℓ 8r[1-3]   [$\frac{4}{4}$]|9|

13 | [Courante (C)]
[untitled]
ℓ 8v^1-9r^2 |25| [$\frac{3}{4}$|11|14|]

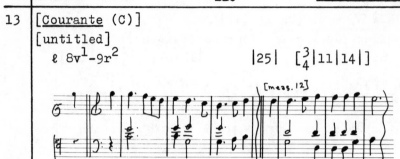

14 | [Courante de la reyne (a)]
Courante /de la /Reyne
ℓ 9v^1-10r^2   C[$\frac{3}{4}$]|7|19|

15 | [GUEDRON, arr: Ces Nymphes dont les regards (a)]
[text between staves:] Ces nimphes dont les re-
gards ...
ℓ 10v^1-2   C|7| [$\frac{4}{4}$|8|]

16 | ℓ 10v^3   In-æternum [intonation, cf #17-19 (G)]
17 | ℓ 11r^1-3   Laudate dominum omnes gentes ...
18 | ℓ 11v^1-2   Gloria [patri]
19 | ℓ 12r^1-3   Sicut |Et in Secula ...

20 | ℓ 12v¹⁻³   domine Saluum fac re-gem...

---

21 | [GUEDRON, arr: C'est trop courir ces eaux (d)]

Cest trop courir ces eaux ...
   ℓ 13r¹⁻³   ^C|14|

---

22 | [Quelle Beauté o mortels (d)]

Quelle beaute O mortels
   ℓ 13v¹⁻³   ^C|7|6| [$\frac{4}{4}$|7|7|

[ℓ lacking?]

---

23 | [Pièce (g) (fragment?)]

Suitte
   ℓ 14r¹⁻³   ^C|4|7|

24 [Je scay Philis (g)]

[text between staves:] Je scay philis qu'en ces bas

Lieux ...

ℓ 14v$^{1-3}$ ^{3}|8|7| [$^3_2$|8|8|

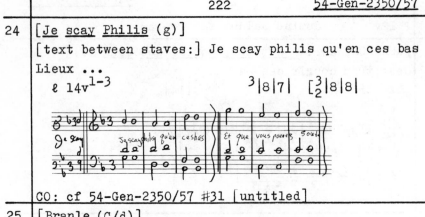

CO: cf 54-Gen-2350/57 #31 [untitled]

25 [Branle (C/d)]

4^e bransle

ℓ 15r$^{1-3}$ [$^4_4$]|17|

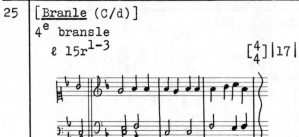

26 [CHANCY, arr: Branle (F/a)]

5e bransle

ℓ 15v$^{1-3}$ C2|3|^3[$^3_4$]12|

27 [Je ne puis éviter ces yeux (d)]

[text between staves:] Je ne puis euiter ces yeux ...

ℓ 16r$^{1-3}$ ^{3}|7|8| [$^3_4$|7|9|

28 | [Ballet nouveau (g)]
ballet /nouueau
ℓ 17v¹⁻³   ^C|8|8|

29 | [Ballet (d)]
Second
ℓ 18r¹⁻³   [4/4|12|

30 | [Branle (fragment) (d)]
3^e bransle
ℓ 18v¹⁻³   [4/4]|13|

[ℓ lacking; MS 2350 ends here. The following
8 ℓ are misbound as the second part of MS 2357, but
were originally part of this ms:]

31 | [Je scay Philis (d)]
[untitled] |fin du |5^e
ℓ 5r$^{1-3}$ [$\frac{3}{4}$]|16|

CO: cf 54-Gen-2350/57 #24, Je scay Philis

32 | [Pièce (d)]
[untitled] |fin
ℓ 5v^1-6r^3 [$\frac{3}{4}$]|35|

33 | [Pièce (g)]
[untitled] |fin
ℓ 6v$^{1-3}$ ^{3}[$\frac{3}{4}$]|16|

34 | [Ballet du soleil (F)]
ballet /du Soleil |fin
ℓ 7r^1-v^3 ^{C}|11|14|

35 | [CORDIER, arr: <u>Branle</u> (d)]

premier /branle /De bocan

ℓ 8r$^{1-3}$ C|12|

CO: cf 54-Gen-2350/57 #9, Bransles de boccan

ℓ 8v^1 metode /pour les /accords [examples
of figured bass]

36 | [<u>Les Baratins</u> (d)]

Courante.

ℓ 8v^2-9r^2 [$\frac{4}{4}$]|4|8|

CO: cf 7-Munich-1511f #11, Les Barantins
cf 55-Redon #8, [untitled]

ℓ 9r^3 par /bemol [continuation of figured
bass examples from ℓ 8v]

ℓ 9v-12r   [blank, ruled]

Provenance: Clermont-Ferrand, France, 1661.

Location: Clermont-Ferrand; Archives départementales du
   Puy-de-Dome, 2 E 976[57].

Description: 43 ℓ.

Notation: Keyboard score (two 6-line staves, 3 systems
   per page, written page by page). Clefs: $C^{1,5,6}$, $G^{2,3}$,
   $F^{3,4,5}$; usually C^6, C^1. Also, French letter score
   (see Ex. 12 in the Commentary).

Scribes: 4-6 unidentified hands, all inexperienced except
   F:
   A #1-5, 7; ℓ. 5v-6r?
   B 6 (same as A?)
   C 8-11
   D 12, 17-20 (same as B?)
   E 13-15
   F 21-23

Marginalia: Numeration by ℓ. in modern hand.

Summary:
   Composers:
     ARTUS: #12.
     CHAMBONNIÈRES: #23.
     ESTY, Guelheur (?): #1.
     GAULTIER: #4.
     LA PIERRE (?): #14.
   Contents:
     #1-19   Miscellaneous simple pieces
     20-23   Full-textured pieces

Inventory:

1 | [La Bourrée de guelheur esty (Guelheur ESTY?) (a)]
La Bourée de guelheur esty [?] |Reprise |fin
ℓ 1r²⁻³   ¢ |5|6|

2 | [Air à chanter au temps en enporte le vent (d)]
Aire a chanter au temp en enporte Le vent [?] |Reprise |fin
ℓ 1v²⁻³ |5|7| [⁴⁄₄|6|8|]

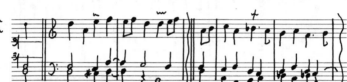

3 | [Courante nouvelle (a)]
Courante Nouuelle |Reprise |fin
ℓ 2r²⁻³   ³|10|10| [³⁄₄|13|15|]

4 [GAULTIER, arr: <u>Gigue</u> (C)]

Gigue de Monsieur gaultier |fin

ℓ 2v$^{2-3}$ ^{C}|5|5| [$^{4}_{4}$|6|6|]

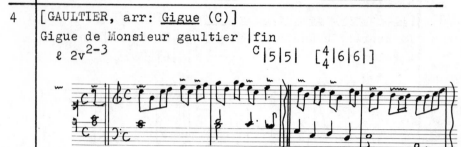

5 [<u>Les</u> <u>Tricottes</u> <u>nouveaux</u> (F)]

Les Tricotte Nouueau |Reprise |fin

ℓ 3r$^{1-2}$ ¢|3|6|

6 [<u>Pièce</u> (d)]

[untitled]

ℓ 3v$^{1-2}$ ¢|8|5| [$^{4}_{4}$|4|5|]

7 [<u>Bourrée</u> (d)]

|fin de La Boureé

ℓ 4r$^{1-2}$ |6|6| [$^{4}_{4}$|7|7|]

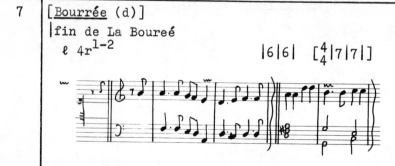

8 | [Les Baratins (d)]
[untitled] |fin
ℓ 4v$^{1-3}$ [$\frac{4}{4}$]|4|4|8|

CO: cf 7-Munich-1511f #11, Les Barantins
    cf 54-Gen-2350/57 #36, Courante

9 | [Pièce (F)]
[untitled] |fin
ℓ 5r$^{1-3}$ [$\frac{4}{4}$]|4|14|

ℓ 5v-6r   Riecle generalle pour bien apprendre
                 accorder Lespinette pour /Madoiselle
                 Claude Redon ce cinquiesme septembre
                 1661 [followed by tuning directions
                 illustrated in French letter score;
                 see Ex 12 in the Commentary]

10 | [La Moutard (Air ancien) (C)]
|fin du Cordon Bleu
ℓ 6v$^{1-2}$ [$\frac{4}{4}$]|11|

CO: cf 27-Gresse #7
    cf 39-Vm7-6301 #14
    cf Terburg
    cf Add-16889 ℓ 99r [lute]
    cf Celle p 140

11 | [Pièce (C)]
[untitled]
ℓ 7r$^{1-2}$ |13| [$\frac{4}{4}$]|7|7|]

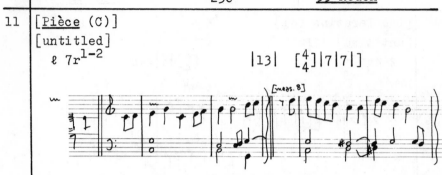

12 | [ARTUS, arr: Gaillarde (d)]
[untitled]
ℓ 7v^1 [$\frac{4}{4}$|3|3|

CO: cf 9-Ihre-284 #85, La Galliard ...
    cf Cassel Suite XIV
ED: cf Lundgren #36, Écorcheville 2-176.

13 | [Pièce (C)]
[untitled]
ℓ 7v$^{2-3}$ |15| [$\frac{4}{4}$|8|8|

14 | [LA PIERRE (?): Bourrée (C)]
La boureé de La piere |fin
ℓ 8r$^{1-3}$ ^{C}|20| [^{C}|8|12|]

15 | [Un Coeur amoureux (C)]

Vn Coeur amoureux Et tendre ne peut sempescher

daymer |Il faut repeter le commencement

  ℓ 8v$^{1-2}$ [$\frac{4}{4}$]|4|6|

16 | [Prélude (C)]

prelude

  ℓ 9r^{1}-v^{1} |24|

17 | [Pièce (F)]

[untitled] |fin

  ℓ 10r$^{1-3}$ ¢|8|16|

ℓ 10v   [blank, ruled]

18 [<u>Ballet</u> (fragment) (C)]
Ballet
ℓ 11r[1]   C|3|2

ℓ 11v   [blank, ruled]

19 [<u>Muniorx</u> (?) (C)]
muniorx [?]
ℓ 12r[1-2]   ¢|6|6| [¢|8|8|]

ℓ 12v   [blank, ruled]

20 [<u>Le</u> <u>Ballet</u> <u>des</u> <u>boufons</u> (fragment) (F)]
Le ballet des boufons
ℓ 13r[1-2]   C|12

ℓ 14r-25r   [blank, ruled]

21 [Courante de madame (Air ancien) (F)]

Courante de Madame |menuetz |fin

ℓ 25v^1-26r^3 $^2_3$[$^6_4$]|7|[$^3_4$]11|¢5|9|

CO: cf 9-Ihre-284 #111, Courant Madam

---

22 [Rondeau (G)]

Rondeau

ℓ 26v^1-27r^3

ℓ 27v-33r   [blank, ruled]

---

23 [CHAMBONNIÈRES: Courante Iris (C)]

Courante de Monsieur de Chambonniere |fin.

ℓ 33v^1-34r^2 ^{3}[$^6_4$]|8|8|

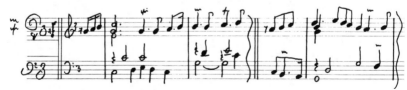

CO: 8-Hintze #15, Courante
   22a-Roper #58, Courante Chambonniere ... double
   23-Tenbury #3, (courante chambonii)
   24-Babell #58, Courante de Mr. de Chambonniere
   33-Rés-89ter #2, Courante. Chambonnieres... Double
   35-Bauyn-I #9, Courante de Mr De Chambonnieres
   36-Parville #61, Courante Chanbonniere
   44-LaPierre p 18, p 34A, Courante Chambonniere...Double

47-Gen-2356 #12, Courante
53-Oldham-2 p 107, Courante de Chamboniere
62-Chamb-I #8, Courante Iris
cf 32-Oldham #17, Double de La Courante Iris

ED: cf Brunold-Tessier #8, Dart-Ch #8, Gilbert p 148.

ℓ 34v-43v   [blank, ruled; some miscellaneous writing
             on ℓ 43v]

Provenance: Paris, 1636.

Facsimile ed.: Marin Mersenne, Harmonie universelle,
after the exemplar at the Bibliothèque des arts et
metiers (Paris), annotated by the author; with an
introduction by François Lesure (Paris: Centre national
de la recherche scientifique, 1963).

Description: 8 separately paginated sections; type-set,
including musical examples.

Summary of relevant contents:
Examples of melodies which are also set elsewhere
for keyboard: Traitez de la voix et des chants.
Keyboard music: Traité des instruments [book 6].

Inventory:
General title:
Harmonie universelle contenant la théorie et la
pratique de la musique.

Separately paginated sections:
[1] Traitez de la nature des sons, et des movvements
de toutes sortes de corps [3 books].
[2] Traité de mechaniqve.
[3] Traitez de la voix et des chants [2 books].
[4] Traitez des consonances, des dissonances, des
Genres, des modes, & de la composition [6 books].
[5] Traitez des instruments ... [6 books]
[Book 6, organ:]

[LOUIS XIII, arr LA BARRE (Pierre III): O beau Soleil (a)]

Chanson composée par le Roy, & mise en tablature par le Sieur de la Barre, Epinette /& Organiste du Roy & de la Reyne.

p 391

ED: Bonfils-31 p 6.

[LA BARRE (Pierre III): 8 Diminutions (a)]

Diminutions des deux premieres Mesures de la Tablature precedente qui ont pour leur /lettre: Tu crois ô beau Soleil, composées par le sieur de la Barre.

p 394-395   8 incipits

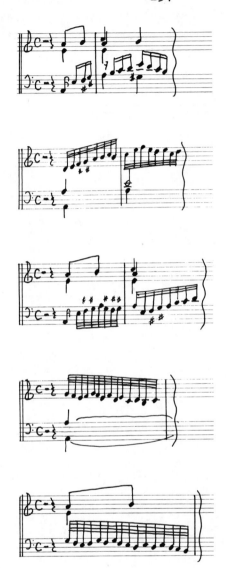

ED: Bonfils-31 p 7.

[6] Livre septiesme des instruments de percussion
    [ie, 7th book on instruments, but paginated separ-
    ately].
[7] Liure de l'vtilité de l'harmonie.
[8] Novvelles Observations.

Provenance: Paris, Robert Ballard; 1643; 2nd ed., 1650.

Facsimile ed.: Jean Denis, Traité de l'accord de l'espinette, 2nd ed., with an introduction by Alan Curtis
   (New York: Da Capo, 1969).

Description: 1st ed.: 24 p. 2nd ed.: 40 p., 1 table.
   Both eds.: type-set, including musical examples in
   the 2nd ed.

Summary: Meantone tuning instructions and other informa-
   tion on harpsichord performance, illustrated in the
   2nd ed. with musical examples. Augmented in the 2nd
   ed. with four chapters on related subjects.

Inventory of 2nd ed.:

p 1 | TRAITÉ DE L'ACCORD
DE L'ESPINETTE,
Auec la comparison de son Clauier
à la Musique vocale.
Augmenté en cette Edition des quatre Chapitres
suiuants.
I.   Traité des Sons & combien il y en a.
II. Traité des Tons de l'Eglise & de leurs es-
        tenduës.
III. Traité des Fugues & comme il les faut traiter.
IV. La manniere de bien jouër de l'Espinette &
        des Orgues.
Dedié à
MONSEIGNEVR
LE MARQVIS DE MORTEMART
Par I. Denis, Organiste de S. Barthelmy, & Maistre
faiseur d'Instruments de Musique.
A PARIS.

Par Robert Ballard, seul Imprimeur
du Roy pour la Musique.
Et se vendent chez l'Autheur, ruë des Arsis
à l'Image Saincte Cecile.
M. DC. L. [1650]

p 2-6	[prefatory material]
p 7-40	[body of text]

p 16-17 | [DENIS: <u>Prélude</u> (E♭)]

Prelude pour sonder si l'Accord est bon par tout.

¢|36| [¢|37|]

ED: Hunt p 203.

58-DUMONT-1652

Provenance: Paris, Robert Ballard; 1652; 2nd ed., 1662.

Locations:

Paris; Bibliothèque nationale, département de la musique:

1---Réserve Vm^1 92: 1652 ed., Superius (2 exemplars), Bassus

2---Réserve Vm^1 93: 1662 ed., Superius, Contra, Tenor, Bassus, Basse-continue

Paris; Bibliothèque Sainte Geneviève:

3---Vm 17: 1652 ed., Tenor

4---Vm 14: 1662 ed., Superius, Contra, Tenor, Bassus, Basse-continue

5---Vm 16: 1662 ed., Tenor

London; British Library [British Museum], Music Room:

6---D 980a: 1652 ed., Tenor, Basse-continue

Summary of locations:

1652 ed.	Superius	Contra	Tenor	Bassus	Basse-cont.
Ex. 1	2	0	0	1	0
Ex. 3	0	0	1	0	0
Ex. 6	0	0	1	0	1
1662 ed.					
Ex. 2	1	1	1	1	1
Ex. 4	1	1	1	1	1
Ex. 5	0	0	1	0	0

Description: 5 partbooks (superius, contra, tenor, bassus, bassus continuus). Folio format, type-set (including keyboard music).

Summary of contents· Accompanied vocal motets with 4 instrumental pieces interspersed, one of which is also printed in keyboard score in the bassus continuus partbook.

241

Inventory of Superius, 1652 ed.:

ℓ i^r | CANTICA
SACRA
II. III. IV. CVM VOCIBVS,
TVM ET INSTRUMENTIS MODVLATA,
Adjectae itidem Litaniae 2. vocib. ad
 libitum
3. & 4. voc.
CVM BASSO-CONTINVO.
Auctore HENRICO DV MONT, Leodiensi
insignis Ecclesiae S. Pauli Parisijs
 Organista.
LIBER PRIMVS.
SVPERIVS
[title vignette]
PARISIIS,
Ex Officina ROBERTI BALLARD, vnici Regiae
Musicae Typographi
M DC. LII [1652]
Et se vendent chez l'Autheur, ruë Sainct
 Anthoine,
proche l'Hotel de Sully.
Auec Priuilege de sa majesté

ℓ i^v | [blank]

ℓ ii^{r-v} | A TRES-HAVTE
ET TRES-PVISSANTE DAME
CHARLOTTE D'AILLY,
VEFVE DE TRES-HAVT
ET TRES-PVISSANT SEIGNEVR
MESSIRE
HONORÉ D'ALBERT,
DVC DE CHAVLNES,
PREMIER MARESCHAL DE FRANCE ...
[signed:] Vostre tres-humble & tres-

	obeïssant serviteur H. DV MONT.
ℓ iii^r	AV LECTEUR ...
ℓ iii^v-33^r	[accompanied vocal motets, superius part, with the following instrumental pieces interspersed:]
ℓ 18^r	... PAVANA ... à 3. Viol.
ℓ 18^v	... SYMPHONIA ... à 3. Viol.
ℓ 29^r	... SYMPHONIA ... à 4. Viol.
ℓ 33^r	... ALLEMANDA GRAVIS ... à Viol B T A C XL Mot.
ℓ 33^v-[34^r]	INDEX ... Acheué d'Imprimer le dixiesme jour du mois de Iuin /de l'an mil six cens cinquante-deux [June 10, 1652] [printer's mark]
ℓ [34^v]	[blank]

Inventory of Bassus continuus, 1652 ed.:

	[same preliminary material and contents; in place of a figured bass part for the last piece, the following keyboard score is given:]

| ℓ 24^v-25^r | [DUMONT: Allemande grave (C)] à 4. Viol. B T A C. XL. Mot. BASSVS-CONTINVVS /ALLEMANDA GRAVIS. |FINIS. /LES MOTETS DE HENRY DV MONT. |

^{C}|15|17|

CO: 35-Bauyn-III #86, Allemande du même
                         Auteur
ED: Bonfils-13 p 4.

Inventory of 1662 ed.:

[exactly the same as the 1652 ed., with
the following exceptions: title vignette
changed; date changed:]
M. DC. LXII [1662]
CVM PRIVILEGIO REGIS
[Index re-set, including different
printer's mark; colophon omitted]

Provenance: Paris, Robert Ballard; 1657; 2nd issue, post
   1678; "troisieme partie" issued in 1661 and 1678.

Locations:
   Paris; Bibliothèque nationale, département de la
   musique:
   1---Réserve Vm^1 94^1 : 1778 issue (Dessus, Haut-taille,
       Basse, Dessus de viole, Basse de viole, Basse-
       continue)
   2---Réserve Vm^{1}94^2: 1778 issue (Troisiesme partie).
   3---Réserve Vm^1 94^3: 1778 issue (Basse de viole).
   Ibid., fonds conservatoire:
   4---Réserve 382: 1657 issue (Dessus, Haut-taille, Basse,
       Dessus de viole, Basse-continue)
   5---Réserve 383: 1657 issue (Haut-taille, Basse-continue).
   6---Réserve 382bis: 1675 issue (Troisiesme partie).
   Paris; Bibliothèque Sainte Geneviève:
   7---Vm 10: 1657 issue (Dessus, Haut-taille, Basse,
       Basse de viole, Basse-continue).
   8---Vm 11: 1657 issue (Haut-taille, Dessus de viole,
       Basse-continue).
   9---Vm 12: 1657 issue (Dessus, Haut-taille, Basse,
       Dessus de viole, Basse de viole, Basse-continue).
   10---Vm 13: 1661 issue (Troisiesme partie).
   London; British Library [British Museum], Music Room:
   11---D.980: 1657 issue (Dessus, Haut-taille, Basse,
       Dessus de viole, Basse de viole, Troisiesme partie).

Summary of locations:

1657	Dessus	Haut-t.	Basse	Des./V.	B./V.	B.-C.	3me
Ex. 4	1	1	1	1	0	1	0
Ex. 5	0	1	0	0	0	1	0
Ex. 6	0	0	0	0	0	0	1

1657	Dessus	Haut-t.	Basse	Des./V.	B./V.	B.-C.	3me
Ex. 7	1	1	1	0	1	1	0
Ex. 8	0	1	0	1	0	1	0
Ex. 9	1	1	1	1	1	1	0
Ex. 10	0	0	0	0	0	0	1
Ex. 11	1	1	1	1	1	0	1
post 1678							
Ex. 1	1	1	1	1	1	1	0
Ex. 2	0	0	0	0	0	0	1
Ex. 3	0	0	0	0	1	0	0

<u>Description</u>: 7 partbooks: Dessus (vocal), Haute-taille
(vocal-instrumental), Basse (vocal), Dessus de viole
ou Bas-dessus (instrumental), Basse de viole ou Basse-
taille (instrumental), Basse-continue (instrumental),
Troisiesme partie pour un dessus de viole ou taille
ou pour une basse de viole touchée à l'octave (instrumental). Upright quarto format, type-set (including
keyboard music).

<u>Summary of contents</u>: Accompanied sacred and secular vocal
music, with instrumental pieces interspersed, two
of which are also printed in keyboard score in the
basse-continue partbook.

<u>Inventory of Dessus, 1657 issue</u>:

ℓ i^r | MESLANGES
A II. III. IV. ET V.
PARTIES,
AVEC LA BASSE-CONTINVË,
CONTENANT
Plusieurs Chansons, Motets, Magnificats,
Preludes, & Allemandes pour l'Orgue
& pour les Violes.
Et les Litanies de la Vierge.
Par le Sieur DV MONT, Organiste de son Altesse

Royale le Duc d'Anjou, Frere vnique du Roy;
& en l'Eglise S. Paul.
LIVRE SECOND.
DESSVS
[title vignette]
A PARIS,
Par ROBERT BALLARD, seul Imprimeur du Roy
pour la Musique, ruë S. Iean de Beauvais,
au Mont Parnasse.
M. DC. LVII. [1657]
AVEC PRIVILEGE DE SA MAIESTE

ℓ iᵛ   [blank]

ℓ iiʳ-iiiᵛ A
MONSIEUR
DE HALVS,
SEIGNEVR
DE COVRBEVOYE,
CONSEILLER DV ROY,
en sa Cour de Parlement de Mets. . . .
[signed:] Vostre tres-humble, & tres-
obeïssant Serviteur,
H. DU MONT.

ℓ ivʳ   AV LECTEUR . . .

ℓ ivᵛ-14ᵛ LES MESLANGES /DE /HENRY DU MONT [Accompanied
vocal chansons]

ℓ 15ʳ   XIX. à 3. Viol. /Pavane

ℓ 15ᵛ-29ʳ [Accompanied sacred vocal compositions]

ℓ 29ᵛ   TABLE DES PIECES . . . FIN

ℓ 30ʳ   EXTRAIT DV PRIVILEGE . . . 1639 . . .

<u>Inventory of Basse-continue, 1657 issue</u>:

ℓ 1^r	[same preliminary material, except:] LES MESLANGES /DE HENRY DU MONT. /A 3. voix & la Basse-Continuë, avec une Quatrième Partie /adjoûtée pour un Dessus de Viole ou Violon, /de laquelle on se servira si l'on veut ...
ℓ 1^v-20^v	[Same vocal chansons as in Dessus partbook, but preceded by preludes (Allemandes or Sarabandes) for viols and continuo; the instrumental pieces are as follows:]
ℓ 1^v	1. Prelude à 2. Pour une Basse & Dessus de Viole |SARABANDE
ℓ 2^v	II. PRELUDE
ℓ 3^v	III. PRELUDE, à 2.
ℓ 4^v	IV. PRELUDE |SARABANDE
ℓ 5^v	V. PRELUDE, à 2.
ℓ 6^v	VI. PRELUDE, à 2.
ℓ 7^v	VII. PRELUDE
ℓ 8^v	VIII. PRELUDE, à 2.
ℓ 9^v	IX. PRELUDE, à 2.
ℓ 10^v	X. PRELUDE, à 2.
ℓ 11^v	XI. PRELUDE, à 2.
ℓ 12^v	XII. PRELUDE |SARABANDE
ℓ 13^v	XIII. PRELUDE OU SARABANDE, à 2.
ℓ 14^v	XIV. PRELUDE, à 2
ℓ 15^v	XV. PRELUDE, à 3
ℓ 16^v	XVI. PRELUDE, à 2
ℓ 17^v	XVII. PRELUDE, à 2

ℓ 18^v	XVIII, PRELUDE, à 2
ℓ 19^r	XIX Piece à 3. Violles |PAVANE
ℓ 19^v	XX Prelude, à 2. lentement
ℓ 21^r-31^r	[Same sacred vocal compositions as in Dessus partbook]

ℓ 31^v-32^r [DUMONT: <u>Allemande</u> (d)]

Allemande pour l'Orgue ou le Clavecin, & pour
3. Violes si l'on veut. |ALLEMANDE |REPRISE
|Suite de l'Allemande.

^{C}|11|13|

CO: cf 35-Bauyn-I #36, Courante de...Chambonnières...
    cf 52-Rés-2671 #41, Les Baricades
    cf 62-Chamb-I #16, les Baricades
ED: Bonfils-13 p 6, Cohen p 16; cf Dart-Ch #16,
    Brunold-Tessier #16.

ℓ 32^v-34^r [DUMONT: <u>Allemande grave</u> (d)]

Allemande grave pour l'Orgue ou le Clavecin,
& pour 3. Violes si l'on veut. /ALLEMANDE GRAVE.
|Suite de L'Allemande grave. |Tournez /pour la
/Reprise |Reprise [etc] |FIN.

^{C}|25|24|

ED: Bonfils-13 p 7.

ℓ 34^v TABLE DES PIECES ... FIN.

<u>Inventory</u> <u>of</u> <u>Troisiesme</u> <u>Partie</u>, <u>1661</u> <u>issue</u>:

> [The following additional partbook was issued,
> containing a third viol part for the Preludes,
> and continuo parts for several of the sacred
> pieces. Nothing more was added for the Alle-
> mandes:]

ℓ i^r

> TROISIEME PARTIE
> ADJOUSTEE
> AUX PRELUDES
> DES MESLANGES
> DE HENRY DV MONT/
> Pour un Dessus de Viole, ou Taille, ou pour
> une Basse de Viole touchée
> à l'Octave.
> Avec la Basse-Continuë des Motets à plusieurs
> Parties pour la commodité
> des Instruments.
> [title vignette (flowers)]
> A PARIS, PAR ROBERT BALLARD, seul Imprimeur de
>   Roy
> pour la musique, ruë S. Jean de Beauvais, au
>   Mont Parnasse.
> M. DC. LXI [1661]
> AVEC PRIVILEGE DE SA MAIESTÉ
>
> [For contents, see the Basse-continue partbook,
> inventoried above]

<u>Distinguishing</u> <u>characteristic</u> <u>of</u> <u>1678</u> <u>issues</u>:

> [After the "TABLE DES PIECES":]
> EXTRAIT DV PRIVILEGE ... 1678 ... Christophe
> Ballard ...

Provenance: London: John Playford, 1663.

Notation: Keyboard score (two 6-line staves, 2 systems per page, written page by page). Clefs: G^3, F^4, sometimes duplicated with C clefs.

Description: v, 55 p. (unnumbered); 8 quires: $[AA]^2$, $A-G^4$.

Summary:

Composers:

ARTUS: #22.
BRYNE: #59-63.
BULL: cf #1.
GIBBS: #35.
JACKSON: #77.
JACOPINO: #29.
LA BARRE: #13-15, 43.
LAWES (William): #7-8?, 9, 45-46, 47-48?, 49.
LOCKE: #38-39, 52?, 54?, 64-69.
MELL: #50.
MOSS: #51.
PRATT: #70, 71?.
ROGERS: #18?, 19, 42.
SANDLEY: #3-6.
TRESURE: cf #13-15.

Contents: Miscellaneous keyboard pieces, some grouped by key and/or in suites:

#1-16   Pieces in G, suites by Sandley, Lawes, anon.
17-29   Pieces in D.
30-40   Miscellaneous.
41-44   Pieces in C.
45-47   Suite (a) by Lawes.
48-58   Miscellaneous.

59-63	Suites by Bryne.
64-74	Miscellaneous.
75-77	Pieces in G.
78-81	Psalm tunes.

Inventory of ca. 1668 issue:

	p i	Musicks Hand-maide Presenting New and Pleasant LESSONS FOR THE Virginals or Harpsycon. [title vignette depicting virginal player on right, facing a viol player and singer, signed:] Guy Vaughan Sculp. London, Printed for John Playford at his Shop in the Temple. 1663.
	p ii	[blank]
	p iii	To all Lovers of Musick. ... JOHN PLAYFORD.
	p iv	[blank]
	p v	A TABLE of the Lessons in this Booke. ... [listing pieces #1-49]
	p 1	Lessons for the Virginalls. [running heading at the top of every page]
1	p 1^1	Preludium [after BULL (G)] ED: Dart-HI #1, cf Dart-BII #221.
2	p 1^2	The Canaries or the Hay [G] ED: Dart-HI #2.
3	p 2$^{1-2}$	An Ayre [SANDLEY (G)] CO: 27-Gresse #24 ED: Dart-HI #2.
4	p 3$^{1-2}$	Corant [SANDLEY (G)] CO: 27-Gresse #25 ED: Dart-HI #4.

5 p 4$^{1-2}$ Saraband [SANDLEY (G)]
      CO: 27-Gresse #26
      ED: Dart-HI #5.

6 p 5$^{1-2}$ A Jegg |Mr Ben: Sandley. [G]
      CO: 27-Gresse #27
      ED: Dart-HI #6.

7 p 6$^{1-2}$ An Ayre [LAWES? (G)]
      ED: Dart-HI #7.

8 p 7$^{1-2}$ Corant [LAWES? (G)]
      ED: Dart-HI #8.

9 p 8$^{1-2}$ Saraband |Mr Wm Lawes [G]
      ED: Dart-HI #9.

10 p 9$^{1-2}$ Selengers Round [G]
      ED: Dart-HI #10.

11 p 10$^{1-2}$ Scotish March. [G]
      ED: Dart-HI #11.

12 p 11$^{1-2}$ Freemans Delight.[G]
      ED: Dart-HI #12.

---

13 [LA BARRE?: <u>Allemande</u> (G)]
  Allmaine
   p 12$^{1-2}$

  ED: Dart-HI #13.

14   [LA BARRE or TRESURE: <u>Courante</u> (G)]

Coranto
    p 13$^{1-2}$

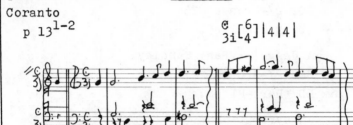

CO: 19-Heardson #69, Corant Labar (Tresor)
ED: Dart-HI #14:

15   [LA BARRE?: <u>Sarabande</u> (G)]

Saraband.
    p 14$^{1-2}$

ED: Dart-HI #15.

16   p 15$^{1-2}$ Corant La Mountague [G]
                ED: Dart-HI #16.

17   p 16$^{1-2}$ The Plesant Spring [D]
                ED: Dart-HI #17.

18   p 17$^{1-2}$ Saraband [ROGERS? (D)]
                ED: Dart-HI #18, Rastall #12.

19   p 18$^{1-2}$ A Jegg: |Mr Ben: Rogers /of Winsor. [D]
                ED: Dart-HI #19, Rastall #13.

20   p 19$^{1-2}$ A Countrie Dance [D]
                ED: Dart-HI #20.

21 | p 20^{1-2} The Grange [D]
ED: Dart-HI #21.

22 | p 21^{1-2} Duke of Yorks march [ARTUS: <u>Bourrée</u>, arr (D)]
CO: cf 7-Munich-1511f #24 [C]
cf 8-Hintze #24
cf 27-Gresse #4 [C]
cf Celle p 18
ED: Dart-HI #22.

23 | p 22^{1-2} Saraband. [D]
ED: Dart-HI #23.

24 | p 23^{1-2} The Kings Delight [D]
ED: Dart-HI #24.

25 | p 24^{1-2} Parthenia [D]
ED: Dart-HI #25.

26 | p 25^{1-2} Coranto La Mounser
ED: Dart-HI #26.

27 | p 26^{1-2} Coranto La Chabott [Air ancien (D)]
ED: Dart-HI #27.

28 | p 27^{1-2} Jocobella [D]
ED: Dart-HI #28.

29 | p 28^{1-2} Italian Rant [JACOPINO, arr (a)]
ED: Dart-HI #29.

30 | p 29^{1-2} Bow Bells [C]
CO: cf 18-Ch-Ch-1236 #73
ED: Dart-HI #30.

31 | p 30^{1-2} Gerard's Mistress [a]
ED: Dart-HI #31.

32 | p 31^{1-2} First Saraband [d]
ED: Dart-HI #32.

33 | p 32^{1-2} Second Saraband [d]
ED: Dart-HI #33.

34 | p 33$^{1-2}$ Glory of the West [a]
ED: Dart-HI #34.

35 | p 34$^{1-2}$ The Lord Monck's March [GIBBS (d)]
ED: Dart-HI #35.

36 | p 35$^{1-2}$ Montrosses March [D]
ED: Dart-HI #36.

37 | p 36$^{1-2}$ Hunsdon House [D]
ED: Dart-HI #37.

38 | p 37$^{1-2}$ The Simerons Dance |By Mr Locke [G]
ED: Dart-HI #38.

39 | p 38$^{1-2}$ An Antick Dance |By M^r. Locke [G]
ED: Dart-HI #39.

40 | p 39$^{1-2}$ The Highlanders March. [F]
ED: Dart-HI #40.

41 | p 40$^{1-2}$ Lady Sands Delight [C]
ED: Dart-HI #41.

42 | p 41$^{1-2}$ Ayre |Mr Ben: Rogers. B.M. [C]
ED: Dart-HI #42, Rastall #14.

---

43 | [LA BARRE: Courante (C)]
Coranto
   p 42$^{1-2}$ $^{C}_{3i}[^3_4]|7|9|$

CO: 16-Cosyn #114, Coranto
    17-Rogers #23, Corrant Beare
    17-Rogers #95, [C]orant
    18-Ch-Ch-1236 #31, Corant
    Drexel-5609 p 12 & 39 [copy of 17-Rogers]
ED: Dart-HI #43, Rastall #15; cf Maas #115, Cofone #23,
    74; cf Sargent #23, 62.

44	p 43$^{1-2}$	The Mitter Rant [C]
		ED: Dart-HI #44.
45	p 44$^{1-2}$	Golden Grove Mr Wm Lawes [a]
		CO: cf 18-Ch-Ch-1236 #80
		ED: Dart-HI #45.
46	p 45$^{1-2}$	Coranto |Mr Wm Lawes. [a]
		ED: Dart-HI #46.
47	p 46$^{1-2}$	Saraband [LAWES? (a)]
		ED: Dart-HI #47.
48	p 47$^{1-2}$	Symphony [LAWES? (g)]
		ED: Dart-HI #48.
49	p 48$^{1-2}$	Saraband Mr Wm Lawes |Finis. [g]
		CO: cf 16-Cosyn #106
		ED: Dart-HI #49; cf Maas #107.
50	p 49$^{1-2}$	A Jigg [MELL (F)]
		ED: Dart-HI #50.
51	p 50$^{1-2}$	A Jigg |By Mr John Mosse [F]
		ED: Dart-HI #51.
52	p 51$^{1-2}$	Apes' Dance [LOCKE (C)]
		ED: Dart-HI #52.
53		[omitted in original numeration]
54	p 52$^{1-2}$	The Bondman's Dance [D]
		ED: Dart-HI #54.
	p 53	The Tunes of Psalms to the Virginal or the Organ
55	p 53^1	The Tune of the 25 Psalm.
		ED: Dart-HI #78.
56	p 53^2	The Tune of the 71 Psalm: called, Yorke↷Tune.
		ED: Dart-HI #79.

57	p 54[1]	The Tune of the 6 Psalm: called, Windsor-Tune.
		ED: Dart-HI #80.
58	p 54[2]	The Tune of the 95 Psalm, or S. Davids-Tune.
		ED: Dart-HI #81.
	p 55	Musick Books lately Printed and Sold by John
		Playford in the Temple...

60-PLAYFORD

Provenance: London, John Playford; 1666.

Notation: Cittern tablature (English-French tuning: b-g-d^1-e^1).

Summary:
  Composers:
    CHAMBONNIÈRES, Jacques-Champion (1601/2-1672)
    COLEMAN, Charles (pre 1636-1664)
    IVES, Simon (1600-1662)
    LAWES, William (1602-1645)
    LOCKE, Matthew (ca. 1622-1677)

  Contents:
      #1-67   Anonymous pieces with descriptive titles.
      68-84   Dance pieces by named composers, almost
                      entirely arrangements.
      85-111   Vocal music with cittern accompaniments.

Inventory of French music:

[title:] | Musick's Delight
         | ON THE CITHREN,
         | Restored and Refined to a more Easie and
         | Pleasant
         | Manner of Playing than formerly; And set forth
         | with
         | Lessons Ala Mode, being the Choicest of our
         | late new Ayres, Corants, Sarabands, Tunes and
         | Jiggs.
         | To which is added several New Songs and Ayres
         | to Sing to the Cithren.
         | By John Playford Philo Musicae.
         | London, Printed By W. G. and sold by J. Play-
         | ford at his Shop in the Temple 1666.

71 [CHAMBONNIÈRES, arr Playford: <u>Sarabande</u> (C)]

Sarabande /La Chamboner

ED: Ex 16 in the Commentary.

61-DUMONT-1668

Provenance: Paris, Robert Ballard; 1668.

Locations:

Paris; Bibliothèque nationale, département de la musique:

1---Réserve Vm^1 96: Altus, Tenor, Bassus-continuus.
Ibid., fonds conservatoire:
2---Cons D. 3620 (1): Altus.

Paris; Bibliothèque Sainte Geneviève:
3--Vm 15: Altus, Tenor, Bassus-continuus.
Paris; Bibliothèque de l'arsenal:
4--Tenor, Bassus-continuus.
London, Royal College of Music Library:
5--186 I.B.9: Altus, Tenor, Bassus-continuus.

Summary of locations:

	Altus	Tenor	Bassus-continuus
Ex. 1	1	1	1
Ex. 2	1	0	0
Ex. 3	1	1	1
Ex. 4	0	1	1
Ex. 5	1	1	1

Description: 3 partbooks: Altus vel superius (vocal-instrumental), Tenor vel cantus (vocal-instrumental), Bassus-continuus (instrumental). Upright quarto format, type-set (including keyboard music).

Summary of contents: Accompanied vocal motets with instrumental pieces interspersed, one of which is also printed in keyboard score in the Bassus-continuus partbook.

Inventory of Altus:

ℓ i^r | MOTETS
A DEVX VOIX,
AVEC
LA BASSE-CONTINVE.
De Mr H. DV MONT, Abbé de Silly,
& Maistre de la Musique de la Chapelle du Roy.
ALTVS, vel SVPERIVS
[title vignette]
A PARIS,
Par ROBERT BALLARD, seul Imprimeur du Roy,
pour la Musique, ruë S. Iean de Beauuais,
au Mont Parnasse.
M. DC. LXVIII. [1668]
AVEC PRIVILEGE DE SA MAIESTÉ

ℓ i^v | [blank]

ℓ ii^r | AV ROY ... [signed:] Tres-humble ... H. DV MONT.

ℓ ii^v-34^r | [Motets, except for the following instrumental pieces:]

ℓ 23^v-24^r | SYMPHONIA

ALLEMANDA

ℓ 34^v | INDEX ...

Inventory of Bassus-continuus:

[Same preliminary material and contents, except that the Allemande is presented in two different versions:]

ℓ 26^v | ALLLEMANDE. [figured bass] |Hujus Allemandae tabulatura reperietur in fine Libri, Altiori gradu.

[and:]

ℓ 36ᵛ-37ʳ [DUMONT: <u>Allemande</u> (a)]

ALLEMANDE |REPRISE |FINIS

ᶜ|10|11|

ED: Bonfils-13 p 13.

Provenance: Paris, Jollain; 1670.

Facsimile ed.: Jacques Champion de Chambonnières: Les Pièces
de clavessin. New York: Broude Brothers, 1967 [2nd issue].

Locations:

Paris; Bibliothèque nationale, département de la
musique:

1---Vm^7 17455 (1): 2nd issue

Ibid., fonds conservatoire:

2---Réserve 250: 1st issue

3---Réserve 251: 2nd issue, bound with 63-Chamb-II

Paris; Bibliothèque Sainte Geneviève:

4---Vm 125: 2nd issue

London; British Library [British Museum], Music Room:

5---k.4.b.1: 2nd issue

Bologna; Civico Museo Bibliografico Musicale:

6---Y84: 2nd issue, bound with 63-Chamb-II

Den Haag; Gemeente Museum:

7---Bound with 63-Chamb-II

Description of Exemplar 1: 1 p.ℓ., vii, 62 p. (i.e., 64:
13-14 repeated in numbering). Oblong quarto format,
23.8 x 17.9 cm. Watermark #7; see also #37, 82x.

Distinguishing characteristics of issues:

1st issue	2nd issue
p. i . . . . is the same as p. v	
ii vi	
iii iii	
iv iv	
v vii	
[63], printed on the verso of 62 is the same as 13*	
[64] 14*	

<u>Marginalia</u>: Ex. 4: on ℓ. i^r, "Ex Libris Ste Genovef
    Parisiensis 1753"; and on p. 40, "B. Ste Gen. Paris."
    Ex. 7: on ℓ. i^r, "20^{tt}" under imprint; then, "Premier
    liure."

<u>Summary</u>: Harpsichord pieces by Chambonnières, in Suites:
    #1-6 (a)
     7-11 (C)
    12-18 (d/D)
    19-23 (F)
    24-30 (g/G)

<u>Inventory</u> <u>of</u> <u>2nd</u> <u>issue</u>:

ℓ 1r	Les
	Pieces de Claussin
	de Monsieur
	de Chambonnieres
	Se Vendent à Paris
	chez Jollain rue St Jacques
	a La Ville de Cologne
	Auec priuilege
	du Roy. 1670
	Liure Premier
	[lower left corner:] Iollain sculpsit
	ED: Brunold-Tessier p XVIX (facsim).
ℓ 1v	[blank]
p i-ii	A Madame
	Madame La Ducheße
	D'Anguien ... [signed:] De Chambonnieres
p iii	Ad Nobilißimum Virum D.
	I Cambonerium ...
	Santolius Victorinus
p iv	Idem ad Eudem ...
	Santolius Victorinus.
p v	**A Monsieur de Chamboniere ...**

p vi | Extrait du priuilege du Roy ... 25 Aoust 1670...pendant l'espace de dix annéés ... ledit sieur de Chanboniere a cedé le priuilege cy dessus a G Jollain.

p vii | Preface ... Demonstration des Marques ...

---

1 | [CHAMBONNIÈRES: <u>Allemande</u> <u>la</u> <u>rare</u> (a)]

Allemande /la Rare |Reprise

p 1^1-2^3 ^{C}|11|14| [^{C}|10|13|]

CO: 32-Oldham #29, Allemande la rare de Mr Chambre
    35-Bauyn-I #110, Allemande La rare de Mr de
                Chambonnieres

ED: Dart-Ch #1, Brunold-Tessier #1.

---

2 | [CHAMBONNIÈRES: <u>Courante</u> (a)]

Courante |Reprise

p 3^1-4^3 ^{3}|7|9| [$^6_4$|7|8|]

CO: 32-Oldham #30, Courante
    35-Bauyn-I #112, Courante de Mr de Chambonnieres

ED: Dart-Ch #2, Brunold-Tessier #2.

2a | [CHAMBONNIÈRES: <u>Double</u> (a)]

Double de la Courante |la 1 fois ... |Reprise

   p 5^1-6^3 ^{3}|8|8| [$^6_4$|7|8|

CO: 32-Oldham #30a, Double de la Courante
     35-Bauyn-I #112a, Double

ED: Dart-Ch #2[a], Brunold-Tessier #2[a].

---

3 | [CHAMBONNIÈRES: <u>Courante</u> (a)]

Courante |Reprise

   p 7^1-8^2 ^{3}|7|10| [$^6_4$|7|8|]

CO: 32-Oldham #27, Aultre Courante
     35-Bauyn-I #116, Courante du meme Auteur
     38-Gen-2348/53 #3, Courante

ED: Dart-Ch #3, Brunold-Tessier #3.

4   [CHAMBONNIERES: Courante (a)]

Courante |Reprise
    p 9¹-10³ $^3[{}^6_4]$|6|8|

CO: 2-Witzendorff #94, Curant Gombonier
    38-Gen-2348/53 #5, Courante
ED: Dart-Ch #4, Brunold-Tessier #4.

5   [CHAMBONNIERES: Sarabande (a)]

Sarabande |Reprise
    p 11¹-12³ $^3[{}^3_4]$|8|16|

CO: 35-Bauyn-I #117, Sarabande de Mr de Chambonnieres
ED: Dart-Ch #5, Brunold-Tessier #5.

6   [CHAMBONNIERES: Gaillarde (a)]

Gaillarde |Reprise |Suitte
    p 13*¹-14*³ $^3[{}^3_4]$|12|20|

CO: 35-Bauyn-I #123, (Gaillarde) de Mr de Chambonnieres
ED: Dart-Ch #6, Brunold-Tessier #6.

7 | [CHAMBONNIERES: <u>Allemande</u> <u>la</u> <u>Dunquerque</u> (C)]

Allemande la /Dunquerque |la 1re fois ... |Reprise

p 13^1-14^3 ^{C}|12|8|

CO: 35-Bauyn-I #3, Allemande La Dunquerque de Mr de
       Chambonnieres

ED: Dart-Ch #7, Brunold-Tessier #7.

8 | [CHAMBONNIERES. <u>Courante</u> <u>Iris</u> (C)]

Courante /Iris |Reprise

p 15^1-16^3 $^3[^6_4]$|8|8|

CO: 8-Hintze #15, Courante
    22a-Roper #58, Courante Chambonniere ... double
    23-Tenbury #3, (courante chambonii)
    24-Babell #58, Courante de Mr. de Chambonniere
    33-Rés-89ter #2, Courante. Chambonnieres...Double
    35-Bauyn-I #9, Courante de Mr De Chambonnieres
    36-Parville #61, Courante Chanbonniere
    44-LaPierre p 18, p 34A, Courante Chambonniere...Double
    47-Gen-2356 #12, Courante
    53-Oldham-2 p 107, Courante de Chamboniere
    55-Redon #23, Courante de Monsieur de Chambon-
                     niere
    cf 32-Oldham #17, Double de La Courante Iris

ED: Dart-Ch #8, Brunold-Tessier #8; cf Gilbert p 148.

9   [CHAMBONNIERES: <u>Courante</u> (C)]

Courante |Reprise

    p 17[1-3] $^3[^6_4]|6|7|$

CO: 22a-Roper #59, 2me Courante ... double
     33-Rés-89ter #3, 2. Courante Chambonnieres ...
                Double
     35-Bauyn-I #23, Courante de Mr de Chambonnieres
     36-Parville #62, Courante Chanbonniere

ED: Dart-Ch #9, Brunold-Tessier #9; cf Gilbert p 150.

---

p 18   [blank, ruled]

---

10   [CHAMBONNIERES: <u>Sarabande</u> <u>de</u> <u>la</u> <u>reyne</u> (C)]

Sarabande /de la Reyne

    p 19[1]-20[3] $^3|31|$ $[^3_4|47|]$

CO: 35-Bauyn-I #19, Sarabande de Mr de Chambonnieres
ED: Dart-Ch #10, Brunold-Tessier #10.

11 | [CHAMBONNIERES: <u>Allemande</u> <u>la</u> <u>loureuse</u> (d)]

Allemande /la Loureuse |La Ire fois ... |Reprise
|suite /de la /Reprise ...

    p 21^1-22^3 ^{C}|8|11| [^{C}|7|11|]

CO: 24-Babell #184, Allemande ... Double
     32-Oldham #23, Allemande La Loureuse
     35-Bauyn-I #30, Allemande la Loureuse de Mr. de
                     Chambonnieres
     36-Parville #21, Allemande la loureuse chanbonniere

ED: Dart-Ch #11, Brunold-Tessier #11.

12 | [CHAMBONNIERES: <u>Courante</u> <u>la</u> <u>toute</u> <u>belle</u> (d)]

Courante la /toute belle |Reprise

    p 23^1-24^3 ^{3}|11| [$^6_4$|10|11|]

CO: 32-Oldham #10, Courante La Toute belle
     35-Bauyn-I #31, Courante La toute belle du même
                     Auteur
     36-Parville #19, Courante Chanbonniere dit la
                     toute belle

ED: Dart-Ch #12, Brunold-Tessier #12.

13 | [CHAMBONNIERES: <u>Courante de madame</u> (d)]

Courante de /Madame |Reprise

    p 25^1-26^3 ^{3}|9|11| [$^6_4$|9|10|

CO: 32-Oldham #11, Courante de Madame
    35-Bauyn-I #34, Autre Courante du meme Auteur
    36-Parville #20, Courante chanbonniere

ED: Dart-Ch #13, Brunold-Tessier #13.

14 | [CHAMBONNIERES: <u>Courante</u> (d)]

Courante |Reprise

    p 27^1-28^3 ^{3}[$^6_4$]|6|9|

CO: 24-Babell #220, Courante
    32-Oldham #13, 3me Courante
    35-Bauyn-I #37, Courante de Monsr. de Chambonniere

ED: Dart-Ch #14, Brunold-Tessier #14.

15 | [CHAMBONNIÈRES: <u>Sarabande</u> (d)]

Sarabande |Reprise

p 29^1-30^3 ^{3}[$^3_4$]|8|16|

CO: 35-Bauyn-I #38, Sarabande de Mr de Chanbonnieres
ED: Dart-Ch #15, Brunold-Tessier #15.

---

16 | [CHAMBONNIÈRES: <u>Les Barricades</u> (d)]

les Baricades |Reprise

p 31^1-32^3 ^{3}|14|15| [$^6_4$|12|15|]

CO: 35-Bauyn-I #36, Courante de Mr. de Chambonnieres
              dit les barricades
    52-Rés-2671 #14, Les Baricades
    cf 59-Dumont-1657 ℓ 31v, Allemande [by Dumont]
ED: Dart-Ch #16, Brunold-Tessier #16; cf Bonfils-13
    p 6, Cohen p 16.

---

17 | [CHAMBONNIÈRES: <u>Gigue la madelainette</u> (D)]

Gigue |Reprise

p 33^1-34^3 ^{3}[$^6_4$]|10|13|

CO: 35-Bauyn-I #56, Gigue (La Madelainette) de Mr. de
              Chambonnieres
ED: Dart-Ch #17, Brunold-Tessier #17.

18 | [CHAMBONNIÈRES: <u>Gigue</u> (D)]

Gigue |Reprise
p 35^1-36^3 ^{3}[$^6_4$]|14|14|

CO: 35-Bauyn-I #58, Gigue de meme Auteur
ED: Dart-Ch #18, Brunold-Tessier #18.

19 | [CHAMBONNIÈRES: <u>Allemande</u> (F)]

Allemande |pour recomencer ....|Reprise
p 37^1-38^3 ^{C}|9|8|

CO: 35-Bauyn-I #60, Allemande de Mr.de Chambonnieres
ED: Dart-Ch #19, Brunold-Tessier #19.

20 | [CHAMBONNIÈRES: <u>Courante</u> (F)]

Courante |Reprise
p 39^1-40^3 ^{3}[$^6_4$]|8|10|

CO: 35-Bauyn-I #65, Courante du meme Auteur
ED: Dart-Ch #20, Brunold-Tessier #20 (cf #101).

21 | [CHAMBONNIERES: <u>Courante</u> (F)]

Courante |Reprise
p 41¹-42³ |7|8| [$^6_4$|7|7|]

CO: 35-Bauyn-I #66, Courante de Mr. de Chambonnieres
ED: Dart-Ch #21, Brunold-Tessier #21.

22 | [CHAMBONNIERES: <u>Courante</u> (F)]

Courante |Reprise
p 43¹-44³   C|7|8| [$^6_4$|6|7|]

CO: 35-Bauyn-I #62, Courante de Mr. de Chambonnieres
    38-Gen-2348/53 #18, Courante
ED: Dart-Ch #22, Brunold-Tessier #22.

23 | [CHAMBONNIERES: <u>Sarabande</u> (F)]

Sarabande |Reprise
p 45¹⁻³   ³[$^3_4$]|8|12|

CO: 35-Bauyn-I #79, Sarabande du même Auteur
    36-Parville #81, Sarabande Chanbonniere
ED: Dart-Ch #23, Brunold-Tessier #23.

p 46   [blank, ruled]

---

24 | [CHAMBONNIERES: <u>Pavane l'entretien des dieux</u> (g)]

Pauane /L'entretien/des Dieux |Suite |2me /partie |3me
partie |Lentement

     p 47^1-49^3 |15|9|17| [$\frac{4}{2}$|15|9|11$\frac{1}{2}$|]

CO: 35-Bauyn-I #107, Pauane de Mr. de Chambonnieres
ED: Dart-Ch #24, Brunold-Tessier #24.

---

p 50   [blank, ruled]

---

25 | [CHAMBONNIERES: <u>Courante</u> (g)]

Courante |Reprise

     p 51^1-52^3 ^{3}|10|8| [$\frac{6}{4}$|9|8|]

ED: Dart-Ch #25, Brunold-Tessier #25.

26 | [CHAMBONNIÈRES: <u>Sarabande</u> (g)]

Sarabande |Reprise |la 1.re fois ...

   p 53[1]-54[3]   ³|8|14|4| [³⁄₄|8|16|4|]

CO: 32-Oldham #25, Sarabande de Monsr de Chambonnieres
    35-Bauyn-I #118, Sarabande [a]

ED: Dart-Ch #26, Brunold-Tessier #26 (cf #133).

27 | [CHAMBONNIÈRES: <u>Courante</u> (g)]

Courante /1 |la 1. ... |Reprise

   p 55[1]-56[3]   ³|10|10| [⁶⁄₄|10|9|

ED: Dart-Ch #27, Brunold-Tessier #27.

28 | [CHAMBONNIÈRES: <u>Sarabande</u> (G)]

Sarabande |Reprise |suite

   p 57[1]-58[3]   ³[³⁄₄]|8|16|

CO: 35-Bauyn-I #95, Sarabande du même Auteur

ED: Dart-Ch #28, Brunold-Tessier #28.

29 | [CHAMBONNIÈRES: <u>Gigue la villageoise</u> (G)]

Gigue.la /Vilageoise |Reprise

p 59¹-60³   ³[$\frac{6}{4}$]|8|14|

CO: 35-Bauyn-I #98, Gigue La villageoise dudit
                    Auteur
    38-Gen-2348/53 #38, Gigue La Villageoise De Mr.
                        Chambonnieres

ED: Dart-Ch #29, Brunold-Tessier #29.

30 | [CHAMBONNIÈRES: <u>Canarie</u> (G)]

Canaris |Reprise

p 61¹-62³   ³[$\frac{6}{4}$]|8|12|

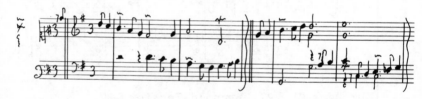

CO: 35-Bauyn-I #99, Canaries de Mr de Chambonnieres
    36-Parville #96, Canaries Chambonniere
    38-Gen-2348/53 #25, Canaries

ED: Dart-Ch #30, Brunold-Tessier #30.

p 63   [blank, unruled]

Provenance: Paris, Jollain; 1670.

Facsimile ed.: see 62-Chamb-I.

Locations:
Paris; Bibliothèque nationale, département de la musique:
1---Vm^7 1851: 1st issue
2---Vm^7 17455 (2): 3rd issue, bound with 62-Chamb-I
    Ibid., fonds conservatoire:
3---Réserve 252: 3rd issue, bound with 62-Chamb-I
    Paris; Bibliotheque Sainte Geneviève:
4---Vm 126: 3rd issue, bound with 62-Chamb-I
    Bologna; Civico Museo Bibliografico Musicale:
5---Y 84: 2nd issue, bound with 62-Chamb-I
    Den Haag; Gemeente Museum:
6---Bound with 62-Chamb-I

Description of Exemplar 2: i, 61 p. Oblong quarto format,
    17.9 x 23.4 cm. Watermark #7.

Distinguishing characteristics of issues:

	1st issue	2nd issue	3rd issue
p i	Title page from 62-Chamb-I before "Liure Premier" had been engraved on it.	Newly engraved title page.	As in 2nd issue.
p ii	From 62-Chamb-I.	Blank.	p. 1.
p iii	From p v of 62-Chamb-I.	From p vii of 62-Chamb-I.	Lacking.
p iv-v	From p vi-vii of 62-Chamb-I.	Lacking.	Lacking.
p 4, 6, 10	Blank upper right corners.	$^($4, 6$^($, 10$^($.	$^($4, $^($6$_($, 10$^($.

p 9^2, meas 4, last note	♩	♩	As in 2nd issue.
p 10^3, meas 1, l h			As in 2nd issue.
p 38^2, meas 4, l h	No note.		As in 2nd issue.
p 40^2, meas 2	No trill or natural in last 2 beats.	Has trill & natural.	As in 2nd issue.
meas 4	No trill.	Has trill.	As in 2nd issue.
p 50^1, meas 1, beat 4, alto	No ornament.	Has ⋀ .	As in 2nd issue.
p 51^2, meas 3, beat 3, alto	8th notes, 1st flatted.	16th notes, 1st & 4th flatted.	As in 2nd issue.
p 60^3, meas 1-2	Separated by a single bar; no sign for petite reprise.	Double bar, has sign.	As in 2nd issue.
p 61	Followed by p 14$^\mathbf{x}$ from 62-Chamb-I.	Last p.	As in 2nd issue.

<u>Marginalia</u>: Ex. 4: p 42, the beginning of a melody with
the text, "lamour [obscured by an ink blot]...al an-
terie fait une lotterie ..."; and p 48, "Courante"
(see Ex 17 in the Commentary).

<u>Summary</u>: Harpsichord pieces by Chambonnières, in Suites:

#1-5 (C)	16-19 (F)
6-10 (d)	20-23 (g)
11-15 (D)	24-30 (G)

<u>Inventory of 3rd issue</u>:

p i | Les
Pieces de Claueßin
de Monsieur

de Chambonnieres
Se Vendent AParis
Chez Jollain rue St Jacques
a La Ville de Cologne
Liure Second
Jollain Sculprit
[above text enclosed in a simple ornamental border]

1   [CHAMBONNIÈRES: Allemande (C)]
Allemande |Reprise
   p 1^1-2^3   C|8|8|

CO: 35.-Bauyn-I #5, Allemande de Mr de Chambonnieres
ED: Dart-Ch #31, Brunold-Tessier #31.

2   [CHAMBONNIÈRES: Courante (C)]
Courante |Reprise
   p 3^1-4^3   3[6/4]|7|10|

ED: Dart-Ch #32, Brunold-Tessier #32.

3 | [CHAMBONNIÈRES: <u>Courante</u> (C)]

Courante |Reprise

p 5^1-6^3 ^{3}[$^6_4$]|5|8|

CO: 35-Bauyn-I #13, Courante de Mr. de Chambonnieres
ED: Dart-Ch #33, Brunold-Tessier #33.

---

4 | [CHAMBONNIÈRES: <u>Gaillarde</u> (C)]

Gaillarde |la 1re fois ... |Reprise |Suitte

p 7^1-8^3 ^{3}[$^3_2$]|8|20|

CO: 35-Bauyn-I #20, Sarabande grave
    cf 33-Rés-89ter #6 [similar theme]
    cf 35-Bauyn-III #63 [similar theme]

ED: Dart-Ch #34, Brunold-Tessier #34 (cf #75); cf
    Gilbert p 157, Roesgen-Chambpion p 145.

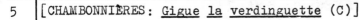

5 [CHAMBONNIÈRES: <u>Gigue la verdinguette</u> (C)]

Gigue La /Verdinguette |Reprise
   p 9^1-10^3 ^{3}|8|11| [$^6_4$|8|10|]]

CO: 33-Rés-89ter #5, Gigue La Verdinguette. Cham-
                     bonnieres ... Double
    35-Bauyn-I #22, Gigue du même Auteur

ED: Dart-Ch #35, Brunold-Tessier #35 (cf p 118);
    cf Gilbert p 154.

6 [CHAMBONNIÈRES: <u>Allemande</u> (d)]

Allemande |la i ... |Reprise ...
   p 11^1-12^3 ^{C}|13|9|

CO: 35-Bauyn-I #29, Allemande de **Mr.** de Chambonnieres
    38-Gen-2348/53 #39, [untitled]

ED: Dart-Ch #36, Brunold-Tessier #36.

7 [CHAMBONNIÈRES: <u>Courante</u> (d)]

Courante |Reprise
   p 13^1-14^3 ^{3}[$^6_4$]|8|7|

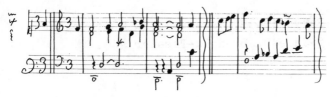

ED: Dart-Ch #37, Brunold-Tessier #37.

8 | [CHAMBONNIÈRES: <u>Courante</u> (d)]

Courante |Reprise

p 15¹-16³ |10|10| [$\frac{6}{4}$|9|9|]

ED: Dart-Ch #38, Brunold-Tessier #38.

9 | [CHAMBONNIÈRES: <u>Courante</u> (d)]

Courante |Reprise

p 17¹-18³   ³[$\frac{6}{4}$|7|9|]

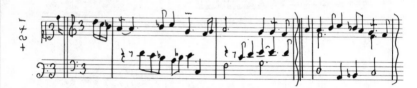

ED: Dart-Ch #39, Brunold-Tessier #39.

10 | [CHAMBONNIÈRES: <u>Sarabande</u> (d)]

Sarabande |Reprise

p 19¹-20² |8|15| [$\frac{3}{4}$|8|16|]

CO: 35-Bauyn-I #39, Sarabande du même Auteur
ED: Dart-Ch #40, Brunold-Tessier #40.

11 | [CHAMBONNIÈRES: <u>Allemande</u> (D)]

Allemande |la i f ... |Reprise ...

   p 21^1-22^3 ^{C}|14|11|

ED: Dart-Ch #41, Brunold-Tessier #41.

12 | [CHAMBONNIÈRES: <u>Courante</u> (D)]

Courante |Reprise

   p 23^1-24^3 $^3[^6_4]$|8|8|

CO: 38-Gen-2348/53 #28, Courante

ED: Dart-Ch #42, Brunold-Tessier #42.

13 | [CHAMBONNIÈRES: <u>Courante</u> (D)]

Courante |Reprise

   p 25^1-26^3 $^3[^6_4]$|7|8|

CO: 35-Bauyn-I #55, Courante de Mr. de Chambonnieres
    38-Gen-2348/53 #29, Courante

ED: Dart-Ch #43, Brunold-Tessier #43.

14 | [CHAMBONNIÈRES: <u>Courante</u> (D)]

Courante |Reprise
    p 27^1-28^3 $^3[^6_4]|6|8|$

CO: 35-Bauyn-I #50, Courante du même Auteur
ED: Dart-Ch #44, Brunold-Tessier #44.

15 | [CHAMBONNIÈRES: <u>Sarabande</u> (D)]

Sarabande |Reprise
    p 29^1-30^3 $^3|4|11|$ $[^6_4|4|8|$

CO: 35-Bauyn-I #53, Sarabande de Mr de Chambonnieres
ED: Dart-Ch #45, Brunold-Tessier #45.

16 | [CHAMBONNIÈRES: <u>Allemande</u> (F)]

Allemande |Reprise
    p 31^1-32^3 $^C|11|11|$ $[^C|10|10|]$

CO: 35-Bauyn-I #61, Allemande du même Auteur
ED: Dart-Ch #46, Brunold-Tessier #46.

17 | [CHAMBONNIÈRES: <u>Courante</u> (F)]

Courante |Reprise
 p 33¹-34³   ³|8|8| [$^6_4$|7|8|]

CO: 35-Bauyn-I #76, Courante de Mr de Chambonnieres
   38-Gen-2348/53 #10, Courante

ED: Dart-Ch #47, Brunold-Tessier #47.

---

18 | [CHAMBONNIÈRES: <u>Courante</u> (F)]

Courante |Reprise
 p 35¹-36³   ³[$^6_4$]|6|7|

CO: 35-Bauyn-I #72, Courante de Mr. de Chambonnieres
   38-Gen-2348/53 #20, Courante

ED: Dart-Ch #48, Brunold-Tessier #48.

---

19 | [CHAMBONNIÈRES: <u>Sarabande</u> (F)]

Sarabande |Reprise
 p 37¹-38³   ³[$^3_4$]|8|16|

CO: 38-Gen-2348/53 #17, Sarabande

ED: Dart-Ch #49, Brunold-Tessier #49.

20 | [CHAMBONNIÈRES: Pavane (g)]
Pauanne |2me /partie |3me partie
p 39^1-41^3 C|10|11|10| [$^4_2$|8|7|6$\frac{1}{2}$|]

CO: 35-Bauyn-I #109, Pauanne de Mr de Chambonnieres
ED: Dart-Ch #50, Brunold-Tessier #50.

---

p 42   [blank, ruled]

---

21 | [CHAMBONNIÈRES: Gigue (g)]
Gigue |Suite |Reprise
p 43^1-44^3 3|26|16| [$^3_4$|26|20|]

CO: 24-Babell #248, Gigue
ED: Dart-Ch #51, Brunold-Tessier #51.

---

22 | [CHAMBONNIÈRES: Courante (g)]
Courante |Reprise
p 45^1-46^3 3|8|11| [$^6_4$|8|10|]

CO: 35-Bauyn-I #103, Courante du mesme Auteur
    38-Gen-2348/53 #1, Courante
ED: Dart-Ch #52, Brunold-Tessier #52.

23 | [CHAMBONNIÈRES: <u>Gigue où il y a un canon</u> (g)]

Gigue ou il y a /vn Canon |Reprise

p 47$^{1-3}$ $^{3}[\frac{3}{4}]$|12|10|

ED: Dart-Ch #53, Brunold-Tessier #53.

p 48   [blank, ruled]

24 | [CHAMBONNIÈRES: <u>Allemande</u> (G)]

Allemande |la 1re fois ... |Reprise

p 49^{1}-50^{3} ^{C}|14|10|

ED: Dart-Ch #54, Brunold-Tessier #54.

25 | [CHAMBONNIÈRES: <u>Gigue</u> (G)]

Gigue |la 1re fois ... |Reprise

p 51^{1}-52^{3} $^{3}[\frac{3}{4}]$|19|16|

ED: Dart-Ch #55, Brunold-Tessier #55.

26 | [CHAMBONNIÈRES: <u>Courante</u> (G)]

Courante |Reprise

p 53^1-54^3 $^3[^6_4]$|8|9|

CO: 23-Tenbury #40, Courante Chambonniere
    24-Babell #87, Courante de Chre.
    32-Oldham #19, Courante
    33-Rés-89ter #34, Courante Chambonnieres ... Double
    35-Bauyn-I #92, Courante de Mr de Chambonnieres
    36-Parville #92, Courante chanbonniere

ED: Dart-Ch #56, Brunold-Tessier #56; cf Gilbert p 190.

27 | [CHAMBONNIÈRES: <u>Courante</u> (G)]

Courante |Reprise

p 55^1-56^3 $^3[^6_4]$|8|8|

CO: 32-Oldham #9, Courante De Monsieur de Chambonnieres
    35-Bauyn-I #88, Courante de Mr de Chambonnieres
    36-Parville #90, Courante Chanbonniere
    38-Gen-2348/53 #36, Courante

ED: Dart-Ch #57, Brunold-Tessier #57.

28 | [CHAMBONNIÈRES: <u>Courante</u> (G)]

Courante |Reprise

 p 57^1-58^3 ^{3}|7|11| [$^6_4$|8|10|]

CO: 32-Oldham #7, Courante de Monsieur de Chambonnieres
  33-Rés-89ter #35, Courante Chambonnieres ... Double
  35-Bauyn-I #91, Courante de Mr de Chambonnieres
  36-Parville #91, Courante Chanbonniere
  38-Gen-2348/53 #33, Courante

ED: Dart-Ch #58, Brunold-Tessier #58; cf Gilbert p 192.

29 | [CHAMBONNIÈRES: <u>Sarabande jeunes zéphirs</u> (G)]

Sarabande /Jeunes Zephirs |Reprise |suitte

 p 59^1-60^3 ^{3}[$^6_4$]|8|16|4|

CO: 5-Munich-1503ℓ #1, Sarrabande de Mons: Chambonnier
  32-Oldham #8, Sarabande de Monsieur de Chambon-
         nieres
  33-Rés-89ter #36, Sarabande Chambonnieres ...
         Double
  35-Bauyn-I #96, Sarabande de Mr de Chambonnieres
  36-Parville #93, Sarabande Chanbonniere
  44-LaPierre p 42, Les Zephirs de Mr de Chanboniere
  45-Dart #55, Sarabande de chamboniere
  cf Philidor p 22, Jeunes Zephirs (de Mr de chan-
        boniere) [for instruments]

ED: Dart-Ch #59, Brunold-Tessier #59; cf Gilbert p 194.

30 | [CHAMBONNIÈRES: Menuet (G)]

Menuet |Reprise

p 61$^{1-3}$ $^3[^3_4]$|8|16|

ED: Dart-Ch #60, Brunold-Tessier #60.

64-LEBÈGUE-I

Provenance: Paris, Baillon; 1677.

Locations:
Paris; Bibliothèque nationale, département de la
musique:
1   Vm^{7}1853: 1st edition, 1st issue
   Ibid., fonds conservatoire:
2   Réserve 632: 1st edition, 4th issue
   Brussels; Conservatoire royal de musique, bibliothèque:
3   15438: 1st edition, 3rd issue (formerly held by the
   Wagener Library in Marburg)
   New Haven, Connecticut; Yale University, John Herrick
   Jackson Music Library:
4   Cupboard, Mc 20 L 49b: 1st edition, 3rd issue
   London; British Library [British Museum], Music Room:
5   K 10a 14: 1st edition, 2nd issue
   Lund, Sweden; Universitetsbibliotek:
6   (Lunds Akademiska Kapell, J.H. Englehart's donation
   Nr. 24): 2nd edition
   Unlocated, formerly in the possession of Henri Prunières:
7   1st edition, 5th issue

Summary of Locations:
1st edition, 1st issue: ex. 1
1st edition, 2nd issue: ex. 5
1st edition, 3rd issue: ex. 3, 4
1st edition, 4th issue: ex. 2
1st edition, 5th issue: ex. 7
2nd edition: ex. 6

Description of Exemplar 1: iii, 90 p. Oblong quarto
format, plate size: 16.8 x 20.5 cm; page size:20.7 x
25 cm. Watermark #66 (cf. #23, 67).

Distinguishing characteristics of 1st edition issues:

	1st issue	2nd issue	3rd issue	4th issue	5th issue
p 1	10 lines of text (see Inventory).	4 lines of text: Les /Pieces de Claussin /Composées par M^r. le Begue Organiste /du Roy et de l'Eglise Sainct Medric -	As in 2nd issue.	As in 2nd issue.	Omitted.
p iii	Privilege dated 1675.	Same.	Same.	Same.	
p 14^2	No "R."	R.	R.	R.	
p 14, meas. 13-16	Clear reading:	Same.	Muddled reading, with erroneous version showing through correction. Original version:	As in 3rd issue.	

p 29, meas. 8	1st and 2nd endings clear	Erroneous version visible as well as corrected reading.	Both versions equally visible, creating a jumble of notes.	As in 3rd issue
p 48	Numbered.	Numbered.	Numbered.	Unnumbered.
p 56	Reprise.	As in 1st issue.	As in 1st issue.	Reprise (e's made from the erroneous c's).
p 58², meas. 3	No S..	No S..	No S..	S..
p 80	Numbered.	Numbered.	Numbered.	Unnumbered.

<u>Characteristics of 2nd edition:</u>

Collation: 1 p.ℓ., 90 p., 1 p.

Summary: Copied from the 1st ed., 3rd issue, except that correct versions of p. 14 (meas. 13-16) and p. 29 (1st ending) are given. The copy is literal, with no changes in clefs, but there are a number of variants in ornamentation. The word "Reprise" is supplied consistently. The Menuet #26 was copied twice (p. 45-47).

Title page: "LIVRE DE /CLAVESSIN /Composé par M^r. LE BÈGUE /Organiste du ROY et de St Medericq /Comme Plusieurs Personnes ignorent la Maniere de joüer ces Pieces ... A. Amsterdam chez /Etienne Roger /le Prix de ce Livre et de Six Florins"

<u>Marginalia</u>: Ex. 2: p iii has 7 lines of text explaining
clefs, beginning, "Quand la clef est en Bemol elle est
marquéé Vn ♭ deuant la notte ...." The names of the
clefs are noted on p 1 and 5.

Ex. 4: front pastedown and end paper has book plate,
"gift of Dame Myra Hess," and 4 paragraph letter in
French with English translation, "A letter sent by M^r
Le begue concerning his preludes ...." (see Commentary).

<u>Summary of Contents</u>: Harpsichord pieces by Lebègue in
Suites:

#1-14 (d/D)	36-44 (C)
15-27 (g/G)	45-51 (F)
28-35 (a/A)	

<u>Inventory of 1st issue</u>:

p i
Les
Pieces de Clauessin
Composées par N.A. LeBegue
Organiste de l'Eglise Sainct Mederic
Se Vendent Chez le S^r. Baillon Maitre faiseur
de Clauessin Rüe Simon le Franc et Chez
l'Autheur dans la mesme Rüe
ᴁParis
Auec Priuilege du Roy
1677
[illustrated, engraved title-page]

p ii [blank]

p iii EXTRAIT DV PRIUILEGE DV ROY ... du 9 Septembre 1675
... pendant l'espace de dix années ...
J'ay taché de mettre les préludes auec toute la fa-
cilité possible ...
Demonstration des Marques [table of ornaments].

1 | [LEBÈGUE: Prélude (d)]

Prelude En d la re sol
  p 1^1-2^3 | |

CO: cf 48-LaBarre-6 #24, Prélude En delaré [similar]
ED: Dufourcq-L p 1.

---

2 | [LEBÈGUE: Allemande (d)]

Allemande |la 1re fois ... |Reprise ...
  p 3^1-4^3 ^{C}|10|11|

CO: 13-Möllersche [copy]
    cf 35-Bauyn-II #63 [similar Allemande by L. Couperin]
    cf 36-Parville #30 [similar Allemande by L. Couperin]
ED: Dufourcq-L p 2; cf Brunold/Dart-Co #63, Curtis-Co #65.

---

3 | [LEBÈGUE: Courante grave (d)]

Courante graue |Reprise
  p 5^1-6^3 ^{3}[$^6_4$]|8|10|

CO: 13-Möllersche [copy]
    45-Dart #2 [copy]
ED: Dufourcq-L p 3.

4 | [LEBÈGUE: <u>Courante gaye</u> (d)]

Courante gaye |Reprise
  p 7^1-8^2 $^3[^6_4]$|8|9|

CO: 13-Möllersche [copy]
    45-Dart #4 [copy]
    48-LaBarre-6 #26, Courante
ED: Dufourcq-L p 3.

4a | [LEBÈGUE: <u>Double</u> (d)]

Double |Reprise
  p9^1-10^3 $^3[^6_4]$|8|9|

CO: 13-Möllersche [copy]
    48-LaBarre-6 #26a, Double
ED: Dufourcq-L p 4.

5 | [LEBÈGUE: <u>Sarabande</u> (d)]

Sarabande |Reprise
  p 11^1-12^3 $^3[^3_4]$|8|16|

CO: 13-Möllersche [copy]

45-Dart #5 [copy]

ED: Dufourcq-L p 5.

---

6 | [LEBÈGUE: <u>Gavotte</u> (d)]

gauotte

  p 13$^{1-3}$ ¢ |4|8|

CO: 13-Möllersche [copy]
    45-Dart #6 [copy]

ED: Dufourcq-L p 6.

---

7 | [LEBÈGUE: <u>Menuet</u> (d)]

Menuet

  p 14$^{1-3}$ ^{3}[$\frac{3}{4}$] |8|16|

CO: 13-Möllersche [copy]
    45-Dart #7 [copy]

ED: Dufourcq-L p 6.

8 | [LEBÈGUE: <u>Canarie</u> (d)]

Canaris |Reprise
  p 15^1-16^3 $^3[^6_4]$ |13|16|

CO: 13-Möllersche [copy]
ED: Dufourcq-L p 7.

9 | [LEBÈGUE: <u>Courante</u> (D)]

Courante En D# |Reprise
  p 17^1-18^2 $[^6_4]$ |6|7|

CO: 13-Möllersche [copy]
    22a-Roper #23 [copy]
ED: Dufourcq-L p 8.

10 | [LEBÈGUE: <u>Sarabande grave</u> (D)]

Sarabande graue |Reprise
  p 19^1-20^3 $^3[^3_4]$ |8|16|

CO: 13-Möllersche [copy]
ED: Dufourcq-L p 8.

11 | [LEBÈGUE: <u>Gigue</u> (D)]

gigue |Reprise

  p 21^1-22^3 $^3[{}^3_4]$|22|25|

CO: 13-Möllersche [copy]
    22a-Roper #17 [copy]

ED: Dufourcq-L p 9.

---

12 | [LEBÈGUE: <u>Chaconne grave</u> (D)]

Chaconne graue |2me Couplet ... 4me

  p 23^1-24^3 $^3[{}^3_4]$|12|8|8|8|

CO: 13-Möllersche [copy]
    22a-Roper #24 [copy]

ED: Dufourcq-L p 10.

---

13 | [LEBÈGUE: <u>Ballet</u> (D)]

Ballet |R.

  p 25$^{1-3}$ $[{}^4_4]$|5|8|

CO: 13-Möllersche [copy]

ED: Dufourcq-L p 11.

14 | [LEBÈGUE: <u>Gavotte</u> (D)]

gauotte |R.
   p 26$^{1-3}$ [$\frac{2}{2}$]|4|8|

CO: 13-Möllersche [copy]
     45-Dart #9, [copy]
ED: Dufourcq-L p 11.

15 | [LEBÈGUE: <u>Prélude</u> (g)]

Prelude En g re sol ut ♭
   p 27^{1}-28^{3} |20|

ED: Dufourcq-L p 12.

16 | [LEBÈGUE: <u>Allemande</u> (g)]

Allemande |1re fois ... |Reprise
   p 29^{1}-30^{3} ^{C}|8|11|

CO: 12-Walther [copy]
     13-Möllersche [copy]
ED: Dufourcq-L p 13.

17 | [LEBÈGUE: <u>Allemande gaye</u> (g)]
Allemande gaye |1re fois ... |Reprise
　　p 31^1-32^2　　　　　　　　C |7|10|

CO: 12-Walther [copy]
　　13-Möllersche [copy]
ED: Dufourcq-L p 14.

18 | [LEBÈGUE: <u>Courante grave</u> (g)]
Courante graue |Reprise
　　p 33^1-34^2　　　　　3[$^6_4$] |8|9|

CO: 12-Walther [copy]
　　13-Möllersche [copy]

ED: Dufourcq-L p 15.

19 | [LEBÈGUE: <u>Courante</u> (g)]
2me Courante
　　p 35^1-36^3　　　　　3[$^6_4$] |7|8|

CO: 12-Walther [copy]
　　13-Möllersche [copy]

ED: Dufourcq-L p 15.

---

20 | [LEBÈGUE: <u>Sarabande grave</u> (g)]

Sarabande graue |Reprise

p 37¹⁻³

CO: 12-Walther [copy]
    13-Möllersche [copy]

ED: Dufourcq-L p 16.

---

21 | [LEBÈGUE: <u>Gavotte</u> (g)]

Gauotte

p 38¹⁻³   ¢|4|8|

CO: 12-Walther [copy]
    13-Möllersche [copy]
    45-Dart #10 [copy]

ED: Dufourcq-L p 16.

22 | [LEBÈGUE: <u>Menuet</u> (g)]

Menuet |Reprise
  p 39$^{1-3}$ $^3[{}^3_4]$|8|16|

CO: 12-Walther [copy]
    13-Möllersche [copy]
    45-Dart #12 [copy]
ED: Dufourcq-L p 17.

---

23 | [LEBÈGUE: <u>Courante</u> (G)]

Courante En g re sol ut #
  p 40$^{1-3}$ $^3[{}^6_4]$|7|9|

CO: 12-Walther [copy]
    13-Möllersche [copy]
ED: Dufourcq-L p 18.

---

24 | [LEBÈGUE: <u>Gigue d'Angleterre</u> (G)]

Gigue d'angleterre fort Viste |1er Couplet ... 4me C
  p 41^1-42^3 $^6_4$|4|6|8|9|

CO: 12-Walther [copy]
    13-Möllersche [copy]
    22a-Roper #20 [copy]
ED: Dufourcq-L p 18.

25 | [LEBÈGUE: <u>Bourrée</u> (G)]

Bourée |R
  p 43¹⁻³

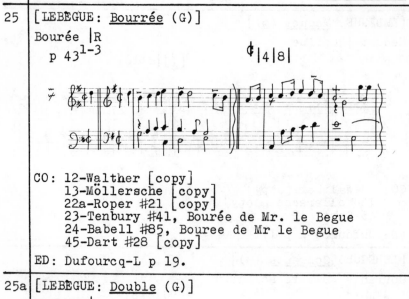

CO: 12-Walther [copy]
    13-Möllersche [copy]
    22a-Roper #21 [copy]
    23-Tenbury #41, Bourée de Mr. le Begue
    24-Babell #85, Bouree de Mr le Begue
    45-Dart #28 [copy]

ED: Dufourcq-L p 19.

25a | [LEBÈGUE: <u>Double</u> (G)]

Double |R
  p 44¹⁻³

CO: 12-Walther [copy]
    13-Möllersche [copy]
    22a-Roper #21a [copy]
    23-Tenbury #41a, Double (du mesme)
    24-Babell #85a, Double

ED: Dufourcq-L p 20.

26 | [LEBÈGUE: <u>Menuet</u> (G)]

2me Menuet [ie, to be played after #27] |R. |2me fois

p 45¹-46³ $^3[^3_4]$|8|16|8|

CO: 12-Walther [copy]
13-Möllersche [copy]
23-Tenbury #42, Menuet Mr Le Begue Serieux
24-Babell #86, Menuet
45-Dart #29 [copy]

ED: Dufourcq-L p 20.

27 | [LEBÈGUE: <u>Menuet</u> (G)]

Menuet

p 47¹⁻³ $^3[^3_4]$|8|16|

CO: 12-Walther [copy]
13-Möllersche [copy]
45-Dart #13 [copy]

ED: Dufourcq-L p 21.

p 48   [blank, ruled]

28 [LEBÈGUE: <u>Prélude</u> (a)]

Prelude En·a·mi·la·re

   p 49¹-50³ |19|

CO: 22a-Roper #9 [copy]

ED: Dufourcq-L p 22.

---

29 [LEBÈGUE: <u>Allemande</u> (a)]

Allemande |1re fois ... |Reprise ...

   p 51¹-52³   ^C|6|8|

CO: 13-Möllersche [copy]
    22a-Roper #10 [copy]
    28-Brussels-926 ℓ 66r, Allemande

ED: Dufourcq-L p 23.

---

30 [LEBÈGUE: <u>Courante</u> (a)]

Courante |Reprise

   p 53¹-54³   3[⁶₄]|8|10|

CO: 13-Möllersche [copy]
    22a-Roper #11 [copy]

ED: Dufourcq-L p 24.

31 | [LEBÈGUE: <u>Courante</u> (a)]

2me Courante

p 55¹-56³ $^3[{}^6_4]|7|9|$

CO: 13-Möllersche [copy]
    45-Dart #15 [copy; incomplete]

ED: Dufourcq-L p 25.

---

32 | [LEBÈGUE: <u>Sarabande</u> <u>grave</u> (a)]

Sarabande graue |Reprise |2me fin

p 57¹-58³ $^3[{}^3_4]|8|12|4|$

CO: 13-Möllersche [copy]
    22a-Roper #12 [copy]
    45-Dart #11 [copy]

ED: Dufourcq-L p 25.

---

33 | [LEBÈGUE: <u>Gigue</u> (a)]

Gigue. |Reprise

p 59¹-60³ $^3[{}^3_4]|25|30|$

CO: 13-Möllersche [copy]

ED: Dufourcq-L p 26.

34 | [LEBÈGUE: <u>Menuet</u> (a)]

Menuet |R
  p 61¹⁻³

CO: 13-Möllersche [copy]
ED: Dufourcq-L p 28.

35 | [LEBÈGUE: <u>Menuet</u> (A)]

2me. Menuet |R
  p 62¹⁻³

CO: 13-Möllersche [copy]
ED: Dufourcq-L p 28.

36 | [LEBÈGUE: <u>Prélude</u> (C)]

Prelude En C sol ut fa
  p 63¹-64² |13|

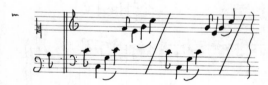

CO: 22a-Roper #2 [copy]
ED: Dufourcq-L p 29.

37 | [LEBÈGUE: <u>Allemande</u> (C)]

Allemande |1re fois ... |Reprise

   p 65^1-66^3   ^C|8|11|

CO: 13-Möllersche [copy]

ED: Dufourcq-L p 30.

---

38 | [LEBÈGUE: <u>Courante</u> (C)]

Courante |Reprise

   p 67^1-68^3 $^3[^6_4]$|8|9|

CO: 13-Möllersche [copy]
    22a-Roper #3 [copy]

ED: Dufourcq-L p 31.

---

39 | [LEBÈGUE: <u>Courante</u> (C)]

2me Courante |R

   p 69^{1-3} $^3[^6_4]$|6|7|

CO: 13-Möllersche [copy]

ED: Dufourcq-L p 32.

39a | [LEBÈGUE: <u>Double</u> (C)]

Double de la Courante |R
   p 70$^{1-3}$ $^{3}[^{6}_{4}]|6|7|$

CO: 13-Möllersche [copy]
ED: Dufourcq-L p 33.

---

40 | [LEBÈGUE: <u>Chaconne</u> (C)]

Chaconne |1er Couplet ... 4me Couplet
   p 71^{1}-72^{3} $^{3}[^{3}_{4}]|16|9|8|9|$

CO: 13-Möllersche [copy]
   22a-Roper #4 [copy]
ED: Dufourcq-L p 34.

---

41 | [LEBÈGUE: <u>Bourrée</u> (C)]

Bourée |R
   p 73$^{1-3}$ ¢ |8|8|

CO: 13-Möllersche [copy]
   22a-Roper #5 [copy]
   45-Dart #26 [copy]
ED: Dufourcq-L p 35.

41a | [LEBÈGUE: <u>Double</u> (C)]

Double |R
  p 74¹⁻³   ¢|8|8|

CO: 13-Möllersche [copy]
    22a-Roper #5a [copy]

ED: Dufourcq-L p 36.

---

42 | [LEBÈGUE: <u>Gigue</u> (C)]

Gigue |1ʳᵉ fois ... Reprise ...
  p 75¹⁻76³   ³[⁶₄]|14|17|

CO: 13-Möllersche [copy]
    22a-Roper #6 [copy]; cf #13

ED: Dufourcq- L p 36.

43 | [LEBÈGUE: <u>Gavotte</u> (C)]

Gauotte |R
   p 77[1-3]   ¢ |4|8|

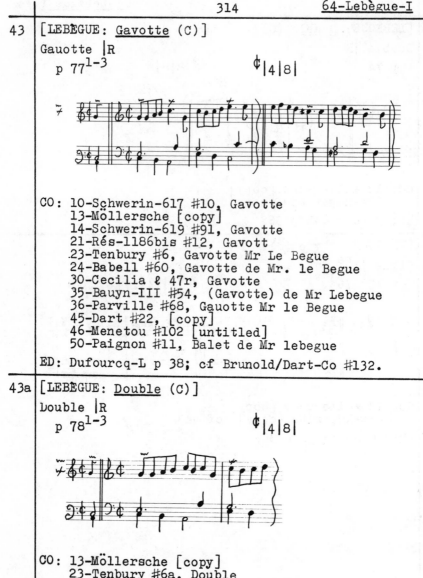

CO: 10-Schwerin-617 #10, Gavotte
    13-Möllersche [copy]
    14-Schwerin-619 #91, Gavotte
    21-Rés-1186bis #12, Gavott
    23-Tenbury #6, Gavotte Mr Le Begue
    24-Babell #60, Gavotte de Mr. le Begue
    30-Cecilia ℓ 47r, Gavotte
    35-Bauyn-III #54, (Gavotte) de Mr Lebegue
    36-Parville #68, Gauotte Mr le Begue
    45-Dart #22, [copy]
    46-Menetou #102 [untitled]
    50-Paignon #11, Balet de Mr lebegue

ED: Dufourcq-L p 38; cf Brunold/Dart-Co #132.

43a | [LEBÈGUE: <u>Double</u> (C)]

Double |R
   p 78[1-3]   ¢ |4|8|

CO: 13-Möllersche [copy]
    23-Tenbury #6a, Double
    24-Babell #60a, Double
    cf 14-Schwerin-619 #91a, [Double]
    cf 35-Bauyn-III #54a, Double par Mr Couperin
    cf 36-Parville #68a, [Double]
    cf 36-Parville #146, Double de la Gavotte de Le
                         Bègue
    cf 50-Paignon #11a, la double

ED: Dufourcq-L p 38; cf Brunold/Dart-Co #132[a].

44 | [LEBÈGUE: <u>Menuet</u> (C)]

Menuet |R
　p 79^{1-3}　　　　　　　　^{3}[\frac{3}{4}] |8|16|

CO: 13-Möllersche [copy]
ED: Dufourcq-L p 39.

---

p 80　　　　　[blank, ruled]

---

45 | [LEBÈGUE: <u>Prélude</u> (F)]

Prelude En•f•ut•fa
　p 81^{1}-82^{3}　　　　　　　|18|

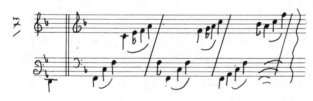

ED: Dufourcq-L p 40.

---

46 | [LEBÈGUE: <u>Allemande</u> (F)]

Allemande |1re fois ... |Reprise ...
　p 83^{1}-84^{3}　　　　　　　^{C}|7|8|

CO: 13-Möllersche [copy]
ED: Dufourcq-L p 41.

47 | [LEBÈGUE: Courante (F)]

Courante |R
p 85¹⁻³

CO: 13-Möllersche [copy]

ED: Dufourcq-L p 42.

48 | [LEBÈGUE: Courante (F)]

Courante |R
p 86¹⁻³

CO: 13-Möllersche [copy]

ED: Dufourcq-L p 42.

49 | [LEBÈGUE: Gigue (F)]

Gigue |Reprise
p 87¹-88³

CO: 13-Möllersche [copy]

ED: Dufourcq-L p 43.

50 | [LEBÈGUE: <u>Sarabande grave</u> (F)]

Sarabande graue |R |petitte Reprise

p 89¹⁻³

CO: 13-Möllersche [copy]

ED: Dufourcq-L p 44.

---

51 | [LEBÈGUE: <u>Gavotte</u> (F)]

Gauotte |R

p 90¹⁻³   ¢ |4|8|

CO: 13-Möllersche [copy]

ED: Dufourcq-L p 45.

---

p 90   fin

Provenance: Paris, Lesclop; 1687.

Locations:

 Paris; Bibliothèque nationale, département de la
 musique, fonds conservatoire:
1 Réserve 633: 1st edition, 1st issue.
 London; British Library [British Museum], Music Room:
2 K. 10a 15: 1st edition, 2nd issue.
 Brussels; Conservatoire royal de musique, bibliothèque:
3 Z. 11.251: 2nd edition.

Description of Exemplar 1: ii, 96 p. [i.e., 97: p. 9 duplicated in numeration]. Oblong quarto format; plate
 size: 17 x 20.7 cm. Watermark #45 (cf. #2).

Distinguishing characteristics of 1st edition issues:

1st issue	2nd issue
p 59 Same as p 59 of 64-Le-bègue-I.	Correct new p 59.
p 73 Correct.	Correct p 73 pasted over erroneous p 75.
p 75 Correct.	Correct p 75 pasted over erroneous ρ 73.

Characteristics of 2nd edition:

 Description: 1 p.ℓ., 47 p. Irregular quarto format;
  plate size: 15.7 x 21 cm.
 Summary: Literal copy of 1st edition, without changes
  in clefs.
 Title page: SECOND LIVRE /DE /Clavecin /Composé par
  M^r LE BEGUE Organiste /du Roy & de St. Medericq
  /A Amsterdam /Chez Estienne Roger /Marchand Lib-
  raire

Marginalia: Ex. 2: Bookplate, "Die steusic Gesellschaft

in Zürich"; p. 39 in lower corner, "Ehrenzelter" (?).
Ex. 3: Library stamp, "Geh. Rath. Wagener Marburg."

Summary of Contents: Harpsichord pieces by Lebègue in
    Suites:

#1-5 (d)	22-27 (A)
6-16 (g, B♭)	28-34 (F)
17-21 (a)	35-44 (G)

Inventory of 1st edition, 2nd issue:

p i | SECOND LIURE
    | DE CLAVES ^{S}IN
    | Composé par M^r. Le Begue
    | Organiste du Roy
    | et de S^t. Medericq
    | et
    | Se vend Chez Le Sieur Lesclop.
    | facteur d'orgues Ruë du Temple
    | au Coin de la Rue CHapon
    | A Paris
    | Auec priuilege du Roy
    | [same illustrated title-page as 64-Lebègue-I]

p ii | [blank]

p 1 | Suitte En de la ré

1 | [LEBÈGUE: Allemande (d)]
  | Allemande |Reprise
  | p 1^1-2^3 ^{C}|6|7|

CO: 11-Ryge #10 [copy:] Allemanda di D.B.H.
    48-LaBarre-6 #36, Allemande
ED: Dufourcq-L p 49; cf Bangert p 26.

2   [LEBÈGUE: <u>Courante</u> (d)]

Courante |R

   p 3^1-4^3 $\frac{3}{2}$|4|3|

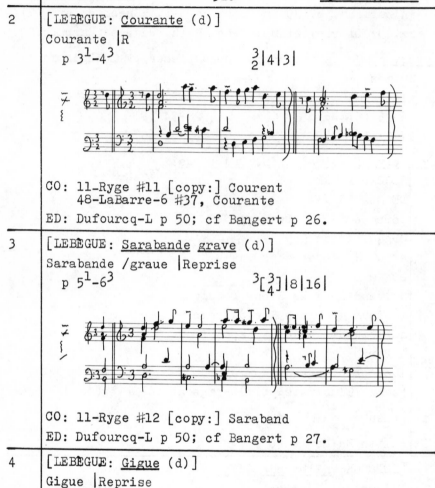

CO: 11-Ryge #11 [copy:] Courent
     48-LaBarre-6 #37, Courante

ED: Dufourcq-L p 50; cf Bangert p 26.

3   [LEBÈGUE: <u>Sarabande grave</u> (d)]

Sarabande /graue |Reprise

   p 5^1-6^3 ^{3}[$\frac{3}{4}$]|8|16|

CO: 11-Ryge #12 [copy:] Saraband

ED: Dufourcq-L p 50; cf Bangert p 27.

4   [LEBÈGUE: <u>Gigue</u> (d)]

Gigue |Reprise

   p 7^1-8^3 $\frac{3}{2}$|10|12|

CO: 11-Ryge #13 [copy:] Gigue

ED: Dufourcq-L p 51; cf Bangert p 28.

5 | [LEBÈGUE: <u>Menuet</u> (d)]

Menuet |Reprise
    p 9¹⁻³ $^3[{3 \atop 4}]$ |8|8|

CO: 22a-Roper #57, menuet
ED: Dufourcq-L p 52.

---

p [9a]   [blank, ruled]

p 10   Suitte En g ré sol ♭

6 | [LEBÈGUE: <u>Allemande</u> (g)]

Allemande |Reprise
    p 10¹-11³ ^{C}|9|11|

CO: 11-Ryge #57 [copy:] Allemand di D.B.H.
    14-Schwerin-619 #1 [copy]
ED: Dufourcq-L p 53; cf Bangert p 51.

7 [LEBÈGUE: <u>Allemande</u> (g)]
2^e Allemande |Reprise
   p 12¹-13³   ^C|6|9|

CO: 14-Schwerin-619 #2 [copy]
ED: Dufourcq-L p 54.

---

8 [LEBÈGUE: <u>Courante</u> (g)]
Courante |Reprise
   p 14¹-15³ $^3[^6_4]$|8|9|

CO: 11-Ryge #58 [copy:] Courent
    14-Schwerin-619 #3 [copy]
ED: Dufourcq-L p 55; cf Bangert p 52.

---

9 [LEBÈGUE: <u>Sarabande</u> (g)]
Sarabande |Reprise |Suitte
   p 16¹-17¹ $^3[^3_4]$|8|16|

CO: 11-Ryge #59 [copy:] Saraband
    14-Schwerin-619 #4 [copy]
ED: Dufourcq-L p 56; cf Bangert p 52.

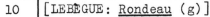

10 | [LEBÈGUE: <u>Rondeau</u> (g)]

Rondeau |Reprise
  p 18¹⁻³   C |4|4|4|

CO: 14-Schwerin-619 #5 [copy]
ED: Dufourcq-L p 56.

11 | [LEBÈGUE: <u>Gigue</u> (g)]

Gigue. |Reprise |Suitte ...
  p 19¹-21² $\frac{3}{2}$ |15|21|

CO: 11-Ryge #60 [copy:] Giqve
    14-Schwerin-619 #6 [copy]
ED: Dufourcq-L p 57; cf Bangert p 53.

12 | [LEBÈGUE: <u>Passacaille</u> (g)]

Passacaille |Suitte ...
  p 22¹-25² $^3[\frac{3}{4}]$ |62|

CO: 14-Scnwerin-619 #7 [copy]
    45-Dart #14 [copy]
ED: Dufourcq-L p 58.

13 | [LEBÈGUE: <u>Menuet</u> (g)]

Menuet |Reprise |Suitte

    p 26^1-27^2 ^{3}[$\frac{3}{4}$]|8|16|

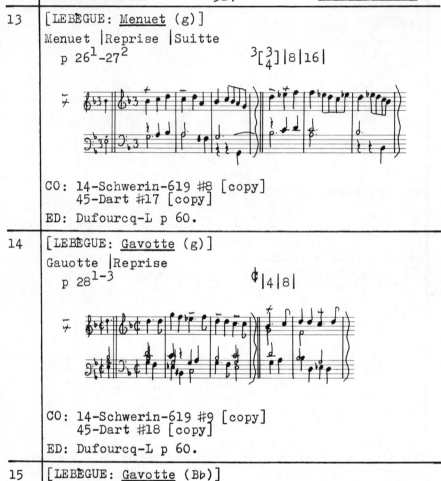

CO: 14-Schwerin-619 #8 [copy]
    45-Dart #17 [copy]

ED: Dufourcq-L p 60.

14 | [LEBÈGUE: <u>Gavotte</u> (g)]

Gauotte |Reprise

    p 28$^{1-3}$ ¢|4|8|

CO: 14-Schwerin-619 #9 [copy]
    45-Dart #18 [copy]

ED: Dufourcq-L p 60.

15 | [LEBÈGUE: <u>Gavotte</u> (B♭)]

Gauotte |Reprise

    p 29$^{1-3}$ ¢|4|8|

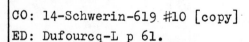

CO: 14-Schwerin-619 #10 [copy]

ED: Dufourcq-L p 61.

16 | [LEBÈGUE: <u>Menuet</u> (B♭)]

Menuet |Reprise
   p 30^1-31^2 ^{3}[$\frac{3}{4}$] |8|8|

CO: 14-Schwerin-619 #11 [copy]
    45-Dart #19 [copy]

ED: Dufourcq-L p 61.

---

p 32   Suitte En A mi la ré

---

17 | [LEBÈGUE: <u>Allemande</u> (a)]

Allemande |Reprise |Suitte
   p 32^1-33^3 ^{C}|9|10|

CO: 14-Schwerin-619 #12 [copy]

ED: Dufourcq-L p 62.

---

18 | [LEBÈGUE: <u>Courante</u> (a)]

Courante |Reprise
   p 34^1-35^3 $\frac{3}{2}$|8|9|

ED: Dufourcq-L p 63.

19 | [LEBÈGUE: <u>Sarabande</u> (a)]

Sarabande |Reprise
p 36¹-37³   ³[³/₄]|8|16|

CO: 14-Schwerin-619 #13 [copy]
ED: Dufourcq-L p 64.

20 | [LEBÈGUE: <u>Gavotte</u> (a)]

Gauotte |Reprise
p 38¹⁻³   ¢|4|8|

CO: 14-Schwerin-619 #14 [copy]
     45-Dart #20 [copy]
ED: Dufourcq-L p 64.

21 | [LEBÈGUE: <u>Menuet</u> (a)]

Menuet |Reprise
p 39¹⁻³   ³[³/₄]|8|8|

CO: 14-Schwerin-619 #15 [copy]
ED: Dufourcq-L p 65.

22 | [LEBÈGUE: <u>Allemande</u> (A)]

Allemande |Reprise
   p 40¹-41³   C |7|10|

CO: 14-Schwerin-619 #16 [copy]
ED: Dufourcq-L p 66.

23 | [LEBÈGUE: <u>Courante</u> (A)]

Courante |Reprise
   p 42¹-43³   ³[⁶₄] |8|9|

CO: 14-Schwerin-619 #17 [copy]
   48-LaBarre-6 #39, Courante En ami La ré #
ED: Dufourcq-L p 67.

24 [LEBÈGUE: Sarabande fort grave (A)]

Sarabande fort graue |Reprise

    p 44^1-45^3 ^{3}[$\frac{3}{4}$] |8|16|

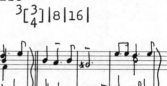

    CO: 14-Schwerin-619 #18 [copy]
        45-Dart #23 [copy]

    ED: Dufourcq-L p 68.

25 [LEBÈGUE: Gigue (A)]

Gigue |Reprise |Suitte

    p 46^1-48^2 $\frac{3}{2}$ |14|17|

    CO: 14-Schwerin-619 #19 [copy]

    ED: Dufourcq-L p 68.

26 [LEBÈGUE: Bourrée (A)]

Bouréé |Reprise

    p 49$^{1-3}$ ^{2}[$\frac{2}{2}$] |8|8|

    CO: 14-Schwerin-619 #20 [copy]

    ED: Dufourcq-L p 70.

26a [LEBÈGUE: Double (A)]

Bourée double |Reprise
   p 50^1-51^2 ^{2}[$^2_2$]|8|8|

CO: 14-Schwerin-619 #20a [copy]

ED: Dufourcq-L p 70.

27 [LEBÈGUE: Canarie (A)]

Cannaris |Reprise |Suitte
   p 52^1-54^2 ^{3}[$^6_4$]|11|18|

ED: Dufourcq-L p 71.

p 55   Suitte En f Vt fa

28 [LEBÈGUE: Allemande (F)]

Allemande |1.ere fois ... |Reprise |Suitte
   p 55^1-56^3 ^{C}|7|9|

ED: Dufourcq-L p 72.

29 | [LEBÈGUE: Courante (F)]

Courante |Reprise
  p 57[1]-58[3] $^3[^6_4]|9|9|$

CO: 48-LaBarre-6 #40, Courante
ED: Dufourcq-L p 73.

30 | [LEBÈGUE: Gigue (F)]

Gigue.|Suitte ...
  p 59[1]-61[1] $^3|15|23|$ $[^3_4|16|24|]$

ED: Ex 18 above; cf Dufourcq-L p 74 (incomplete).

31 | [LEBÈGUE: Sarabande (F)]

Sarabande |Reprise
  p 61[2]-62[3] $^3[^3_4]|8|16|$

CO: 14-Schwerin-619 #21 [copy]
ED: Dufourcq-L p 74.

32 | [LEBÈGUE: Menuet (F)]

Menuet |Reprise
   p 63[1-3]   ³[³⁄₄]|8|8|

CO: 14-Schwerin-619 #22 [copy]
    24-Babell #9, 2me menuet
ED: Dufourcq-L p 75.

33 | [LEBÈGUE: Menuet (F)]

Menuet |Reprise
   p 64[1-3]   ³[³⁄₄]|8|16|

CO: 14-Schwerin-619 #23 [copy]
    24-Babell #8, Menuet de Mr. Le Begue ...
    45-Dart #25 [copy]
ED: Dufourcq-L p 75.

34 | [LEBÈGUE: Chaconne (F)]

Chaconne |Suitte ...
   p 65[1]-70[3]   ³[³⁄₄]|105|

CO: 14-Schwerin-619 #30 [copy]
ED: Dufourcq-L p 76.

35 | [LEBÈGUE: _Allemande_ (G)]

Allemande |Reprise
   p 71¹-72²   C|8|11|

CO: 22a-Roper #22 [copy]
   cf 11-Ryge #65 (similar Buxtehude Allemande)
ED: Dufourcq-L p 79; cf Bangert p 13.

36 | [LEBÈGUE: _Courante_ (G)]

Courante |Reprise
   p 73¹-74³   ³[⁶₄]|8|9|

CO: cf 11-Ryge #66 (similar Buxtehude Courante)
ED: Dufourcq-L p 80; cf Bangert p 13.

37 | [LEBÈGUE: _Sarabande grave_ (G)]

Sarabande graue |Reprise |Suitte |2ᵉ Rep
   p 75¹-76²   ³[³₄]|8|16|4|

CO: cf 11-Ryge #67 (similar Buxtehude Sarabande)
ED: Dufourcq-L p 81; cf Bangert p 14.

38 | [LEBÈGUE: <u>Chaconne grave</u> (G)]

Chaconne graue |j.^{er} Couplet ... |Suitte ... |6.^{e}

   p 77^{1}-83^{2} ^{3}|16|19|16|20|20|25| [$^{3}_{4}$|116|]

CO: 14-Schwerin-619 #27 [copy]

ED: Dufourcq-L p 82.

---

39 | [LEBÈGUE: <u>Menuet</u> (G)]

Menuet |Reprise

   p 84$^{1-3}$ ^{3}[$^{3}_{4}$]|8|8|

CO: 14-Schwerin-619 #24 [copy]

ED: Dufourcq-L p 86.

---

40 | [LEBÈGUE: <u>Gigue</u> (G)]

Gigue |Reprise |Suitte

   p 85^{1}-87^{3} ^{3}|25|25| [$^{3}_{4}$|26|26|]

ED: Dufourcq-L p 86.

41   [LEBÈGUE: <u>Bourrée</u> (G)]

Bouréé |Reprise

   p 88$^{1-3}$ ¢|8|8|

CO: 14-Schwerin-619 #25 [copy]

ED: Dufourcq-L p 87.

42   [LEBÈGUE: <u>Air de hautbois</u> (G)]

Air de Hautbois |Reprise

   p 89^{1}-90^{3} $^{2}[\frac{2}{2}]$|9|16|

CO: 14-Schwerin-619 #26 [copy]

     45-Dart #27 [copy]

ED: Dufourcq-L p 88.

43   [LEBÈGUE: <u>Gavotte</u> (G)]

Gauotte |Reprise |2^{e} Rep

   p 91$^{1-3}$ $^{2}[\frac{2}{2}]$|4|8|4|

CO: 14-Schwerin-619 #28 [copy]

ED: Dufourcq-L p 88.

43a | [LEBÈGUE: <u>Double</u> (G)]

Double |Reprise |2.^e Rep |Suitte

   p 92^1-93^1 ^{2}[$\frac{2}{2}$] |4|8|4|

CO: 14-Schwerin-619 #28a [copy]

ED: Dufourcq-L p 89.

44 | [LEBÈGUE: <u>Petite</u> <u>Chaconne</u> (G)]

Petitte /Chaconne |Suitte ...

   p 94^1-96^3 ^{3}[$\frac{3}{4}$] |4|44|

CO: 14-Schwerin-619 #29 [copy]

ED: Dufourcq-L p 90.

p 96   fin

Provenance: Paris, author; 1680.

Locations:

Paris; Bibliothèque nationale, département de la musique:

1   $Vm^8u.9$

Ibid., fonds conservatoire:

2   Réserve 912

Description of Exemplar 1: 1 p.ℓ., 1-10[a], 72 p. [i.e., 77: 5 blank unnumbered p.: 15a, 28a, 48a, 52a, 59a]. Engraved; irregular format; plate size: 10.8 x 17.5 cm. Watermark #35.

Facsimile edition: Perrine, Pièces de luth en musique (Geneva: Minkoff, 1973).

Summary:

Composers

GAULTIER, Ennemond "le vieux" (ca. 1575-1651)

GAULTIER, Denis "le jeune" (1597/03-1672)

Contents:

#1-10	Pieces attr. to E. Gaultier (d)
11-19	Pieces attr. to D. Gaultier (d)
20-21	Pieces attr. to E. Gaultier (a)
22-27	Pieces attr. to D. Gaultier (a)
28-30	Pieces attr. to E. Gaultier (a, c, C)

Inventory:

ℓ i^r | Pieces de Luth en Musique
auec des Regles pour les toucher parfaitem^t
sur le Luth, et sur le Claussin
Dediées
A Monsieur de Bartillat
Par le Sr Perrine

A Paris chez l'Auteur ruë des Victoires proche la
porte Montmartre chez Mr Fertier.

ℓ i^v [blank]

p 1-3 A Monsieur de Bartillat /Conseiller du Roy en tous
Ses Conseils, - /et Garde de son Tresor Royal ...
[signed:] Vôtre tres humble et tres /ôbeissant Ser-
uiteur /Perrine.

p 4-9 Aduertissment ...

p 10 Extrait du Priulege du Roy ... 9^e Mars 1680 ...

p 10 [a] [blank, ruled, with clefs and small "4" at the top
of the page; this same plate was used for each
blank page in the book].

1   [GAULTIER (E), tr PERRINE: <u>Courante</u> <u>l'immortelle</u> (d)]
l'jmmortelle du vieux Gaultier. Courante
     p 1¹-2²   ³[$\frac{3}{4}$]|12|16|

CO: cf 24-Babell #226, Courante L'Immortelle
    cf 33-Rés-89ter #29, Courante du Vieux Gautier.
                        L'Immortelle.
    cf 45-Dart #40, Limortelle [g]
    cf Stockholm-176 ℓ 4v, l'Immortelle Courante du
                        V. Gautier
    cf Skara #20,   Courant Monsr Gautier
    cf Stockholm-2 p 32, Courant immortele de Mons:
                        Gautie
    cf Ottobeuren p 142, L'Immortelle Courrante de
                        Suitte du mesme
ED: cf Gilbert p 182, Souris-G #81, Souris-G #66.

2 | [GAULTIER (E), tr PERRINE: <u>Allemande</u>, <u>Tombeau de</u>
<u>Mesangeau</u> (d)]

Allemande ou Tombeau de Mezangeau de V.G.

p 3^1-4^2 ^{C}|9|13|

ED: Souris-G #10.

---

3 | [GAULTIER (E), tr PERRINE: <u>Allemande</u>, <u>Testament</u> (d)]

Allemande ou Testament du V.G. |Cette piece se
joüe encore en gigue. tournez

p 5^1-6^2 ^{C}|8|9|

3a | Gigue du V.G. [same as #3, except for time signature]

p 7^1-8^2 $^{\mathcal{C}}$|8|9|

ED: Souris-G #57.

---

4 | [GAULTIER (E), tr PERRINE: <u>Courante</u> (d)]

Courante du V.G.

p 9^1-10^2 $^3[\frac{3}{4}]$|14|16|

ED: Souris-G #12.

| 5 | [GAULTIER (E), tr PERRINE: <u>Courante</u> (d)] |

Courante du v.g.

p 11¹-12²   ³[¾] |12|14|

ED: Souris-G #13.

| 6 | [GAULTIER (E), tr PERRINE: <u>Canarie</u> (d)] |

Canaris du v.G.

p 13¹-15²   ³[¾] |16|24|16|

ED: Souris-G #67.

[p 15a: blank; cf p 10a]

7 | [GAULTIER (E), tr PERRINE: <u>Allemande la poste</u> (d)]
Allemande du V.G. |cette piece se joüe encore en
gigue. tournez
    p 16^1-17^2 ^{C}|8|9|

7a | Gigue du v.G. [same as #7, except for time signature]
    p 18^1-19^2 ₵|8|9|

CO: cf 33-Rés-89ter #28, Gigue du Vieux Gautier
ED: Souris-G #63; cf Souris-G #85, Gilbert p 185.

8 | [GAULTIER (E), tr PERRINE: <u>Courante</u> (d)]
Courante du v.G.
    p 20^1-21^2 ^{3}[$\frac{3}{4}$]|12|17|

ED: Souris-G #68.

9 | [GAULTIER (E), tr PERRINE: <u>Courante</u> (d)]
Courante du v.G.
    p 22^1-23^2 $^\flat$[$\frac{3}{4}$]|14|14|

ED: Souris-G #69.

10 | [GAULTIER (E), tr PERRINE: <u>Gigue</u> (<u>Carillon</u>) (d)]

Gigue du v.G.
p 24^1-25^2 ¢|10|10|

ED: Souris-G #72; cf #64.

11 | [GAULTIER (D), tr PERRINE: <u>Fantaisie</u> (d)]

Fantaisies du Jeune Gaultier
p 26^1-28^2 C|29|

ED: Tessier-G #85.

[p 28a: blank, ruled; cf p 10a]

12 | [GAULTIER (D), tr PERRINE: <u>Gigue</u> (d)]

Gigue du J.g.
p 29^1-30^2 ¢|10|10|

ED: Tessier-G #84.

13 | [GAULTIER (D), tr PERRINE: <u>Courante</u> (d)]

Courante du j.G.

p 31^1-32^2 ^{3}[$\frac{3}{4}$]|12|14|

ED: Tessier-G #81.

---

14 | [GAULTIER (D), tr PERRINE: <u>Courante la royale</u> (d)]

Courante du j.G.

p 33^1-35^1 ^{3}[$\frac{3}{4}$]|14|20|

ED: Tessier-G #86.

---

15 | [GAULTIER (D), tr PERRINE: <u>Courante</u> (d)]

Courante du j.G.

p 35^2-36^2 ^{3}[$\frac{3}{4}$]|14|14|

ED: cf Souris-G #25 (similar Courante).

16 | [GAULTIER (D), tr PERRINE: <u>Sarabande</u> (d)]

Sarabande du J.G.

  p 37^1-38^2 $^3[^3_4]$|16|12|

CO: cf 33-Rés-89ter #30, Sarabande Gautier le Jeune

ED: Tessier-G #83; cf Gilbert p 184, Tessier-G p 125.

17 | [GAULTIER (D or E), tr PERRINE: <u>Courante la Lyonnoise</u>
(<u>la plaintive</u>) (d)]

Courante du j.G.

  p 39^1-40^2 $^3[^3_4]$|12|14|

ED: Tessier-G #82, Souris-G #27.

18 | [GAULTIER (D or E), tr PERRINE: <u>Courante le canon</u> (d)]

Le Canon, du jeune Gaultier

  p 41^1-42^2 $^3[^3_4]$|12|12|

CO: cf Stockholm-2 p 34, Le Canon Courante du Gautier
    cf Stockholm-176 ℓ 5v, Le Canon Courante du Gautier

ED: Tessier-G #80, Souris-G #20.

19 | [GAULTIER (D), tr PERRINE: <u>Allemande</u> <u>grave</u> (<u>tombeau</u>) (d)]

Allemande graue du J.G. ou Son Tombeau.

p 43^1-46^1 ^{C}|14|14|

ED: Tessier-G #87 (in b).

---

p 46   fin des pieces en D. la. ré

---

20 | [GAULTIER (E), tr PERRINE: <u>Courante</u> (<u>Volte</u>) <u>les</u> <u>larmes</u> (a)]

Courante du V.G. ou les Larmes

p 47^1-48^2 $^3[\frac{3}{4}]$|17|16|

CO: cf 33-Rés-89ter #25, Courante du Vieux Gautier [d]
    cf 36-Parville #17, Courante du Vieux gautier [d]
ED: Souris-G #51; cf Gilbert p 180, Souris-G #78.

[p 48a: blank, ruled; cf p 10a]

21 | [GAULTIER (E), tr PERRINE: <u>Courante</u> (a)]

Courante du v.G.

p 49$^{1-2}$ $^3[^3_4]$ |9|17|

ED: Souris-G #70.

22 | [GAULTIER (D), tr PERRINE: <u>Pavane</u> (a)]

Pauane du Jeune Gaultier

p 50^1-52^2 ^{C}|11|10|12|

23 | [GAULTIER (D), tr PERRINE: <u>Courante</u> (a)]

Courante du J.G.

p 53$^{1-2}$ $^3[^3_4]$ |12|18|

23a | [GAULTIER (D), tr PERRINE: <u>Double</u> (a)]

double |double
    p 53^2-54^2, 56$^{1-2}$ ^{3}[$\frac{3}{4}$]|12|18|

---

24 | [GAULTIER (D or E), tr PERRINE: <u>Allemande</u>, <u>le</u> <u>tom-beau</u> <u>de</u> <u>l'enclos</u> (a)]

Allemande ou Tombeau de Lenclos du J.G.
    p 57^1-59^1 ^{C}|9|10|

CO: cf Darmstadt-18 ℓ 8v, Allemande von der Lauten
                        abgesetzt ... Gautier
ED: Tessier-G #54, Souris-G #11.

25 | [GAULTIER (D), tr PERRINE: <u>Sarabande</u> (a)]

Sarabande du même
    p 59$^{1-2}$ ^{3}[$\frac{3}{4}$]|8|12|

ED: Tessier-G #46.

[p 59a: blank, ruled; cf p 10a]

26 | [GAULTIER (D), tr PERRINE: <u>Courante</u>, <u>la belle tene-</u>
<u>breuse</u> (a)]

Courante ou la belle Tenebreuse du J.G.

p 60^1-61^2 ^{3}[$^3_4$]|14|14|

ED: Tessier-G #51.

27 | [GAULTIER (D), tr PERRINE: <u>Chaconne</u> (<u>Sarabande</u>) (a)]

Sarabande du J.G.

p 62^1-67^2 ^{3}|8|4|12|12|[etc] [$^3_4$|93|]

ED: Tessier-G #56.

28 | [GAULTIER (E), tr PERRINE: <u>Courante</u> <u>la</u> <u>petite</u> <u>bergère</u>
(a)]

Courante du V.G.

p 68^1-69^2 ^{3}[$^3_4$]|16|16|

CO: cf 33-Rés-89ter #26, Courante du Vieux Gautier
ED: Souris-G #33; cf Souris-G #80, Gilbert p 181.

29 | [GAULTIER (E), tr PERRINE: <u>Sarabande</u> (c)]

Sarabande du vieux Gaultier

p 70^1-71^2 $^3[{}^3_4]$|16|20|

ED: Souris-G #71.

30 | [GAULTIER (E), tr PERRINE: <u>Pièce</u> (C)]

Piece du V.G.

p 72$^{1-2}$ ${}^6_4$|4|4|4|

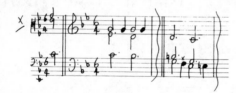

ED: Souris-G #73.

Provenance: Paris, author; 1682.

Locations:
    Paris; Bibliothèque nationale, département de la
    musique:
  1   Réserve Vmb 16$^{(1-2)}$.
    Paris; Bibliothèque Sainte Geneviève:
  2   Vm 128, Vm 129 (<u>olim</u> V 562).

Description: 2 vols. v. I: 2 p.ℓ., 24 p. v. II: 22 p.
    Both vols.: preliminary material typeset, music en-
    graved; plate size: 16 x 24.5 cm. Oblong quarto format.
    Watermark #27.

Marginalia: Ex. 2: "20. Ex Libris Sancta Genevefae Parisi-
    ensis 1753" on title page and a few insignificant
    words throughout the volumes.

Summary of contents: Pieces by Nicolas Gigault, 1624/5-
    1707:
    v. I: Variations on noëls.
    v. II: Miscellaneous sacred and secular keyboard
           pieces, including more noëls.

Inventory:
ℓ i^{r}

    LIVRE DE MVSIQVE
    DEDIE A LA TRES S^{TE} VIERGE
    PAR GIGAVLT ORGANISTE DE S. NICOLAS
    DES CHAMPS A PARIS.
    CONTENANT
    LES CANTIQUES SACREZ QVI SE CHANTENT EN L'HON-
      NEVR DE SON
    DEVIN ENFANTEMENT,
    DIVERSIFIEZ DE PLUSIEURS MANIERES A II. III.
    ET IV. PARTIES QVI PEU
    vent estre touchez sur l'Orgue & sur le Clauessin:

aussi sur le Luth, les Violles, Vio̅
lons, Flutes & autres Instruments de Musique.
Une Piece Diatonique en forme d'Allemande
marquée simple, & avec les Ports de Voix:
Pour servir de Guide & d'Instruction pour les

former & adapter à toutes sortes de Pieces,
Le tout divisé en deux parties
Et se vendent,
A Paris chez l'AUTEUR,   près de S. Nicolas
   des Champs.
AVEC PRIVILEGE DV ROY
[p 1, bottom:] graueés par Bonneuil

ℓ i^V   [blank]

ℓ ii^r   A /LA TRES SAINTE /VIERGE ...

ℓ ii^V   AVERTISSEMENT /Amy Lecture, je vous expose des
Noëls que j'ay dediez à la Tres sainte Vierge
... je me suis attaché de les mettre en Musique,
& ce pour estre touchez sur tous les instru-
mens portez par l'affiche dans les mouvemens
que l'Eglise leur a donné, sans rien changer.
I'en ay fait plusieurs à deux, parce que non
seulement cela exprime nettement & plus facile-
ment le chant sur l'Orgue & le Clavessin par
le dégagement des parties, mais aussi cela se
peut plus aisement   sur le Luth, la
Harpe & la Consonante, Quant aux Violles,
Violons, & Fluttes ...
  Il y a plusieurs personnes qui seroient
bien aises d'avoir quelque tendresse dans
leur touché. Pour cela j'ay disposé une piece
Diatonique décrite en deux manieres, l'une
simple & l'autre composée de ports de voix

pour donner l'idée & l'usage de les appliquer
à toutes autres sortes de pieces. I'ay mar-
qué les tremblemens   avec de petites croix
pour les personnes qui n'ont pas encore la
practique de mettre où il faut....
EXTRAIT DV PRIVILEGE DV ROY ... 26 Novembre
1682 ... Achevé d'imprimer pour la premiere
fois le 5. jour de Decembre 1682.

p 1-4	Condit r a 4 partyes |Noel noel &C |a 2 partyes |a 2 partyes | a 3 partyes |a 3 p. en dialogue | a 3. p. 2 dessus
p 5	Ce qui Se touche en quelque lieux auant a la uenue de noel /a 2. p. |a 3. partyes |a 3. en dialogue |a 3. 2 dessus |a 4. a 2 ceurs
p 6-10	a la uenue de noel a 2. p. |a 2 p [etc] CO: cf 7-Munich-1511f #25 cf 44-LaPierre p 17
p 11-13	voicy le Jour solemnel a 2.p. [etc]
p 14-16	une uierge pucelle a 2. p [etc]
p 17-19	or nous dites marie a 2. p [etc]
p 20-23	or uoyla noel passé a 2 p.
p 24^1	Estant Cesar Auguste [fragment]
p 24$^{2-3}$	peuples Catholiques [fragment]
v II, ℓ i^r	[same as v I, with "II" added:] II LIVRE DE MVSIQVE ...
ℓ i^v	[blank]
ℓ ii^{r-v}	[same as v I]
p 1	Conditor
p 3[ie 2]^1	Prosa /mittit ad virginem

p 3[ie 2]^2	naturam
p 3[ie 2]^3	Eci qui
p 4[ie 3]$^{1-2}$	accede nuncia. a 2
p 4[ie 3]$^{2-3}$	audi. Et Suscipit 2 3
p 5[ie 4]^1	natura premitur. a 2.
p 5[ie 4]^2	mittit ad uirginem a 2
p 5[ie 4]^3	mittat ad uirginem a 4
p 5 [sic]	a 3. 2 dessus
p 6-11^1	laissez paistre nos bestes a 2 p. [etc]
p 11^2-16^2	Ou sen uont ces gays bergers a 2.p.

p 16^3-17^3 [GIGAULT: <u>Allemande</u> (d)]

Allemande par fugue |reprise

^{C}|14|12|3|

p 18^1-19^3 [GIGAULT: <u>Double</u> (d)]

la mesme allemande auec les ports de voix|reprise

^{C}|13|12|3|

p 20	Chantons Je vous prie noel a 2 [etc]
p 21	noel pour lamour de marie ...

p 22$^{1-2}$	les bourgeois de Chastres et de [sic]
p 22$^{2-3}$	uous qui desirez sas fin

68-d'ANGLEBERT

Provenance: Paris, author; 1689.

Facsimile ed.: Jean Henry d'Anglebert: Pièces de Clavecin.
New York: Broude Brothers, 1965 [1st ed., 2nd issue].

Locations:

Paris; Bibliothèque nationale, départment de la
musique:

1---Vm^7 1854: 1st edition, 1st issue.

Ibid., fonds conservatoire:

2---Réserve 89 (olim 18440): 1st edition, 1st issue.

3---Réserve 89bis (olim 18439): 1st edition, 1st issue.

London; British Library [British Museum], Music Room:

4---e 382: 1st edition, 1st issue.

Brussels; Bibliothèque royale Albert 1er, département
de la musique:

5---Fétis 2941 FPC: 1st edition, 2nd issue.

Rochester, New York; Eastman School of Music, Sibley
Library:

6---Vault M22 A589: 2nd edition.

New Haven, Connecticut; Yale University, John Herrick
Jackson Music Library:

7---cupboard Mc 20 An 4a: 3rd edition

Bologna; Civico Museo bibliografico musicale:

8---V 79: 1st edition, 1st issue.

Den Haag; Gemeente Museum:

9---1st edition, issue not ascertained.

Vienna; Österreichische Nationalbibliothek, Musiksammlung:

10---[1st edition reported; not examined]

Paris; private collection of André Meyer:

11---[1st edition reported; not examined]

Troyes; Bibliothèque municipale:

12---[1st edition reported; not examined]

New York; New York Public Library, Library and Museum
for the Performing Arts, Music Division:
13---[1st edition reported; not examined]
Washington, D.C.; Library of Congress:
14---[1st edition reported; not examined]
Munich; Bayerische Staatsbibliothek, Musiksammlung:
15---[3rd edition reported; not examined]
Berlin; Deutsche Staatsbibliothek, Musikabteilung:
16---[3rd edition reported, missing since the Second
World War]

Summary of locations:
1st edition, 1st issue: Ex. 1-4, 8; cf 9-14
1st edition, 2nd issue: Ex. 5; cf 9-14.
2nd edition: Ex. 6.
3rd edition: Ex. 7; cf 15-16.

Description of 1st edition, 1st issue: vii(numbered [a]-f),
128 p. Oblong quarto format, plate size: 19 x 21.5
cm. Watermark #75 (cf. #8, 55, 57, 82, 99).

Distinguishing characteristics of 1st edition issues:

	1st issue	2nd issue
p a (im-print)	"...Rüe Ste. Anne ..." "Au bout de la Rue du hazard"	"...Rüe St. Honoré..." No notation.
p 127	"Fin du premier Livre"	No notation.
p 128	No notation.	"Fin du Ier Livre /Reveu et corrigé"

Characteristics of 2nd edition:
Identical to 1st edition, 2nd issue, with the sub-
stitution of an entirely new typeset title-page:
PIECES DE CLAVECIN
COMPOSEES
PAR J·HENRY D'ANGLEBERT,
ORDINAIRE DE LA MUSIQUE DE LA CHAMBRE DU ROY, AVEC LA
MANIERE DE LES JOUER.

Diverses Chaconnes, Ouvertures, & autres Airs de
   Monsieur DE LULLY
mis sur cet Instrument.
Quelques Fugues pour l'Orgue.
Et les Principes de l'Accompagnement.
[printer's mark]
Chez CHRISTOPHE BALLARD, seul Imprimeur du Roy pour la
Musique, ruë S. Jean de Beauvais, au Mont-Parnasse.
M. DCCIII. [1703]
Avec Privilege de Sa Majesté [nb: privilege statement
   from 1689 remains on p f (see Inventory, below)].

Marginalia: Ex. 2: Considerable contemporary marginalia
   and an engraving inserted at the beginning; p 26,
   one meas. added at the end, tied to final chord;
   p 58^3 meas. 4, little mark over g (fingering?);
   p 59^3 meas. 5, tenor g added to chord in r.h.; p 61,
   several ornaments added; p 61^1 meas. 6, g added;
   p 76^2, "2e fois" crossed out and "pet. repr." added.
   Ex. 3: Some pencil notations by A. Dethoux, 1839.
   Ex. 6: Miscellaneous notations by previous owners
   on title page: signature dated 1705 (tracing #110);
   "Victoria Zietkiewicz /à Aug: Braun," etc. Ex 8:
   title page, "1689" after imprint.

Summary of Contents: Pieces by Jean-Baptise d'Anglebert
   (1628-1691), including some transcribed from works
   by Lully and arrangements of popular melodies.

#1-16	Suite (G)	58-62	Organ fugues
17-37	Suite (g)	63	Quatour
38-49	Suite (d)	64	Principes de l'Ac-
50-57	Suite (D)		compagnement

Inventory of 1st edition, 1st issue:
p a   Pieces de clavecin
           Composées par J.-Henry d'Anglebert
           Ordinaire de la Musique de la Chambre du Roy

avec la maniere de les Joüer.
Diverses Chaconnes, Ouvertures et autres Airs
de Monsieur de Lully mis sur cet Instrum.^{t}
Quelques Fugues pour l'Orgue.
Et
les Principes de l'Accompagnement.
Livre premier.
AVEC PRIVILEGE DU ROY.
 AParis Chez l'Autheur Rüe Ste Anne près S.^{t}
  Roch
Au bout de la Rue du hazard.

p aa	[blank]
p b-c	A son Altesse Serenissime /Madame la Princeße de Conty /Fille du Roy ... [signed:] D.! Anglebert
	[Portrait inserted in some exemplars, in varying locations in preliminary pages, with inscription:] IEAN HENRY D'ANGLEBERT ORDINAIRE DE LA MUSIQUE DE LA CHAMBRE DU ROY POUR LE CLAVECIN [signed below:] P. Mignard pinxit ... C Vermeulen Sculp. [verso blank]
p d	Preface ...
p e	Marques des Agréments et leur Signification ...
p f	Extrait du Privilege du Roy ... pendant le temps de huit années ... Registré sur le Liure de la Communauté le Ier /decembre 1689.

1 | [d'ANGLEBERT: <u>Prélude</u> (G)]

Prelude
   p 1¹-2³ |11|

CO: 33-Rés-89ter #32, Prelude d'Anglebert
ED: Gilbert p 2, cf p 202; Roesgen-Champion p 2, cf p 151.

2 | [d'ANGLEBERT: <u>Allemande</u> (G)]

Allemande |Ire fois ... |Reprise ...
   p 3¹-4³   C|9|9|

ED: Gilbert p 4, Roesgen-Champion p 4.

3 | [d'ANGLEBERT: <u>Courante</u> (G)]

Courante |1re fois... |Reprise ...
   p 5¹-6³   ³[6/4]|8|11|3|

CO: cf 35-Bauyn-II #86 (similar Courante)
ED: Gilbert p 6, Roesgen-Champion p 6.

3a | [d'ANGLEBERT: <u>Double</u> (G)]

Double de la Courante |Reprise ...

    p 7^1-8^3 $3[^6_4]$|8|11|3|

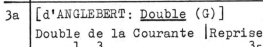
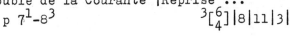

ED: Gilbert p 8, Roesgen-Champion p 8.

4 | [d'ANGLEBERT: <u>Courante</u> (G)]

2^e Courante |1re fois ... |Reprise ...

    p 9^1-10^3 $3[^6_4]$|8|10|2|

ED: Gilbert p 10, Roesgen-Champion p 10.

5 | [d'ANGLEBERT: <u>Courante</u> (G)]

3^e Courante |1re fois ... |Reprise ...

    p 11^1-12^3 $3[^6_4]$|8|9|3|

ED: Gilbert p 12, Roesgen-Champion p 12.

6 [d'ANGLEBERT: <u>Sarabande</u> (G)]

Sarabande /Lentement |Reprise |Ire fois ...
     p 13^1-14^3 ^{3}[$\frac{3}{4}$]|16|16|4|

ED: Gilbert p 14, Roesgen-Champion p 14.

7 [d'ANGLEBERT: <u>Gigue</u> (G)]

Gigue |Ire fois ... |Reprise
     p 15^1-16^3 $\frac{12}{8}$ |9|10|

ED: Gilbert p 16, Roesgen-Champion p 16.

8 [d'ANGLEBERT: <u>Gaillarde</u> (G)]

Gaillarde /Lentement |Ire fois ... |Reprise |fin
     p 17^1-18^3 $\frac{3}{2}$|8|16|

CO: 33-Rés-89ter #38, Galliard D'Anglebert
ED: Gilbert p 20, Roesgen-Champion p 18.

9 | [d'ANGLEBERT: Chaconne Rondeau (G)]

Chaconne Rondeau |Ire fois ... |4e Couplet |fin

p 19¹-22³   ³|8|16|24|24 [etc] [$\frac{3}{4}$|97|]

ED: Gilbert p 22, Roesgen-Champion p 20.

---

10 | [d'ANGLEBERT: Gavotte (G)]

Gavotte /Lentement

p 23¹⁻³   C|4|8|

CO: 33-Rés-89ter #39, Gavotte d'Anglebert

ED: Gilbert p 26, Roesgen-Champion p 24.

---

11 | [d'ANGLEBERT: Menuet (G)]

Menuet |Reprise

p 24¹⁻³   ³[$\frac{3}{4}$]|16|16|

CO: 33-Rés-89ter #40, Menuet d'Anglebert

ED: Gilbert p 27, Roesgen-Champion p 25.

12 | [LULLY, arr d'ANGLEBERT: <u>Ouverture</u> from <u>Cadmus</u> (1673) (G)]

Ouverture de Cadmus

   p 25^1-26^3 ¢|11|^{3}53| [$^¢$|11|$\frac{3}{4}$|54|]

ED: Gilbert p 88, Roesgen-Champion p 26.

13 | [LULLY, arr d'ANGLEBERT: <u>Symphonie</u> from <u>Roland</u> (1685) V-2 (G)]

Ritournelle des Feés de Rolland. Mr de Lully /Lentement |Ire fois ...

   p 27$^{1-3}$ ^{3}|6|24| [$\frac{3}{4}$|6|25|]

ED: Gilbert p 114, Roesgen-Champion p 28.

14 | [LULLY, arr d'ANGLEBERT: <u>Menuet</u> <u>dans</u> <u>nos</u> <u>bois</u> from <u>Trios</u> <u>pour</u> <u>le</u> <u>coucher</u> <u>du</u> <u>roi</u> (G)]

Menuet dans nos bois.   M^r. de Lully./Lentement Reprise fin
p 28$^{1-3}$ $^3[\frac{3}{4}]$ |8|16|

CO: 36-Parville #109, Menuet dans nos bois. Mr. de
Lully
51-LaBarre-11 p 205, Dans nos bois de Mr de lully
cf 27-Gresse #20, Air Dans un bois
cf 27-Gresse #52, [untitled]

ED: Gilbert p 112, Roesgen-Champion p 29.

15 | [LULLY, arr d'ANGLEBERT: <u>Chaconne</u> from <u>Phaéton</u> (1683) II-5 (G)]

Chaconne de Phaeton M^r. de Lully |po^r recomencer |fin
p 29^1-33^3 ^{3}|137| [$\frac{3}{4}$|143|]

CO: cf 14-Schwerin-619 #61, Chaconne de Phäeton
cf 24-Babell #263, Chaconne de Phaeton
cf 43-Gen-2354 #1, Chaconne de phaEton
cf 44-LaPierre p 24, 45A, Chaconne de Phaéton
cf 46-Menetou #9, chaconne

ED: Gilbert p 100, Roesgen-Champion p 30.

16 | [d'ANGLEBERT: <u>Gigue</u> (G)]
2e. Gigue. on la joüe auant la Gaillarde apres la 1re
Gigue /Gayement |Ire fois ...
   p 34$^{1-3}$ ^{C}|9|11|

CO: 33-Rés-89ter #37, Gigue d'Anglebert
ED: Gilbert p 18, Roesgen-Champion p 35.

17 | [d'ANGLEBERT: <u>Prélude</u> (g)]
Prelude
   p 35^1-36^3 |8|

CO: 33-Rés-89ter #42a, prelude d'Anglebert
ED: Gilbert p 28, cf p 20?; Roesgen-Champion p 36.

18 | [d'ANGLEBERT: <u>Allemande</u> (g)]
Allemande |Ire fois ... |Reprise
   p 37^1-38^3 ^{C}|9|11|

ED: Gilbert p 30, Roesgen-Champion p 38.

19 | [d'ANGLEBERT: Courante (g)]
Courante |Ire fois ... |Reprise
p 39^1-40^3 $^3[^6_4]$|8|9|

ED: Gilbert p 32, Roesgen-Champion p 40.

20 | [d'ANGLEBERT: Courante (g)]
2^e. Courante |Ire fois ... |Reprise
p 41^1-42^3 $^3[^6_4]$|10|10|

ED: Gilbert p 33, Roesgen-Champion p 41.

21 | [LULLY, arr d'ANGLEBERT: Courante (g)]
Courante M^r. de Lully |Ire fois ... |Reprise
p 43^{1-3} $^3[^6_4]$|9|7|

CO: 33-Rés-89ter #42d, Courante
    36-Parville #41, Courante de Mr Lully
    46-Menetou.#117, Courante de Mr de lully
ED: Gilbert p 96, cf p 95; Roesgen-Champion p 42.

21a | [d'ANGLEBERT: <u>Double</u> (g)]

Double de la Courante |Ire fois ... |Reprise

    p 44¹⁻³   ³[$^6_4$]|9|7|

CO: 33-Rés-89ter #42e, Double dela Courante
    36-Parville #41a, Double De La courante Lully

ED: Gilbert p 97, Roesgen-Champion p 43.

22 | [d'ANGLEBERT: <u>Sarabande</u> (g)]

Sarabande /Lentement |Reprise |Ire fois ... |Fin

    p 45¹⁻³   ³[$^3_4$]|8|16|

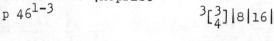

ED: Gilbert p 35, Roesgen-Champion p 44.

23 | [LULLY, arr d'ANGLEBERT: <u>Dieu des enfers</u> from <u>La</u>
<u>Naissance de Vénus</u> (1665) II-6 (g)]

Sarabande. Dieu des Enfers Mr de Lully /Lentement
|Ire fois ... |Reprise

    p 46¹⁻³   ³[$^3_4$]|8|16|

CO: 36-Parville #141, Dieu des Enfers
    cf 24-Babell #247, 2me Sarabande

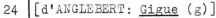

ED: Gilbert p 98, Roesgen-Champion p 45.

---

24 | [d'ANGLEBERT: <u>Gigue</u> (g)]

Gigue |Ire fois ... |Reprise ...

 p 47^{1}-48^{3} $\frac{12}{8}$|9|9|

ED: Gilbert p 36, Roesgen-Champion p 46.

---

25 | [LULLY, arr d'ANGLEBERT: <u>Gigue</u> (g)]

Gigue.Mr de Lully |Reprise

 p 49$^{1-3}$ $^{3}[^{6}_{4}]$|8|12|

ED: Gilbert p 99, Roesgen-Champion p 48.

---

26 | [d'ANGLEBERT: <u>Gaillarde (Sarabande)</u> (g)]

Gaillarde /Lentement |Ire fois ... |Reprise ...

 p 50$^{1-3}$ $\frac{3}{2}$|8|12|4|

CO: 32-Oldham #12, Sarabande, façon de Gaillarde.
      D'anglebert

ED: Gilbert p 38, Roesgen-Champion p 49.

27 | [d'ANGLEBERT: <u>Passacaille</u> (g)]
Passacaille |Ire fois ... |Suite de La Passacaille
|pour /recomencer |pour finir
   p 51¹-54¹   ³|1|4|4| [etc] [$\frac{3}{2}$|85|]

CO: 33-Rés-89ter #44, Passacagle D'Anglebert
    cf Chigi-27 ℓ 36v [untitled]
ED: Gilbert p 40, Roesgen-Champion p 51.

28 | [LULLY, arr d'ANGLEBERT: <u>Menuet la jeune Iris</u> from
<u>Trios pour le coucher du roi</u> (g)]
Menuet la Jeune Iris. Mr de Lully. /Lentement |Ire
fois ... |Reprise
   p 54²⁻³   ³[$\frac{3}{4}$]|8|9|5|

ED: Gilbert p 113, Roesgen-Champion p 56.

29 | [ANON, arr d'ANGLEBERT: <u>Gavotte où estes vous allé</u> (g)]
Gavotte. Ou estes vous allé. Air ancien /Lentement
|Reprise ...
   p 55¹⁻²   ²[$\frac{2}{2}$]|8|8|

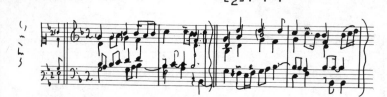

ED: Gilbert p 120, Roesgen-Champion p 57.

30 | [ANON, arr d'ANGLEBERT: <u>Gavotte</u> <u>le</u> <u>beau</u> <u>berger</u> <u>Tirsis</u> (g)]

Gavotte. le beau berger Tirsis Air ancien /Lentement Reprise
p 55^3 ^{2}[$\frac{2}{2}$]|4|8|

ED: Gilbert p 121, Roesgen-Champion p 58.

31 | [ANON, arr d'ANGLEBERT: <u>Vaudeville</u> <u>la</u> <u>bergère</u> <u>Anette</u> (g)]

La Bergere Anette. Vaudeuille
p 56$^{2-3}$ ^{3}[$\frac{3}{4}$]|6|18|

CO: 36-Parville #142, Le Bergere Anette
ED: Gilbert p 122, Roesgen-Champion p 59.

32 | [LULLY, arr d'ANGLEBERT: <u>Ouverture</u> from <u>Le Carnaval</u> (1668, 1675) (g)]

Ouverture de la Mascarade M^r. de Lully |Ire fois ...
|Reprise |Lentement
p 57^1-58^3 ^{2}[$^2_2$]|13|37|

CO: 33-Rés-89ter #42b, Ouuertuor dela Mascarade.
ED: Gilbert p 90, Roesgen-Champion p 60.

33 | [LULLY, arr d'ANGLEBERT: <u>Second</u> <u>Air</u> (<u>sourdines</u>) from <u>Armide</u> (1686) II-4 (g)]

Les Sourdines d'Armide M^r. de Lully /Lentement |Ire
fois ... |Reprise ...
p 59$^{1-3}$ $^6_4$|7|12|

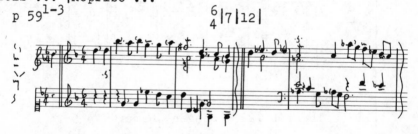

CO: cf 14-Schwerin-619 #64, Sourdinet damide
    cf 23-Tenbury #49, Air d'Armide
    cf 24-Babell #124, Air d'Armide Sourdines tres Doux
    cf 36-Parville #115, Air d'Armide
    cf 36-Parville #149, Sourdinnes de'Amide
    cf 49-ResF-933 #2, Sourdines d'Armide
ED: Gilbert p 115, Roesgen-Champion p 62.

34 | [LULLY, arr d'ANGLEBERT: <u>Les Songes agréables</u> from
<u>Atys</u> (1676) III-4 (g)]

Les Songes agreables d'Atys M<u>r</u>. de Lully |1<u>re</u> fois ...
|Reprise ...
 p 60¹⁻³ $3[\frac{3}{4}]|9|20|$

CO: 33-Rés-89ter #43, Air de Ballet. les Songes
                      agreables
     cf 14-Schwerin-619 #53, Songes Agreables Datis
     cf 24-Babell #131, Les Songes Agreables
     cf 36-Parville #117, Les Songes agreables d'Atys
     cf 46-Menetou #114, Les Songes agreables d'atis

ED: Gilbert p 116, Roesgen-Champion p 63.

35 | [LULLY, arr d'ANGLEBERT: <u>Entrée d'Apollon</u> from <u>Le</u>
<u>Triomphe de l'amour</u> (1681) (g)]

Air d'Apollon du Triomphe de l'Amour M<u>r</u>. de Lully
/Lentement |1<u>re</u> fois ... |Reprise
 p 61¹-62¹ $2[\frac{2}{2}]|9|19|7|$

CO: cf 14-Schwerin-619 #56, Ouverture dapollon du
                          Triomphe de Lamour
     cf 24-Babell #129, Entrée d'Apollon
     cf 30-Cecilia ℓ 52r, Dessante dopollon
     cf 36-Parville #43, Entree dapollon
     cf 46-Menetou #100, entree dappollon
     cf Stockholm-176 ℓ 14v, Entreé d'Apollon
     cf Saizenay-I p 222, Entrée d'Apollon

ED: Gilbert p 118, Roesgen-Champion p 64.

36 [ANON, arr d'ANGLEBERT: <u>Vaudeville menuet de Poitou</u> (g)]

Menuet de Poitou /Vaudeuille |Reprise

   p 62$^{2-3}$ $^3[^3_4]|6|14|$

CO: 36-Parville #143, menuet de Poitou

ED: Gilbert p 123, Roesgen-Champion p 66.

37 [LULLY, arr d'ANGLEBERT: <u>Passacaille</u> from <u>Armide</u> (1686) V-2 (g)]

Passacaille d'Armide Mr de Lully |Ire fois ... |Suite de la Passacaille ...

   p 63^1-66^3 $^3|24|4|12|4|$ [etc] $[^3_4|110|]]$

CO: cf 14-Schwerin-619 #63, Passacaille Darmide
    cf 24-Babell #138, Passacaille D'Armide
    cf 31-Madrid-1360 #27, La Chacona
    cf 49-RésF-933 #1, Passacaille D'armide
    cf Minorite ℓ 44v, Passacaille armide

ED: Gilbert p 108, Roesgen-Champion p 67.

38 | [d'ANGLEBERT: Prélude (d)]

Prelude

p 67^1-70^3 |9|

CO: 33-Rés-89ter #23, Prelude d'Anglebert

ED: Gilbert p 45 (with partial facsimile), Roesgen-
    Champion p 71; cf Gilbert p 204.

---

39 | [d'ANGLEBERT: Allemande (d)]

Allemande |Ire fois ... |Reprise ...

p 71^1-72^3 ^{C}|10|10|

CO: 12-Walther [copy]

ED: Gilbert p 50, Roesgen-Champion p 76.

---

40 | [d'ANGLEBERT: Courante (d)]

Courante |Ire fois ... |Reprise

p 73$^{1-3}$ $^3[^6_4]$|8|8|

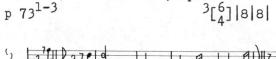

CO: 12-Walther [copy]
    cf 35-Bauyn-III #46 (similar Courante)

ED: Gilbert p 52, Roesgen-Champion p 78.

40a	[d'ANGLEBERT: <u>Double</u> (d)] Double de la Courante... |Reprise p 74$^{1-3}$ $^3[^6_4]$|8|8|  CO: 12-Walther [copy] ED: Gilbert p 53, Roesgen-Champion p 79.
41	[d'ANGLEBERT: <u>Courante</u> (d)] 2.^{e} Courante |Ire fois ... |Reprise... |au Commencement p 75^1-76^3 $^3[^6_4]$|9|12|12|2|  CO: 12-Walther [copy] ED: Gilbert p 54, Roesgen-Champion p 80.
42	[d'ANGLEBERT: <u>Sarabande grave</u> (d)] Sarabande graue /Lentement |Ire fois ... |Reprise p 77$^{1-3}$ $^3[^3_4]$|8|16|  CO: 12-Walther [copy] ED: Gilbert p 56, Roesgen-Champion p 81.

43 | [d'ANGLEBERT: <u>Sarabande</u> (d)]

Sarabande /Lentement |Ire fois ... |Reprise ...

p 78¹⁻³　　　　　　　　　$\frac{3}{4}$[$\frac{3}{4}$]|12|16|

CO: 12-Walther [copy]
　　33-Rés-89ter #24, Sarabande d'Anglebert
ED: Gilbert p 57, Roesgen-Champion p 82.

44 | [d'ANGLEBERT: <u>Gigue</u> (d)]

Gigue |Ire fois ... |Reprise

p 79¹-80³　　　　　　$\frac{6}{4}$[$\frac{6}{8}$]|16|18|

CO: 12-Walther [copy]
ED: Gilbert p 58, Roesgen-Champion p 84.

45 | [d'ANGLEBERT: <u>Gaillarde</u> (d)]

Gaillarde /Lentement |Ire fois ... |pour recommencer
... |Fin

p 81¹-82³　　　　　　$\frac{3}{2}$|8|16|4|

CO: 12-Walther [copy]
ED: Gilbert p 60, Roesgen-Champion p 86.

46 | [d'ANGLEBERT: <u>Gavotte</u> (d)]

Gauotte |Reprise

p 83$^{1-3}$ $^2[^2_2]|8|12|$

ED: Gilbert p 62, Roesgen-Champion p 88.

47 | [d'ANGLEBERT: <u>Menuet</u> (d)]

Menuet |Reprise

p 84$^{1-3}$ $^3[^3_4]|16|20|]$

ED: Gilbert p 63, Roesgen-Champion p 89.

48 | [LULLY, arr d'ANGLEBERT: <u>Ouverture</u> from **Proserpine**
(1680)(d)]

Ouuerture de Prosperine M^r. de Lully |Ire fois ...
|Reprise |Suite de l'Ouuerture de Prosperine ...

p 85^1-87^3 $\mathbb{C}|11|^6_422|^C12|^{\mathbb{C}}1|$

CO: cf 46-Menetou #92, entree De prosperine
ED: Gilbert p 92, Roesgen-Champion p 90.

49 | [d'ANGLEBERT: <u>Variations</u> <u>sur</u> <u>les</u> <u>folies</u> <u>d'Espagne</u> (d)]
Variations sur les folies d'Espagne |Ier Couplet ...
22.e Couplet
p 88^{1}-98^{3} ^{3}|16|16| [etc] [$\frac{3}{4}$|351|]

CO: 15-Berlin-30206 p 40 [copy]
33-Rés-89ter #21, Variations sur les follies
d'Espagne d'Anglebert
ED: Gilbert p 64, Roesgen-Champion p 93.

50 | [d'ANGLEBERT: <u>Allemande</u> (D)]
Allemande /gayement |Ire fois ... |Reprise ...
p 99^{1}-100^{3} ^{C}|12|11|

ED: Gilbert p 76, Roesgen-Champion p 106.

51 | [d'ANGLEBERT: <u>Courante</u> (D)]
Courante |Ire fois ... |Reprise ...
p 101$^{1-3}$ ^{3}[$\frac{6}{4}$]|9|8|

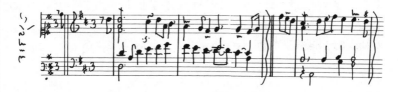

ED: Gilbert p 78, Roesgen-Champion p 108.

52 | [d'ANGLEBERT: <u>Courante</u> (D)]

2^{e}. Courante |Ire fois ... |Reprise ...

p 102$^{1-3}$ $^3[^6_4]$|9|9|

ED: Gilbert p 79, Roesgen-Champion p 109.

53 | [d'ANGLEBERT: <u>Sarabande</u> (D)]

Sarabande |Reprise

p 103$^{1-3}$ $^3[^3_4]$|12|16|

ED: Gilbert p 80, Roesgen-Champion p 110.

54 | [d'ANGLEBERT: <u>Gigue</u> (D)]

Gigue /guayement |Ire fois ... |Reprise ...

p 104$^{1-3}$ $^3[^3_4]$|16|20|

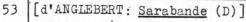

ED: Gilbert p 81, Roesgen-Champion p 111.

55 | [LULLY, arr d'ANGLEBERT: <u>Chaconne</u> from <u>Acis</u> <u>et</u> <u>Gala-</u>
<u>thée</u> (1686) II-5 (D)]

Chaconne de Galatée Mr de Lully /Lentement
   p 105$^{1-3}$ ^{3}[$\frac{3}{4}$]|40|

CO: 51-LaBarre-11 p 206, Chaconne de Galatée de Mr
                           de Lully
    cf 14-Schwerin-619 #123, Chaconne de Galothe
    cf 23-Tenbury #75, Chaconne de Galatée
    cf 24-Babell #97, Chaconne de Galatée
    cf 36-Parville #29, Chaconne de galatée
    cf 49-RésF-933 #4 [untitled]

ED: Gilbert p 106, Roesgen-Champion p 112.

56 | [d'ANGLEBERT: <u>Chaconne</u> <u>rondeau</u> (D)]

Chaconne Rondeau |Ire fois ... Double |fin... |premier
Couplet ... |5e Couplet
   p 106^{1}-108^{3} ^{3}|8|8|16| [etc] [$\frac{3}{4}$|95|]]

ED: Gilbert p 82, Roesgen-Champion p 114.

57 [d'ANGLEBERT: Tombeau de Mr. de Chambonnières (D)]

Tombeau de M^r. de Chambonnieres /fort lentement

|Ire. fois ...

p 109^1-110^3 $\frac{3}{2}$|8|16|

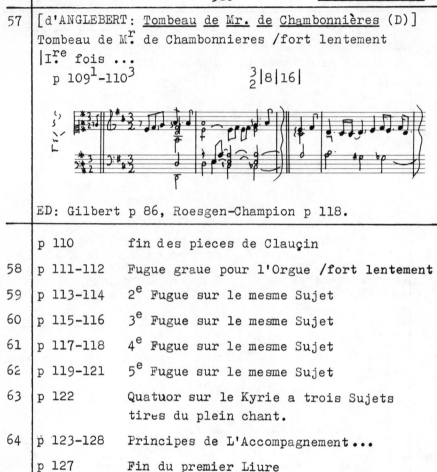

ED: Gilbert p 86, Roesgen-Champion p 118.

	p 110	fin des pieces de Clauçin
58	p 111-112	Fugue graue pour l'Orgue /**fort lentement**
59	p 113-114	2^e Fugue sur le mesme Sujet
60	p 115-116	3e Fugue sur le mesme Sujet
61	p 117-118	4e Fugue sur le mesme Sujet
62	p 119-121	5e Fugue sur le mesme Sujet
63	p 122	Quatuor sur le Kyrie a trois Sujets tires du plein chant.
64	p 123-128	Principes de L'Accompagnement...
	p 127	Fin du premier Liure
	p 128	feüille adjoutée
	p [129]	[blank]